A BRIEF HISTORY OF
LAGER

A BRIEF HISTORY OF

LAGER

500 YEARS OF THE
WORLD'S FAVOURITE BEER

MARK DREDGE

To Grandad.

An Hachette UK Company
www.hachette.co.uk

First published in Great Britain in 2019 by
Kyle Books, an imprint of Kyle Cathie Ltd
Carmelite House
50 Victoria Embankment
London EC4Y 0DZ

www.kylebooks.co.uk

ISBN: 978 0 85783 5 239

Distributed in the US by Hachette Book Group, 1290 Avenue of the Americas,
4th and 5th Floors, New York, NY 10104

Distributed in Canada by Canadian Manda Group, 664 Annette St., Toronto,
Ontario, Canada M6S 2C8

Publisher: Joanna Copestick
Editorial Director: Judith Hannam
Editor: Tara O'Sullivan
Editorial Assistant: Sarah Kyle
Designer: Paul Palmer-Edwards
Production: Nic Jones

A Cataloguing in Publication record for this title is available from the British Library

Printed and bound in UK

10 9 8 7 6 5 4 3 2 1

CONTENTS

PROLOGUE

I'm 15 metres underground in cellars that were dug in the fourteenth century. This far below ground it's freezing cold. The air is sweet with fermentation, woody with the aromas of old oak barrels and, thanks to a quirk in the old ventilation system that has a pipe next to a log-fired kiln, it also smells smoky. The walls around me are bright white, the wet floor is a deep red, and blue hose pipes connect to banks of cylindrical silver tanks. In the next cellar, men in overalls and thick sweaters lift wooden barrels to fill them with beer, their heavy exhalations hanging in the still, cold air. There must be a hundred or more of these barrels, all painted red around the rim with the word "Schlenkerla" branded onto them.

These cellars are dug deep into Stephensburg, a hill in the Franconian city of Bamberg, a few hours north of Munich. They've been used to store beer at a naturally low temperature for hundreds of years. Matthias Trum, the sixth-generation owner of Brauerei Heller, better known as Schlenkerla, opens a tap on the side of a 5,000-litre tank and pours me a glass of beer.

It's deep brown and cloudy, and a thick cream-coloured foam rises from it. It's smooth, robust, caramelized like charred dark fruits, and it's really, really smoky. Smoky like glowing wood embers, like your jacket the morning after a bonfire, like sausages on a barbecue, like your beer has been set on fire. Not many beers taste like this.

After climbing a long and steep rock staircase, Matthias shows me why the beer is so smoky: they make their own malted barley and it's heated directly by burning beechwood fires, with the malt sucking up the smoke. Hundreds of years ago, most malt was made this way, meaning most beer was smoky. Today malt is kilned with indirect heat and without fire and smoke. Schlenkerla maintains the traditional, old process.

Later I walk back down the hill on a snowy January afternoon to the brewery's tavern in the middle of the town. With its black-and-white medieval front and dark-green window shutters, this has been a tavern since 1405, and by 1485 a barrel-making cooper lived there, meaning brewing probably also took place. The beer was brewed in the tavern and then transported in barrels up to the cellars in the hill where it was fermented and stored in the cold, sometimes for several months, before being taken back to the tavern to be drunk. In this part of Germany, long, cold storing was the normal way of making the everyday beers – and they made what we'd now call "lager" beers.

The German word for "to store" is *lagern* – and these beers were "lagered". It's believed the process of putting beer in cold cellars underground started somewhere around what's now Franconia or towards the border of Bavaria and Bohemia to the east. Cold lagered beer was born in a cellar in this specific part of the world, where the cold temperature is just as important as the lagering – the natural refrigeration left a better-tasting and more consistent beer than one stored in ever-changing ambient conditions. The only place that was reliably cold year-round were underground cellars.

Schlenkerla has been using cellars dug into the hillsides for centuries, and their process of brewing in the tavern and then taking the beer up the hill continued in more or less the same way (certainly from after the 1670s, anyway) until the 1930s, when the brewhouse was moved to above the cellars, making the tavern just the place for eating and drinking.

Today the tavern feels like a place where time has stopped: it's paused a few centuries ago, somewhere after midday and before midnight (it's impossible to tell when you're in here). It's handsomely cathedral-like, cloistered with dark wood and white walls; the grey stone floors have been worn shiny; beechwood burns in the fireplaces; the bar has a copper surface with two wooden barrels on it, both tilted, and one has a burnished gold tap in its round belly. Those barrels had been filled in the brewery cellars and brought down here to be drunk.

I get a half-litre of their Rauchbier Märzen. *Rauchbier* means "smoke beer", while Märzen has its origins as a beer brewed in March and then stored in cold cellars, emerging in September or October, transformed by its time underground. It's very dark-brown-maroon in the glass, almost opaque. The smoke is intense: evocative and ethereal as an aroma, but challenging, unusual and unexpected in a beer. It's full-bodied and smooth, not light and fizzy. It's cool, not cold. It's malty like toasted bread, fruity like roasted plums. It's more filling than refreshing and it's satiating in a savoury, wood-smoked, umami kind of way, which makes it more like a foodstuff than a quenching beer.

Say the word "beer" to most people and they picture a glass of sparkling, golden yellow liquid with a bright white foam on top. That's your quintessential glass of modern lager, a drink that's refreshingly simple, clean, balanced and usually served cold and fizzy. But this dark, smooth, nourishing Rauchbier is also a lager, and 500 years ago this is what all lagers might have been like.

This book is a search for the answers to several questions: what are the earliest origins of lager? Why and how did it go from smoky and dark to crisp and yellow? Why and how was pale lager able to become a drink that's brewed and drunk everywhere in the world? Bamberg is an epicentre of lager, a city of old traditions and also modern brewing, and a place where we can see the trajectory of lager's history in tight focus. It's the perfect starting point for me to learn the story of this great drink.

By the end of my second glass of Schlenkerla's Rauchbier the smoke seems to have spread from my glass and into the air around me. My senses have been filled with the wonderful aromas of wood smoke, and I'm wrapped in a cosy blanket of the tavern's wood-fired warmth. I've gone from being challenged by the taste to craving more, but there are other beers I want to drink in Bamberg, a city with nine breweries.

I walk from the centre of the old part of Bamberg and head east. I love this town. It has cobbled old streets in a medieval layout, there's a market square, the buildings have black-and-white facades and orange roofs, there's a large cathedral and old monastery (where Bamberg's first brewery was located as early as 1015 – it now houses the Franconian Brewery Museum). Seven hills lead in and out (it's a Franconian Rome), two rivers converge, and above one of them sits the most picturesque sight in the city: the old town hall, a chocolate-box building hanging off a bridge and over the river.

Bamberg is surrounded by natural advantages for brewing. Barley grows all around this part of Germany, and today there are two major maltings in the town, taking that local barley and transforming it into different malts (two breweries – Schlenkerla and Spezial – also make their own). Hop fields are to the south, and bales of hops from the harvest used to be distributed regionally from Bamberg. If it's not a field of barley or hops then it's probably a forest, providing wood for brewing vessels, barrels and the fuel to run the brewhouses. In those seven hills, cellars were dug. There's good, clean brewing water in Bamberg, while the rivers provided a distribution network. And nearby lakes froze in winter, giving ice to further cool the cellars.

Mahrs Bräu is my next stop. Since 1895 it's been in the Michel family, and it's been a brewery since 1670 where, like Schlenkerla, they had cellars dug into Stephensberg. The brewery and tavern are next to each other, and I can smell the brew as I push through a heavy door into a traditional taproom with dark wooden floors, wood-panelled walls with stags' heads on them, and a wood fire.

There are three wooden barrels behind the bar. I take a beer called aU, a name shortened colloquially from "Ungespundet".[1]

---

1 It's pronounced as if to say "I'd like a U" (that's not "ay you", it's "ah oooh"). This is made more understandable when you see that the beer's full name is sometimes written as *Mahrs Bräu Kellerbier*

A chunky glass of a hazy amber lager with smooth white foam is placed in front of me. The man on the table next to me is served an aU at the same time. He lifts up his glass, looks at it intently, lovingly, admiring the glowing colour. He smiles, takes one gulp, then a second, sinking a third of his beer before smacking his lips and letting out a deeply satisfied and seemingly involuntary sigh of pleasure. My reaction is exactly the same.

This is another beer that's not much like the lagers the world is familiar with. It's robust in both malt and hop, toasty, a little sweet, smooth, medium-bodied and bitter. If the smoky Schlenkerla Rauchbier Märzen tastes something like lager 500 years ago, this amber aU represents the second evolution – the revolution of lager – from the middle of the 1800s, as lager started to get lighter in colour and lost its smokiness. It's a wonderful beer, and it's easy to see how drinkers might have moved from the heavier and more filling smoky dark lagers to this leaner and cleaner one.

Lagers then transformed again, and by the end of the nineteenth century were even lighter and brighter, influenced by the Pilsner beers of Pilsen in nearby Bohemia, now the Czech Republic. Mahrs brew a Pils, so to drink through lager's chronological history, I order one of them.

It's a brilliant golden colour with a thick cloud-like white foam. It's elegantly fruity and floral with aromatic German hops. It's gentle in carbonation, then dry and bitter. Anyone in the world could pick up this golden lager and understand it, even if it has a fuller flavour and aroma than most Pilsners.

This kind of simple, refreshing pale beer is what lager is to most people, and there's an assumption that lager has always been this way, but those cold, fizzy, yellow beers are a modern taste. Even in the middle and later decades of the nineteenth century lager remained relatively dark and sweet; when lager was first brewed domestically in North America it would've been dark and sweet; when it was first brewed in Britain or Brazil or Japan it was dark and sweet. Those bright, light, golden brews were arguably pioneered not in its birthplaces of Bavaria or Bohemia but in cities like St Louis or Milwaukee or even Mexico City or Tokyo or Amsterdam: as it travelled, and time passed, beer changed.

For much of beer's 10,000-year history it was seen as a kind of sustenance, an additional liquid supplement to a limited diet, and drunk more for nutritious value than to get you drunk (there was schnapps or cheap spirits for that). As food got lighter and more varied, and as people could afford a more diverse diet, we came to drink more for the pleasure of the liquid itself, and came to

---

Ungespundet-Lager Hefetrüb. The *Ungespundet* part of the name means "unbunged" and comes from the time when wooden barrels would've been filled in the cold cellar and bunged shut to allow carbonation to build in the barrel; an unbunged beer would have had a gentler carbonation. *aU* is a classic kind of *Kellerbier*, or cellar beer, which is popular in this region and originated as a beer drawn directly from the cellars, where it was fresh and usually a little cloudy with yeast.

value something lighter. It's like bread: the dense, dark loaves of the eighteenth century were heavy with calories, but when we could get those calories from elsewhere the bread got lighter. Heavy, darker beers transformed into golden, refreshing ones around the turn of the twentieth century.

Before lager was widely drunk, beer around the world was predominantly British-influenced ale, which was typically strong in flavour and alcohol content. As lager became popular, it changed what "beer" was to most drinkers. This leads us to defining what lager is.

LAGER VERSUS ALE

All beer is beer, whether it's pale ale or stout or Pilsner or wheat beer or whatever else. Beer is the top of the family tree, which can be split into three, with many different beer styles branching out from each.

Lager is a whole family of styles, including Pilsner, pale Helles, dark Dunkel, smoky Rauchbier, dry Asian lagers. American lager is its own style (think Budweiser), as is the hoppy New Zealand Pilsner or the amber-coloured lagers of Mexico. There are dozens of types of lager, and what specifically makes them a lager is the particular species of yeast used to brew it. That yeast is known as *saccharomyces pastorianus* (or *saccharomyces carlsbergenis*, which is named after Carlsberg brewery, while *pastorianus* is named after Louis Pasteur – we'll see why later). There are numerous strains of *S. pastorianus*, and in simple terms the yeast prefers to work in cold conditions and was once notable for being "bottom-fermenting" or "lower fermenting", which makes more sense when we look at "top-fermenting" ale yeasts.

Ale is another family, and within that family tree are stouts (like Guinness). There are white ales, golden ales, IPAs, red ales, brown ales, wheat beers, most Belgian beers. Like lager, it's a particular species of yeast, known as *saccharomyces cerevisiae*,[2] which makes it an ale. There are many strains of *S. cerevisiae*, and the yeast prefers to work in ambient and warmer conditions and would rise as thick foam to the top of the fermentation vessel, giving it the classification of "top-fermenting". Lager yeast wasn't visibly active on the top of the vessel, hence being called "lower fermenting."

The third family is more complicated, but we'll call it "sour" or "wild", because it includes beers that are often intentionally sour. These will be made with

---

2 This is a family of many different yeast strains. Some can be used to make beer; others make bread, wine, *sake* and to produce industrial ethanol, which might be used in all sorts of things, ranging from hand sanitizer to rocket fuel. *Saccharomyces* translates as "sugar fungus", with the name relating to yeast that consumes sugars and turns them into alcohol.

wild yeasts (a primary one is known as *brettanomyces*) and bacteria (the same kind of bacteria that makes yogurt tangy), often in a "mixed fermentation": a variety of different yeasts in the same beer. If lager is bottom-fermenting and ale is top-fermenting then "wild" goes in all sorts of different directions, and has a kind of hard-to-control and -understand lawlessness.

Once upon a time all beer was "mixed fermentation", meaning it was made with numerous strains of yeast and possibly bacteria. It was typically drunk young – a week or two after brewing – before sourness or unwanted funky flavours came through. It was only late in the nineteenth century that technology and science allowed for "pure" fermentation with a single strain of healthy yeast, giving a more useful distinction of lager and ale. For the purpose of this book we can mostly forget about wild beer.

At its simplest, three things define a lager: a specific kind of brewing yeast, cold temperatures and being long-stored or long-"lagered".

Early Bavarian beers were brewed in similar ways to British ales: brewers mixed malt and water in a wooden vessel, drawing sweetness, colour and flavour from the grain, before moving the sweet "wort" into a copper pan and boiling it with bitter and aromatic hops. Then the bitter-sweet liquid moved into large, open-topped wooden tuns to ferment. This is where lager differed from ale because it fermented underground in the cold (8°C/46°F) for a week or two (ale fermented quicker in warmer temperatures) and then it was transferred even deeper underground where it was even colder (0–4°C/32–39°F). It was there stored in large enclosed wooden lagering barrels, sometimes big enough to hold up to 5,000 litres in each, and it was lagered for three to ten months. When the beer was ready it was poured into smaller wooden barrels to go to the tavern.

Long-storage wasn't unique to Bavaria, and British brewers had huge wooden vats (bigger-than-your-house-huge, capable of holding millions of pints in each) in which they left their ale for many months before transferring it to smaller wooden barrels to serve from. Storing beer was important to allow the flavours to mature, softening the rough edges of its rudimentary production. The important difference between the old British ales and the Bavarian lagers is that the Bavarians deliberately tried to keep their beer cold in the underground cellars.

Before beer production became commercial, most cellars were just underneath houses but, as brewing increased in scale, the cellars came to be built in hillsides or beneath large areas of open land. The natural temperature of these cellars or caves was 8°C (46°F), ideal for the special kind of yeast that had evolved in the region.

Yeast is temperamental when it comes to temperature, with ale yeast preferring warmer conditions than the cold-loving lager yeasts. Historically, there was a mixed culture of yeast and bacteria in all beers and so when brewers started digging cellars, a Darwinian survival of the fittest took over: the yeast that liked being cold thrived, while the warm-loving yeasts and bacteria went into hibernation. (This is especially important in relation to the bacteria, as at low temperatures it was less likely to turn a beer sour – just as food stays fresher in a refrigerator compared to when it's left out in the kitchen.) Nature was then nurtured by the brewers, who deliberately selected yeast from good barrels of beer to be re-used. Over time, the warm-loving yeasts were domesticated out of the beers of Bavaria.

The combination of special cold-loving, bottom-fermenting yeast and cold cellars became the standard way of fermenting beer in Bavaria – but *only* in and around Bavaria until well into the nineteenth century, with the rest of the beer-brewing countries making ale styles in ambient temperatures. Then lager production (at this time it was still mostly dark and sweet, but no longer smoky) moved through central Europe, where new kinds of lagers were made, like the particularly popular pale and bitter Pilsners. It's from there that lager brewing and drinking began to dramatically increase. It was made in northern Europe, the US, South America, southeast Asia and Australia, and everywhere it went it came to replace old-style ales. By the end of the twentieth century something like 90 per cent of all beer was lager. Today lager is the world's most global drink, brewed in virtually every country, and that simultaneously makes it the most local drink, with everywhere having its own lager.

THE WORLD'S LOCAL DRINK

We can effectively split lager's lifespan into three distinct phases. Pre-industrialization (for lager that means before the 1830s), which was a few hundred years of localized, empirical and idiosyncratic production, often led by monks and kings, where the practice of storing it gave birth to cold-lagered beers. Then from the early 1830s to the late 1880s were six decades of industrial, technical and scientific developments led by private brewers who became incredibly wealthy industrialists, building palaces and empires of liquid gold, who set the direction for the future of consistent, quality-led, large-scale global lager brewing, which would progress into the twentieth century. The third phase came from the 1950s onwards. The world had changed, it had modernized, and beer's development was now shaped more by what was happening in the home than the brewhouse, with suburbanization, supermarkets, car ownership, fridge-freezers, televisions and mass-marketing all changing consumer habits. Then as beer became global, the industry became marked by mergers, takeovers and consolidation, and the beer itself became increasingly less diverse, leaving the simple pale lagers that we are all familiar with.

Today's lagers are not like they were 500 years ago. The need for efficiency, volume and speed has turned a process that took seven months into one of as little as seven days. It's made dark beers light, flat beers fizzy, sweet beers dry, cloudy beers clear, and those developments allowed lager to become the most loved of drinks, and yet also one of the most misunderstood.

This is the story of how a beer brewed in a cold cellar somewhere in Bavaria became the world's favourite drink.

CHAPTER ONE

THE BIRTH OF LAGER

THE PRINCE OF BEER

"Emma, wake up!" I yell, running into the bedroom too early on a Saturday morning. "Emma, I've found someone I have to speak to about the history of lager!" – and I start listing all the things I've just pieced together about this man's incredible family history.

He's from the House of Wittelsbach, who have been making beer for over seven hundred years. His ancestor signed a law decreeing that Bavarian beer could only be made with barley, hops and water. Another ancestor banned brewing in the summer. The family opened what became the most famous pub in the world. The wedding of this man's great-great-grandfather started Oktoberfest. His family had the monopoly of wheat beer brewing in Bavaria for over two hundred years. One of their family homes had a big deer park next to it, which has since become the biggest beer garden in the world. One great-uncle, King Ludwig II, who almost bankrupted Bavaria by building castles like Neuschwanstein, the same castles that would later inspire Walt Disney, also granted university status to what is now the world's foremost brewing school, housed in the world's oldest brewery. In the late 1800s that same castle-loving great-uncle brought lederhosen – the world's greatest beer-drinking pants – back into fashion. And this man I want to meet brews beer in a castle. *An actual castle.*

By the time I've finished jumping around excitedly Emma has sort of woken up.

"Lederhosen? What?" she says, not having following much of what I've just said. "Who's he?"

"Well, that's the problem. He's the Prince of Bavaria."

****

Did he just say what I think he said?

I'm sitting outside a thirteenth-century castle, sweating in the summer's heatwave. There's a dried-up moat beneath my feet, and above me the hot July sun is barely shaded by the huge old chestnut trees. I'm drinking my third glass of dark lager, there's medieval music ringing in my ears because a loud parade has just gone past on its way to a jousting tournament,[3] I'm talking to a prince and I'm generally feeling a bit overwhelmed, so it takes a moment to process what I've just heard.

Several months earlier, after my royal realisation, I'd sent a speculative and hopeful email to König Ludwig Schloßbrauerei in Kaltenberg and requested a meeting with Prince Luitpold of Bavaria. He personally emailed me back with a suggested meeting date. And now I'm here and I've been talking to the white-haired and energetic Prince Luitpold for an hour, and we've had some beers, and I'm pretty certain he's just told me that he has a copy of the original Bavarian beer purity law in his office.

It's called the *Reinheitsgebot* – *Rhine-heights-ga-Boat*, or something like that – and learning more about it is one of the main reasons that I'm here. It was a "purity law" that said beer in Bavaria could only be brewed with barley, hops and water. Germany and great beer are synonymous, and it is this purity law that's arguably responsible for that reputation. It also, along with a later rule that prohibited brewing in the summer, had the knock-on impact of making lager the beer of Bavaria: lager, or bottom-fermented beer, would be theirs alone for over three hundred years before every other nation in the world would start to produce their own versions of this Bavarian drink. The *Reinheitsgebot* is one of the most important documents in the history of brewing. And he has a copy upstairs?

"Can I see it?" I blurt out excitedly.

The Prince leads me through the courtyard of Kaltenberg Castle. Right now there are people dressed in full suits of armour with maidens swooning around them, which makes this moment even more surreal. The Prince lives in this castle and he's brewed beer here since the 1970s (though I don't think the maidens are perpetually swooning around).

We walk up an iron staircase, down a long white corridor with a stone floor, towards a dark, heavy, ornate door, which creaks open in exactly the way you'd expect a very old castle door to creak.

I spin inside the Prince's office, which looks like the kind of turret where the Princess sleeps, only it's lined with bookcases and beer memorabilia. It is a uniquely beer-specific fairy tale. This is unreal, I think to myself exactly as I realize I wasn't supposed to actually go inside his office, and that he's ushering me down another stone-floored corridor and into a room with a large wooden

---

3   I'm at their annual *Ritterturnier* (the Knights' Tournament), a medieval festival that takes place in the castle grounds over three weekends in July. It's bonkers. They've even built a large stadium just for the jousting. There are old crafts on display, they sell dark beer from large clay mugs, and the food is mainly roasted meat.

table, not quite the kind where the King sits at one end and the Queen at the other and they eat grandiose banquets, but similar, just with more beer stuff and brewing awards. Prince Luitpold places a heavy, thick, wide, worn-edged grey-bound book on the table.

This is not what I was expecting to see.

He opens to the first page, a black-and-white line illustration of two men in full armour holding a coat of arms. These are Prince Luitpold's ancestors: Duke Wilhem IV, who signed the law, and Duke Louis X, his brother and co-regent. Red script at the top of the page announces that this is the Land Ordinance of Upper and Lower Bavaria from 1516.

He turns through the pages and pages of script. I thought this was just a single-page beer law, so I'm confused about why it's such a big book. I explain that the image I have of the *Reinheitsgebot* is a large scroll-like manuscript with a long title, a big wax seal, the royal signature at the bottom and a few stains that look like someone has rested their beer mug on it.

"That was created by marketing!" says the Prince, with an I've-heard-that-one-before kind of laugh.

"When parts of Bavaria merged in the early 1500s", he explains, "they had to make a new law book, which was printed and handed out to all the courts." He turns to a random page: "This rule is about the accounting of the church." He turns more pages, scanning the script: "This is how to prepare rabbits and small animals . . . how to colour your clothes, to dye them . . . making saddles . . ." The beer law was just one small law in a big book full of all kinds of different laws or activities important at the time of creating the new region of Bavaria. It wasn't even called the *Reinheitsgebot* until 1919, and it wasn't until several decades after that that it became a marketable tradition.

"Here it is," says the Prince, opening out a double page of handsomely hand-inked text. "It says 'How beer shall be served and brewed in summer and winter in the countryside.' That's the title of this law.

"It starts about the price of beer. This is mostly what the law is about. From St Michael's Day to St George's Day one *maß* [a little over a modern litre] or one *kopf* [a bowl-shaped container a little smaller than one *maß*], is not to exceed one *Pfennig*. And then in summer it shouldn't be more than two *Pfennig*." His finger moves down a paragraph. "Look here: *gersten, hopffen und wasser . . .*"

That's barley, hops and water, and it says that in Bavaria, beer can only be brewed with those three ingredients. It's a very simple law that sought to make beer a better, safer and more reliable drink in terms of ingredients and price, and it's probably the most important document in the history of German brewing: no mandate of beer is as well known as this around the world.

But the *Reinheitsgebot* wasn't a magical moment that somehow created lager. It didn't give a recipe; it didn't give any other regulations about how the beer should be made or served or anything else; it didn't even include yeast, an essential ingredient in beer. What it did do was define beer at a time when it had no real definition. It also ensured that brewers utilized the processes and conditions that best suited the development of lager.

Lagered beers – beers stored in cool cellars for an extended time – were brewed at least two hundred years before the *Reinheitsgebot* was signed, and made somewhere between the western edge of Bohemia and Nuremberg in what's now Franconia, north Bavaria. So the purity law didn't lead to the first lager being brewed, it didn't create a revolution of brewing and it didn't have an impact outside of Bavaria – it *wouldn't* have an impact outside of Bavaria until the middle of the nineteenth century. But it did make lagered beers the beers of that region.

Before we get to the hows and whys of that, let's look at what beer was like before the 1500s.

BEER BEFORE LAGER

Beer links all the way back to the beginning of civilization, around 10,000 years ago, and it shares a parallel history with farming. Among the earliest crops planted were grains. If you had grain and water you could turn it into three important foodstuffs based on how much water you mixed with the crushed grain: a small amount of water made a dough for bread or a kind of biscuit; a little more water gave a porridge-like consistency; even more water and you got a liquid, and in that liquid were lots of sugars that airborne yeast would ferment into alcohol. This beer was not golden, clear and fizzy, nor was it served cold: it would likely have been chunky like a barley soup and probably not very alcoholic, as it would've been drunk fresh before any sourness developed.

I'm not going to go into much more of the really old history, or even the stories of the Mesopotamians or Egyptians (the first great brewing cultures), because so much stuff happened in those ancient years and much of it is unknown or irrelevant to lager, so instead we can jump to around the twelfth century.

In Europe in the early Middle Ages, beer was brewed almost exclusively in the home and by women. Some larger estates, like monasteries, royal residences and the homes of noblemen, had breweries that produced beer for their household and staff, though the wealthy were just as likely to be drinking wine. It's the monasteries we're most interested in to begin with.

Monks were the first to establish proper processes and principles for brewing, and monasteries were the only places where brewing took place on any kind of commercial scale, with the monks brewing for themselves, their guests and for pilgrims. Monastic brewing is how several of Bavaria's most famous breweries began – Weihenstephan in Freising, Augustiner and Paulaner in Munich – and the name Munich is a derivation from "near the monks", showing their importance to the development of the city.

In *Beeronomics*, Johan Swinnen suggests the monasteries were "glorified frat houses": all the guys together, drinking several litres of beer a day. That beer gave additional nutrition and flavour to the monks' diets, it tasted good (certainly better than water) and it had spiritual and medicinal roles. You might not think about heading to a monastery today to get a beer (a few Belgian monasteries aside), but hundreds of years ago, it was the place to go.

It was European monks who really systematized the brewing process, through, for example, labour separation, with malting being done by a professional, and the job of the brewer often combining with the craft of the cooper, which made sense when the brewing vessels, the fermentation vessels and the barrels for storing and serving the beer were all made of wood.

In the thirteenth century, copper began to become an important brewing material for boiling the liquid (and remained so until overtaken by stainless steel in the twentieth century). Copper is malleable, can be seamlessly formed (meaning no leaks) into large pans and conducts heat well. Some early copper pans were large enough initially to brew around 1,000 litres at a time. By the 1500s this capacity had quadrupled (in 1540 one copper in Hamburg held 8,750 litres), and in the mid-1800s a single copper was capable of making over 25,000 litres at a time.

The set-up of a monastic brewery from the 1400s is shown in numerous works of art. A robed brewing monk stirs a large copper cauldron filled with bubbling liquid that sits on a brick hearth and is lit directly by a wood fire. Next to him are wooden vessels shaped like buckets, in which the grain and water have probably been steeped, somewhere nearby (though not always shown) are open wooden barrels for fermenting the beer, and there are closed barrels for storing or serving it. It was a simple process, and since then little has fundamentally changed.

From around the year 1300, as towns grew and the monasteries couldn't produce enough beer, private breweries were founded. Leuven and Antwerp were primary brewing cities in Belgium; Gouda, in the Netherlands, had 350 breweries in 1480; Hamburg and Bremen were large brewing cities and also exported a large amount of beer. Hamburg in particular was *the* beer city of the fourteenth century and almost half of all "master artisans" registered in the city were brewers. Brewers' guilds had formed, too. Munich had one by 1280, as did other cities, and this is a clear sign of how brewing was beginning to professionalize and become profitable as a secular occupation.

Beer then would've varied enormously, but several basic types existed, with much regional variation: brown or red beer was made with roasted barley malt and would likely have been sweet, tart, and smoky from the malt, which was made over wood fire; white beer was typically made with air-dried barley malt, so was pale and not smoky, as well as lighter in colour, sweet, and somewhere between tart and acidic; and wheat beers would have been brewed mostly with wheat, probably making them quite thick and sweet and also tart.

Beer didn't always contain hops, and other herbs and spices were often used in their place, especially (around the Middle Ages, anyway) in the wheat beers of Northern Europe. An important transition in brewing would be marked by the exclusive use of hops, which is what happened between the thirteenth and seventeenth centuries. This was a defining moment in beer's history, one comparable to the introduction of formal brewing processes in the monasteries, and thanks to the anti-bacterial qualities in hops, beer could last for longer without souring.

Between the fifteenth and seventeenth centuries, beer began to have a larger and more central role in the daily diet, with everyone from "monks and nuns to small children to building labourers" drinking beer, as Richard Unger puts it in Swinnen's *The Economics of Beer*. Alcohol in general was used by the working classes as pleasing relief after tiring work, while the spread of taverns and inns led to socializing with food and drink as one of the few leisure activities. Beer was considered a foodstuff, and in North Germany in the mid-fourteenth century it was promoted with the slogan, "A Beer Equals Half a Meal."

People also drank to get drunk: "The sixteenth century is considered by all sources to be the greatest period of drunkenness in German history," says Gregory Austin in *Alcohol in Western Society from Antiquity to 1800*. In Hamburg, a city with 520 professional brewers in 1500, the average annual consumption of beer was 320 litres; by 1615 this had more than doubled to 700.

It is "no exaggeration to say that alcohol was the anaesthetic of the pre-industrial workplace," writes Austin. "Indeed, far from undermining productivity, it may even have boosted output by inuring the work force against fatigue of working from sun-up to sundown in conditions of unspeakable misery." Work was in fields, all year round; it was strenuous, with long numbing hours, and in the home there was rarely any heating apart from the hearth. Beer and other alcohol made the hardships of life a bit more bearable.

Brewing was still a rudimentary endeavour, more about following passed-along processes than understanding exactly what was happening: the methods of production were much the same in 1650 as in 1450; there was just an increase in scale. Brewing was practical but not yet scientific, but enough was known about it to give us some clues about production, specifically in relation to how lager and lagering developed, and the awareness of specific yeast types.

The brewing ordinances of Nuremberg of 1303–25 indicate that a dark, hopped, bottom-fermented beer was brewed in Franconia at the beginning of the fourteenth century, and that bottom fermentation had probably been known in Bavaria since the beginning of the fifteenth century, possibly brought there from Cheb on the Franconia–Bohemia border. It's believed that bottom-fermentation spread down through Bavaria, and by the fifteenth century it was becoming a more standard way of brewing.

In 1420, Munich declared that all beer must be well fermented by top-fermentation and not sold for seven days, which tells us two things: they distinguished between top- and bottom-fermentation, and they sold top-fermented beer young, but not *too* young. That same year, a brewer got permission to use bottom-fermenting yeast and that gives us one of the earliest known mentions of bottom-fermenting yeast.

In Hamburg in 1483 there was a regulation that said beer had to leave the brewer's cellar within eight days of being put into barrels (reduced to three days in summer): this was to ensure a proper fermentation, but also that it be drunk before it went sour. Again, we learn two things: they understood that warm weather made the beer go sour quicker and, because of the short timings, we can assume they were brewing top-fermented beers at ambient temperatures.

The city of Nabburg, east of Nuremberg, gives us another early mention of lager yeast, as Corran notes in *A History of Brewing*: "One brews the warm or top fermentation; but first in 1474 one attempted to brew by the cold bottom fermentation and to preserve part of the brew for the summer." This yet again tells us two things: they know that bottom fermentation and cold work together, and they knew to store the beer. This is one of the first references to mention the yeast, the cold temperature *and* maturation, the three key processes in lager brewing.

All of this leads to one big question: why did they need a purity law at all?

BARLEY, HOPS, WATER . . . AND OX BLADDER?

The *Reinheitsgebot* wasn't the first German beer purity law.

In 1156, a decree was passed in Augsburg by Emperor Frederick Barbarossa (who's not one of Prince Luitpold's ancestors) declaring that "a brewer who makes bad beer or pours an unjust measure shall be punished: his beer shall be destroyed or distributed at no charge to the poor." In 1293, the city of Nuremberg instituted a purity law, with several other cities adding them in the fourteenth century.

In 1363, Munich City Council began to supervise and regulate brewing throughout the city, partly to make sure beer was produced within the city and so could be taxed, but also to ensure it was healthy. In 1447, the "Munich purity law" ordered that brewers may use only barley, hops and water for their beers – this has become one of the world's longest-running food laws. In 1469, a Regensburg ruling said only barley malt, water and hops for beer.

In 1487, the ruler of Bavaria-Munich,[4] Duke Albrecht IV, made brewers in his duchy swear on a public oath to the Munich purity law of 1447; this was the first major impact that the House of Wittelsbach had had on beer quality. At that time the price was also fixed, and a team of beer inspectors had the role of inspecting inns or taverns to ensure they were complying. Altogether this ruling brought control of brewing under the city's authorities.

****

In 1493, Duke George of Bavaria-Landshut instituted a *Biersatzordnung*, or "beer regulation", to his duchy, and included malt in it, which therefore permitted the use of wheat (malt is the product of the malting process and it's commonly done to barley and wheat). His fourteen-page law was much more detailed than the 1447 or the 1516 laws, and it covered beer, wine and mead, and looked to control the ingredients, the quality, the price and the taxes, and even included details like how to fill a barrel with beer. The law excluded yeast from the ingredient list but it didn't leave it out completely, explaining how brewers could sell their yeast, known as "germ", and there was a distinction made between beer yeast and wine yeast. The punishment for not following any of these rules was "pain of chastisement of body and goods".

In 1503, Duke George died with no heir, which triggered the Landshut War of Succession. This ended in 1505, with the result that Duke Albrecht IV of Bavaria-Munich was able to reunite the divided Bavaria (minus a few southern districts and a new duchy of Palatinate-Neuburg), making one new duchy with Munich as its capital.

---

4 Bavaria had been split up and divided and passed around the ruling Wittelsbach family many times, with each duchy ruled separately and passing to the male heir. The great dynasty family ruled in Bavaria from 1180 until 1918, and there's a lot of family history I'll overlook, but important for this story is that at the end of the 1400s Bavaria had numerous divisions (Munich, Landshut, Ingolstadt and Straubing), but when they were all eventually brought together a new law book was necessary.

When Duke Albrecht IV died in 1508, his fifteen-year-old son Wilhelm IV ascended the throne of the newly-reformed Bavaria, and over the next years would work on a new law book. It's this book, signed and distributed in 1516, which had the famous beer purity law inside of it. Wilhelm IV is thought to have compared his father's Munich purity law to the more extensive Landshut one and had to pick one of them: he went with his father's simpler one, and this became the new Bavarian law.

The important words in the *Reinheitsgebot* regarding the ingredients are these: "We wish to emphasize that in future in all cities, markets and in the country, the only ingredients used for the brewing of beer must be barley, hops and water."

That one small line in a large law book written 500 years ago came to have a big impact on brewing and what we drink today, both in Germany and around the world. It's the "barley, hops and water" part that is the famous element, though as we've seen the law also concerns itself with the price of beer and how it changes with the brewing seasons. It also gives the punishment for any law-breaking, whether by brewer or tavern owner: "Anyone who knowingly violates this decree shall be punished by the court by having each of these beer barrels removed from his possession."

The law only applied in Bavaria, with the rest of what we now call Germany able to brew with whatever ingredients it wanted. So why did Bavaria want or need to implement this law?

"It was for protection," says Prince Luitpold. "It was protecting bread from beer production. It was protecting people from poisonous plants. And it was protecting people from the price of beer." (It also, more cynically, was important for controlling tax and the trade of important raw ingredients).

By declaring that only barley was to be used in beer, the law saved wheat for baking bread, creating a more stable price for two staple foodstuffs in the early sixteenth century. "In Bavaria, beer is not drunk," it was said: "beer is eaten." This was especially so among the lower classes: by the mid-1840s it was estimated that at least 40,000 people in and around Munich – about half the population – got their nutrition primarily from beer and bread. By choosing barley, the lawmakers were effectively selecting bottom-fermentation, as barley beers were typically made with bottom-fermenting yeast and stored in cellars.

The protection against poison was pertinent, because beer was an everyday and all-day drink of Bavaria, where the combination of water, barley and hops tasted better and was more nutritious (and potentially less contaminated) than water alone, so a guarantee of quality for this staple liquid was vital.

"The use of hops in beer was one of the most important events," says Richard Unger in *Beer in the Middle Ages and the Renaissance*. "When brewers learned to do this on a large scale, it transformed the industry," because alongside the bitterness and flavour hops give to beer, their anti-bacterial qualities meant that a hopped beer would last longer than an unhopped one.[5] Hops allowed beer to become one of "the few foods that would keep for months without becoming inedible". And being left for months was important for the production of lager.

Before hops, anything could've gone into a brew, and many different ingredients were added to create a more powerful taste: bog myrtle, mugwort, yarrow, wild rosemary, carrot seeds, lavender, acorns, juniper, marjoram, thyme, plums, fir rind, burnet, elderflowers, rose hips, honey, ginger, gentian roots, bitter oranges, lemons, oregano and cardamom, often used with hops as part of a larger spice mix (known as "gruit", this spice mix was tightly controlled in Northern Europe, and brewers had to buy it from a central gruit merchant). Tavern owners were also known to spice their beers using anything from chicory to caraway seeds if they were turning sour.

But not all the things added to beer were delicious. Some were dangerous or disgusting, while brewers and publicans sometimes attempted to induce a greater intoxicating effect with potentially poisonous, psychotropic or hallucinogenic ingredients like henbane, mandrake, resinous pinewood soot, hemp, poppy, ivy, wormwood, and even the gall bladder of ox.

According to the doctor Johan Peter Frank, writing in Mannheim in 1783, "the wickedness of [tavern owners] knew but few bounds. They made beer more potent by adding poppy or tobacco and made stale beer palatable with every kind of noxious trick, all with devastating effects on the health of the population at large." Liberally adulterating a staple daily drink made it unsafe for a significant amount of the population, underlining the need for the purity laws.

As for water, you can't make beer without it. There's no alternative liquid option, and the water source was simply whatever could be drawn from the local wells. As this was sometimes of dubious healthfulness, cities became more aware of clean drinking liquids like beer, which had been boiled and therefore sterilized during its production.[6]

The Bavarian law's wording doesn't mention yeast, and there's a fallacy that brewers didn't know about yeast at this time. That's not true: we've already seen definite mentions of brewing yeast in the fourteenth and fifteenth centuries, when they already had a basic understanding of how it behaved. One theory for its omission is that brewers possibly thought it didn't remain in the beer, being either

---

5 The anti-bacterial qualities of hops are interesting. They can't stop all bacteria, meaning that the beer will eventually go sour, but they can neutralize the really bad varieties that could be potentially dangerous to health. In the Middle Ages, hops were sometimes added to wine to stop it going sour.

scooped off the top of the fermentation vessel (in top-fermenting ale) or left in the bottom (with bottom-fermenting lager). But this is just a conjecture and not proven – and in any case it would have been an incorrect belief, as the yeast would almost certainly have found its way into the mug of beer when someone drank it.

Another reason we know German brewers had at least a basic understanding of yeast is because of Hugh Hefner, the founder of *Playboy* magazine.

Sort of, anyway. Many surnames come from jobs, and among the most common German surnames today are Müller (miller), Schmidt (blacksmith), Schneider (tailor), Fischer (fisherman), Becker (baker), Koch (cook), Hoffmann (courtier), Wagner (wainwright), Krüger (innkeeper), and so on. The surname Hefener, or Hefner, has a direct translation as Yeaster.

The Hefener collected the *zeug* that remained at the bottom of the beer tank after fermentation. *Zeug* means "stuff", showing that the brewers back then knew something was there, and that it included yeast, but didn't quite know exactly what the rest of it was (in fact it was a mix of yeast and grain proteins and hop particles). The good yeast from a tasty batch of beer was effectively harvested and moved into the *Zeug-Wanne*, or "stuff vat", from which it could be transferred to the next batch of beer, with the Hefener or the brewer choosing the good yeast to re-use in the next batch. This nurtured selection would combine with the cold natural environment to become an important factor in the development of lager. Nuremberg even had a guild of Hefeners who were responsible for maintaining a stock of (likely dried) yeast over the summer when brewing was not permitted, and then providing sufficient yeast when brewing was resumed in the cooler months (we'll look at the significance of this soon).

In 1551 yeast was included in an updated version of Bavaria's beer purity law, but it would be more than 300 years before scientists began to properly understand brewing yeast, how it worked and how to control it. When finally they did it would become the greatest discovery in beer's 10,000-year history – we'll come to that later.

Lager existed before the *Reinheitsgebot* was signed, but so did many other kinds of beers in the region; from 1516, that law ensured that the ingredients

---

6 This is a good time to bring up a common misconception: that people drank beer because it was safer than water. Fundamentally this is true, because when you brew beer you boil it. But think about it: if the only function is to make water safer, then they could've just boiled it. That's a lot easier than making beer, which required them to grow or buy the grain, to malt it, then crush it, then mix it with water, then boil it with hops, then add some yeast and leave it for a few days. That's hard work. Instead, people made beer because it tasted better than water, had more nutrients than just water, and got them a little bit drunk; all important things. But perhaps the more relevant reason was that by turning water (and grain and hops) into beer, it could last longer as raw ingredients: the sweetness taken from the grain turned into alcohol, which is a preservative, while hops further helped with their anti-bacterial qualities. So beer wasn't simply made to make water safe, but to keep it safe, and safe for longer.

and processes combined to make lager the beer of Bavaria. But *only* of Bavaria. Nowhere else where beer was made in significant volumes – Britain, the Netherlands, North Germany, Belgium – could you drink what we'd now call lager, making it a minuscule percentage of all beer drunk in the world. But by the 500th anniversary of the *Reinheitsgebot*, lager would account for 90 per cent of all beer in the world, with each of those countless different lagers able to be traced somehow back to Bavaria and the law issued by the House of Wittelsbach in 1516.

What the *Reinheitsgebot* did was define what a beer was in Bavaria, and by association what it couldn't be. "The purity law really was an important thing," says Prince Luitpold of his ancestors' contribution to the history of brewing, and it came "without them knowing that that was important. This is really just a law book. That's kind of an amazing thing."

But in 1553 an additional law would be written, and it would, arguably, have an even greater impact on the history of lager than the *Reinheitsgebot*.[7]

WINTERBIER AND SOMMERBIER; BRAUNBIER AND WEISSBIER

Braunbier was what everyone drank in Bavaria, with variations based on differences between the brewers: it would've had different levels of sweetness, bitterness, smokiness and alcohol (and probably acidity, too); it would've had different levels of brownness (not that anyone could see the colour through the stone mugs); it would've had differing qualities, like levels of carbonation or fullness of body, and its overall character would've been inconsistent because there was no brewing apparatus or technology to help brewers understand their beer in a scientific way.

Without science, brewers were trying to improve their processes and the quality of their beer empirically – over centuries, skills, secrets, techniques and tricks to help make tasty beers had been passed on from brewer to brewer. For our story, one of the more important discoveries was that beer tasted better when it was brewed in the cooler months, when it could be fermented at lower temperatures, and when it was then stored and matured in cold cellars for an extended period.

---

7 With rose-tinted retrospect we can think of the purity of Bavarian beer, but in fact there were numerous examples of beers made in the region using ingredients beyond water, barley, hops and yeast. There were beers with juniper and other spices; sugar and honey; oats; bitter oranges, gentian root, and more. The rules were also updated and changed a few times, including in 1551 when coriander and bay leaves were allowed by ducal decree, and then in 1616, salt, juniper and caraway seeds were accepted.

In 1553 this knowledge had become significant enough that Duke Albrecht V (the son of Duke Wilhem IV, the one who signed the *Reinheitsgebot*), formally instated a brewing season that required *Braunbier* to be brewed only between St Michael's Day and St George's Day: that is, 29 September to 23 April. This is where the cold cellars come in, since brewers needed to store large volumes of beer for potentially many months, and it leads us on to *Winterbier* and *Sommerbier*, both *Braunbiers*, using the same ingredients, just in different volumes and with differing production times.

Winterbier was brewed in the winter and then drunk in that same winter brewing season, where it was matured or lagered in the cellars for one to three months (for example, it might've been brewed in early November and drunk in late December or into January). It was matured in small barrels and drunk as a "*Schenkbier*", meaning "tap beer", for everyday and quick drinking, which made it important that the beer become bright and sparkling as quickly as possible.

Sommerbier was also brewed in the winter (since of course you could only brew in the winter), and made in the first three months of the new year, after which it was left in the cellars in large wooden barrels (up to 5,000 litres in size) for between three and nine months, making it a true "*Lagerbier*". *Sommerbier* was drunk between May and October.

Sommerbier was stronger in alcohol, drier and less sweet (probably due to the additional time for the yeast to metabolize sugar), and more heavily hopped than *Winterbier*, giving it a greater stability for its winter-long maturation (beers to be served in September were also more heavily hopped than those due for drinking in June, for example, and barrels of beer were blended in the cellars for consistency before being put into smaller barrels for serving from). *Sommerbier* was more expensive because it was stronger and generally tasted better.

Brewers had to judge their production carefully. If for whatever reason they failed to produce enough lager beer for the late spring and summer months they suffered economically. September was a challenging cross-over month where they might have run out of *Sommerbier* but had yet to start brewing their *Winterbier*.

Most cellars were roughly 10 metres underground, and at that depth you'll naturally have a constant temperature of 8°C (46°F), which is exactly the temperature that lager yeast likes to work at, and too cold for ale yeast to dominate or for bacteria to spoil the beer (8°C is also exactly the optimum temperature for drinking beer). As an additional measure to keep the cellars cool, brewers would've planted chestnut trees above them to give extra shade (and create nice gardens to sit in and drink). Later on, as production and therefore cellars grew, they had to harvest ice from lakes, ponds, canals or man-made frames, which would be left in the cellars in large blocks. This was most important in the warm months when brewing couldn't take place, because brewers had large volumes of beer in those cellars that had to remain cold when external temperatures were rising.

Whether *Winter* or *Sommer*, when the beer was ready, it was drawn from larger casks into smaller ones "which are immediately carried out to the publican, and on the same day drank by his customers: so that every publican must be supplied with beer every day from the Brewery," explains Booth in his 1834 book *The Art of Brewing* – we'll hear more from him later.

From 1850 the summer brewing prohibition was lifted, because the large-scale use of ice to cool cellars allowed greater and safer year-round brewing control, and then from the 1870s artificial refrigeration removed the need for ice altogether.[8] But in the sixteenth century all that was still a long way away.

LIQUID BREAD AND BEER RIOTS

"This beverage is a primary necessity for the Bavarian population," writes the French ambassador to Munich in 1844, and "for a large segment of the working class, beer is the principal food, and it is considered as nourishing as bread itself."

In the mid-nineteenth century, a litre mug of *Braunbier* contained around 400 calories. Beer could ease hunger with its nourishing qualities; its smokiness, bitterness and sweetness seasoned bland and repetitive meals; and drinking a litre of lager made you feel a lot better than eating half a kilogram of stodgy potatoes or dense bread.

"The whole country suffers from deficiency of nourishing and stimulating food," writes an American correspondent in Munich for *Atlantic Monthly* in 1864. "They attempt rather to allay the gnawings at their stomachs by potations of beer, and the appetite grows by what it feeds on." Even the poor, he writes, are seldom seen at their work without a mug of beer standing near them[9] . . . The most common manifestation of Bavarian beer-drinking is a perpetual tast-

---

8 The widespread use of ice meant that technically beer could've been brewed year-round, giving a consistent cold temperature, but the yeast was only one part of the problem: the other was the malt. Today, malt is made on a large scale and stored in large sacks or silos ready for use. Hundreds of years ago – even 100 years ago – the malt was prepared in the day or two before the brew took place. As part of the malting process, the grain is steeped in water and allowed to germinate, but if maltsters couldn't control the temperature of that germination it could get too warm and germinate too quickly. If it wasn't possible to make malt in the summer, you couldn't make beer.

9 This might seem comical now, but beer really was an everyday drink that people consumed in a similar way to how we drink tea, coffee or soft drinks. Intoxication wasn't the aim (in general), and they paced their drinking in the same way as we might drink a coffee every couple of hours. Plus, beer was low-alcohol and a very standard drink; if they wanted to get drunk then they'd have schnapps.

ing, and not a pouring-down of the liquid a glass at a time. These people seem to have the art of doing this thing so gradually and quietly that the soothing liquor passes gently into the circulation, and produces an effect very different from that which would result from swallowing it a glass at a draught, enabling them to drink without visible effect a much larger quantity in the aggregate. By "larger quantity" our correspondent is not being flippant, as "torrents of this foaming liquid rush daily through the channels of human bodies made originally too small to admit half the quantity," where

> A man is scarcely reckoned with real beer-drinkers until he drinks six masses [one mass is one litre] – twenty-four of our common tumblers [250ml/8.5oz each]; ten masses are not uncommon; twenty to thirty masses – eighty to one hundred and twenty of our dinner-glasses – are drunk by some.

Beer was drunk in breweries and taverns, giving the working-class communities a vital social space at a time when housing was overcrowded and grim. Beer and the tavern were simple distractions from the hardships of life.

If you wanted to fit into lower-class society you had to drink beer, but the working classes weren't earning much money, and food shortages led to food prices rising faster than salaries. In the 1840s, around half of Munich's male population (excluding day labourers, unemployed or illegal workers) worked as journeymen, primarily in building the ever-growing city. These men averaged a daily salary of 40–50 *kreuzers*, out of which they'd have to pay for accommodation, which for a single man was frequently a straw bed in a small, shared room with no windows and filled with foul air and probably some rodents, and cost 3–5 *kreuzers* a day. Beer was around six *kreuzers* per *maß*, with an unmarried journeyman likely having at least two or three a day. For food, he'd likely spend 8–10 *kreuzers* on bread and potatoes, plus maybe the occasional sausage, and smoke heavily, leaving very little spare money for anything else. Because of this, the price of beer – the *Biersatz* – was sensitive to the people who most depended upon it.

The *Biersatz* changed each season, and was determined by the grain harvest. The Interior and Finance Ministries controlled the price in order to collect the appropriate taxes (in the 1840s beer accounted for one-sixth of Bavaria's tax receipts). Typically at that time, *Winterbier* was one *kreuzer* cheaper than *Sommerbier*, but this varied from season to season. The new price would come into effect on 1 May for *Sommerbier* and 1 October for *Winterbier*. But in the spring of 1844, there was a problem.

Wages were stagnant in the city, and there had been a sustained period of tension and discontent, with many of the working classes feeling decisions were being made without their interests in mind. Journeymen and soldiers complained about the ostentatious lifestyles of the wealthy brewers, bakers, butchers and public officials. Numerous anonymous threatening letters had warned about the consequences of a price rise for *Sommerbier*. When it was announced that the price was to increase from 6 to 6.5 *kreuzer*, those threatening letters turned into a planned revolt.

1 May 1844 should've been a big celebration, because as well as the change of beer season the social event of the year was taking place: King Ludwig's daughter, Princess Hildegarde, was to be married (the King's own wedding, thirty-four years earlier, had been responsible for what became Oktoberfest). But many working-class men had no interest in the nuptials.

Later that day, according to one account, a group of soldiers were in the Maderbräu brewery on the outskirts of the city when a man named Korbinian Steiglmayer complained loudly about being asked for 26 *kreuzer* for four litres of beer, and poorly served to boot. He refused to pay. Other drinkers, threatening to destroy everything in Maderbräu unless the beer price came down and the quality improved, smashed glasses, opened the kegs and broke tables and chairs. From somewhere a whistle was blown, and all the soldiers and workers knew what that meant. Within hours around 2,000 men were rioting and attacking breweries and taverns across Munich.

They rioted for three days. Infantrymen were called in, but some of them were the ones actually fighting. "I am sure almost a third of the people were soldiers," explains a reporter in the *Northampton Mercury*, who seems incredulous that it was all about a price rise of one sixth of an English penny, but then adds that "a Bavarian gets up in the morning a beer barrel, and goes to bed a barrel of beer."

By 3 May all of Munich's thirty-three breweries had been damaged (the brewer from the Löwenbräukeller had to escape through the window of his house and climb down a sheet); even bakeries and butchers were targeted. "The Bavarians are a gruff but good-natured people and they would sooner chop firewood than start an uprising," wrote a French correspondent, "but take away or water down their beer and they will rebel far more wildly than any other people."

After the first day of rioting, the beer price had actually been lowered to six *kreuzers*, but they were fighting for more than just beer now. It was for bread and meat, too, and a general sense of inequality in the city. Finally, on 4 May, the King lowered the price of the beer even further at the Hofbräuhaus, the Royal Court's Brewery, so that "the workers and the military can afford to buy a healthy and inexpensive drink", says Attenbockum in *The Munich Hofbraühaus*.

The Hofbräuhaus was owned by the royal family and would go on to become the most famous pub in the world. We're going to drink there soon, but before we do, let's go to the most famous beer festival in the world.

OKTOBERFEST: THE MOST FAMOUS FESTIVAL IN THE WORLD

"The first Oktoberfest was the wedding party of my great-great-grandfather," says Prinz von Luitpold. Not many people can say that their great-great-grandparents once threw a party so great that people continued to celebrate it for over 200 years.

The wedding of Crown Prince Ludwig and Therese Charlotte Luise of Saxony-Hildburghausen took place on 12 October 1810, in the courtyard chapel of the royal residence. The following day, 6,000 people from the upper-middle class were invited to a dinner and dance, while for everyone else food and drink was provided at the Marienplatz, the Promenadenplatz, in the Neuhauser Gasse and at the Anger, where 32,065 bread rolls, 3,992 pounds of Swiss cheese, 400 kilos of mutton, 8,120 cervelat sausages and 13,300 pairs of smoked sausage were distributed for free, accompanied by 23,200 litres of beer and 400 litres of Austrian white wine, all while 150 musicians played. You can see why the locals might have been interested in this becoming an annual thing, but while the free food and beer was nice, the event that the majority of Münchners were really looking forward to came on 17 October.

From the 1400s and up until sometime between the 1760s and 1790, there had existed a "scarlet race" in Munich, in which the winner of a prestigious horse race won a piece of scarlet, at that time a precious colour only worn by the wealthy or royalty. It was proposed that the tradition of the scarlet race be revived for the wedding.

There were 30 horses competing on the racetrack, which was surrounded by almost all of the 40,000 population of Munich, attracted to both the race and the presence of the royal newlyweds. The 3,370m race was won in 18 minutes and 14 seconds by Franz Baumgartner (some reports say that it was his idea in the first place to hold the race).

As Dering and Eymold describe in their book *Das Oktoberfest: 1810–2010*, the week-long wedding celebration was "an all-Bavarian homage to the king" and "the national euphoria was so great that, at the suggestion of the bourgeois military, the grounds were soon named after the newly wed Crown Princess Therese" – Theresienwiese, or Therese's Meadow. Today it's colloquially known as simply Wiesn.

In 1811, the "*Oktober-Festen*" combined the horse race with an agricultural fair. "It was an exhibition of animals, an exhibition of everything that grows in the field: just a big national agricultural fair with prizes for the farmers," says Prinz Luitpold – the unspoken aim, at a time when most people just ate potatoes, to improve the quality of other produce. There was also a shooting competition, a bowling alley and wheelbarrow races. Local innkeepers put up booths around the horse track to sell beer and food to those attending.

By 1819 there were twelve beer suppliers to the festival, plus one wine grower, two coffee shops, three liquor dealers, four pastry chefs, six cooks, some bakers, a fruit dealer and women walking around selling cheese, nuts and radishes. Until the first indoor stalls came in the 1820s visitors would sit on benches outside. Soon there were also fairgrounds and attractions.

Through the 1860s beer started to become a greater focus at Oktoberfest, with people now seeing it as a festival for drinking. In 1871 Germany became a unified country, which enabled the event to grow. The following year, 1872, was the first time Oktoberfest moved forward into September, and ever since then it's finished on the first Sunday in October.

1872 was also significant for beer reasons: a special beer was sold there for the first time, although it wasn't originally supposed to be drunk there. This beer, called Märzen, was brewed in March, set down with the fresh promise of spring, and then stored through the summer to be tapped in October, emerging out of the cellars as a final and special *Sommerbier*.

It had been a hot summer and people at Oktoberfest were thirstier than usual, meaning that supplies of regular lager were low. Michael Schottenhamel, one of the tent owners, spoke to Joseph Sedlmayr of Franziskaner-Leist Brauerei, who offered him this new Märzen "brewed in Viennese style", which was paler in colour and drier to drink than the darker, fuller-bodied Munich *lagerbiers*. It was a celebratory beer worthy of Oktoberfest, but at 12 *kreuzers* a mug instead of nine *kreuzers* it was going to be much more expensive. People paid the money, and subsequently the beer was advertised as Oktoberfest-Märzenbier. It remained the main beer of the festival until the 1950s, when it got lighter.

As the festival developed through the late nineteenth century, the focus was on the Wirtsbudenring, where eighteen or twenty beer stalls were run by taverns, each one newly constructed every year by carpenters. The first *Bierburg*, or Beer Castle, was built in 1895 by the now-closed Thomasbräuerei and had a hall large enough for 800 people. The following year saw the opening of the Schottenhamel *Bierburg*. In 1907 it was decided to get rid of the ring of inns and it became a *straße* of castles; by 1910 all of the largest breweries had their own beer castles, with Pschorr Bräuerei's big enough for 12,000 people.

One of my favourite stories involves the "Bayrischer Herkules", otherwise known as Hans Steyrer. He's said to have juggled cannonballs, lifted a 500lb stone on just one finger and, using only his thumb and forefinger, lifted a 40-litre barrel of beer from the floor to the table. In 1879 he took over a tent at Oktoberfest and served "Oktoberfest Kraftbier", a play on words meaning "powerful beer", which he sold alongside powerful cheese, powerful meat and powerful broth. He also created what became a new tradition: the entry of the innkeepers.

On the first day of 1887's Oktoberfest, Steyrer paraded through the streets of Munich towards the Wiesn in a richly decorated personal flotilla of eight carriages loaded with the strong man, his family, his waitresses and his beer. His private pageant was stopped by the police, and he was charged with gross mischief and disturbing public order and security and fined 100 gold marks. He did it again the next year and soon other tent innkeepers started to arrive in the same extravagant manner. Today, on the morning of the opening ceremony of Oktoberfest, all the innkeepers arrive by horse and cart in a large parade, dragging big carriages loaded with wooden barrels on a 7-kilometre route, which takes two hours and involves 9,000 people. (Before we move on, take a moment and image search Hans Steyrer, because he had the most magnificent moustache, which flared out from the sides of his mouth like two bushy squirrel tails.)

Another lasting tradition began in 1950 when Oktoberfest properly resumed after the war. Munich's mayor, Thomas Wimmer, tapped the first barrel in the Schottenhamel tent and shouted "*O'zapft is!*", "It's tapped!" – and then everyone could start drinking. With this celebration beer became, as Jeffrey Gaab says in his history of the Hofbräuhaus, "a symbol of the renewing strength" of Munich, and Oktoberfest became the world-famous festival it is today.

O' zapft is!

The official opening still takes place in the Schottenhamel tent when, at exactly midday on the penultimate Saturday of September, the Mayor of Munich takes a heavy wooden hammer in one hand and a golden beer tap in the other, lines them up, and thumps the tap into the large barrel of Spaten beer. They then declare "*O'zapft is!*" A thunderous, booming, vibrating gun salute will be heard by everyone in Munich while the mayor is filling a large stone mug with fresh Spaten beer. And the greatest beer-drinking event begins.

Even if you've never been to Oktoberfest, you probably have an idea of what it's like: lots of people drinking large glasses of beer, pretzels, music and everyone dressed in traditional outfits – that sort of thing. What you might not appreciate is the enormity of it all.

It takes place on what used to be a wonderful meadow but is now a great slab of gravel and concrete so huge you could lay out seventy-seven football fields on it.

The *Wirtsbudenstraße* is now a 1-kilometre-long boulevard of beer running from the entrance all the way to a large Ferris wheel at the end. Along it are food vendors and stalls and the sweet smell of caramelized nuts, pretzels and doughnuts. But it's what's on either side of the *Wirtsbudenstraße* that's really important: the fourteen big tents. The word "tent" under-sells it somewhat, because the *smallest* can seat 3,000 people and the biggest, the Hofbräu-Festzelt, has space for 10,000 people – it's 85m long by 62m wide and 13m tall. Each of the fourteen tents is rented for the duration of Oktoberfest, often by a family that has run it for many generations. Each tent will only pour one type of beer, brewed especially for the festival by one of the Big Six Munich breweries (Augustiner, Hacker-Pschorr, Hofbräuhaus, Löwenbräu, Paulaner and Spaten). Märzen was the favourite beer of Oktoberfest until 1953, when the Augustiner brewery sold Wiesnedelstoff, a lighter-coloured lager that would become the new kind of *Oktoberfestbier*. Today the lager is around 6 per cent ABV and bright gold in colour, like a stronger version of a typical Munich Helles.

From waiters to beer pourers to cooks to cleaners to office staff, it takes up to 500 people to run each tent, and in total, during the sixteen days of the festival, around 13,000 people will be employed at Oktoberfest. Over six million people will drink more than seven million litres of beer, and they'll eat a lot, too. There's food in all tents, and there's over 140 food vendors around the festival. The most popular beer hall dish is *hendl*, spit-roast chicken, and around 500,000 birds are cooked and cut in half to serve a million portions each year. Hundreds of thousands of sausages are eaten, knee-knocking quantities of pig knuckles, and God-knows-how-many pretzels (but, anecdotally, you'll be lucky to find a single vegetable on the entire, enormous festival grounds).

And the beer tents only cover *half* the festival grounds; the other half is a spinning, whirling, blasting, screaming funfair of rides, amusements and arcades (don't go anywhere near them after too many beers . . .).

****

I'm here with my dad. In the last few years he's become a regular drinking buddy for me, and this is our time when we get to hang out as mates as well as father and son, and I love that. This is his first time at Oktoberfest.

We start in the Löwenbräu tent, a massive hall with a sunshine-yellow roof. Inside, the noise is amazing: in the middle of it the brass band is playing a traditional song, but that sound is overwhelmed by thousands of people chatting and laughing. On the benches lined up all the way to the back there must be 5,000 people. On either side are the beer taps, pouring from giant serving tanks (each must be refilled every night) into giant glasses, gushing with gold and then frothing over with thick, white foam. A sign on the wall says "*Bierprise*

€11.50". In 2018 it went above €11 a *maß* for the first time.[10]

"*Achtung!*" A woman carrying a tray of eight spit-roasted half chickens passes by at a ferocious speed. Right behind her a server has her arms wrapped around ten one-litre mugs of beer, weaving among the crowd like a rugby player charging out of the scrum.

We find space to sit next to an old couple and order two beers. Dad and I raise our mugs and say cheers to each other, then to the others on our table, then we take some photos to send to Mum. And then, finally, we drink. It's a warm September day, and this fresh *maß* of lager is beautiful to look at and taste.

From somewhere a cheer grows. It's the rising cheering of something exciting happening with the prospect of something more exciting to come. And then I see: a young guy stands on the bench downing the beer in his mug. Chug, chug, chug: he wipes his chin and raises his empty glass in the air triumphantly as the cheers turn into a roar. He takes in the glory for a few seconds before a yellow-vested security guard with arms the girth of a beer stein marches to the table. It's a heroic self-immolation as he's removed to a mixture of cheers and boos.

The brass band is playing the most calm and yet uplifting tunes – somehow a mix of traditional German with theatrical and inspirational Hollywood: Hansel and Gretel meets Hans Zimmer. And then every fifteen minutes or so they play the most famous drinking song there is: "*Ein Prosit*". (I'd pay a large amount of money to actually hear Hans Zimmer play "*Ein Prosit*".)

Ein Prosit, Ein Prosit
Der Gemütlichkeit
Ein Prosit, Ein Prosit
Der Gemütlichkeit.
Oans, zwoa, drei, G'suffa!

A toast, a toast
To *Gemütlichkeit*
A toast, a toast
To *Gemütlichkeit.*
One, two, three, drink!

Every time it plays conversations pause, you bash the chunky mugs in uncoordinated unison, you sing along and you drink a big gulp of beer. The more the

---

10 Water, by the way, was around €5 for a half-litre bottle. And coffee, if you dared to ask for one, would cost you over €7 a cup. You drink beer at Oktoberfest (and if you feel like you've had enough beer then all the tents will also serve you a *maß* of alcohol-free beer).

song plays, the more you drink. It's the ultimate drinking song; the ultimate make-you-drink song.

Gemütlichkeit is the important word there. It's one of those untranslatable German words. It conveys a sense of coziness, of familiar comfort, of acceptance and belonging, of a relaxed state of mind, and it's the definitive of the Bavarian drinking experience. It's something that resonates around the world even though most of us don't have a specific word for it – but we do know how it feels to be comfortable, content and happy somewhere surrounded by others, especially after a couple of beers.

We go to an Augustiner tent next, where they pour all the beer from 200-litre wooden barrels, and each barrel is emptied in just a few minutes. In here the music is more upbeat, and it's a unifying sound, bringing us all together in the same way the beer brings us together. *Gemütlichkeit* again.

When our beers are empty we go across *Wirtsbudenstraße* and into the Hofbräu tent, the biggest tent of all. It's bright in the afternoon sun, hop flower garlands hang from the vast ceiling, and in the middle of it all spins the Angel Alois holding a harp, taking a short break from his residence in the Hofbräu-haus to oversee the drinking in the festival tent (we'll meet Alois soon). There's a constant flow of waitresses carrying full beers and trays loaded with food. The music never stops – and if it does, people just sing their own songs. Dad and I both sit and drink with big smiles. You can't *not* smile when you're here.

Next is the Hacker-Pschorr tent, with its ceiling painted sky blue – no matter the time of day, you think and feel like it's sunny. We eat currywurst and roast chicken and drink another beer before taking a little break to wander around and ride on the Ferris wheel to get a view over the whole festival grounds. As the sun is beginning to set all the lights are on and it's impossible to comprehend or explain just how big it is. If you go to Oktoberfest, go on the Ferris wheel.

We finish in the Schottenhamel tent.[11] This is where the opening ceremony takes place every year, and it's a legendary tent that's been in the same family since 1867 (when it was a small booth with fifty seats – now they can fit almost 10,000 in). We toast our beers again.

This is my fifth beer and I still love it. After the first half a beer you feel the excitement of it all. You love the taste, the place, the sounds and sights, and by the end of that first beer, with the alcohol tingling through you, you feel like a superhero. Untouchable. Like you can drink this beer forever. The first mouthful of the second *maß* is the best-tasting beer of the day, and specifically one of

---

11 The completists among you might be concerned that I only had five of the six Oktoberfest beers, but don't worry, because we returned the next day and drank several more, including the missing Paulaner. I wouldn't have been able to leave Oktoberfest without having had at least one beer from each of the six breweries.

the greatest beers in the world – it's fresh, it's cold and the effects of the first mug have crescendoed into a glorious warm feeling. By the second half of the second mug you'll know you've been drinking a 6 per cent ABV beer and you might slow down a little – pace yourself, you know, and get some food – so the last few gulps are a little warmer and flatter. Then the third mug comes and, because you've had a snack and because this new fresh beer is so refreshing and crisp, you drink the first half like you haven't had a beer in a month. There's a chance you won't remember the end of the third beer, though, because that one has a way of just disappearing into the music and talking and fun of the festival, but somehow it leaves you thirsty. It's a magic trick how that happens; how you can have had three litres of beer and still want more. The fourth stein feels lighter – or you've got stronger, which is equally likely – and tastes like the freshest beer of the day, for the first few mouthfuls at least. The rest of that beer, and the next one or two or however many you manage, all spin into a blur of neon and brass band and pretzels and lederhosen. And while you may not remember all of it, you'll certainly never forget Oktoberfest.

It's just anthem music now. That's when people stand on the benches, that's when the sipping turns to swigging, when the talking turns to singing. Oktoberfest is a different place at 9 p.m. to the one it was at 3 p.m. It's brilliantly noisy and drunk and fun – it was brilliantly noisy and drunk and fun six hours ago, but now it's just much, much more of all of those things. The alcohol has kicked in and kicked away all the inhibitions, all the things that say we shouldn't dance on the table, shouldn't talk to strangers, shouldn't love singing to pop songs – it's all gone and everything has lifted. And while I'm here at the one in Munich, the same thing is happening simultaneously at Oktoberfest events all around the world, where everyone is together and enjoying the brilliance of the world's most social drink.

When *Ein Prosit* plays again, Dad and I sing loudly and crash our glasses together. *Oans, zwoa, drei, G'suffa!*

THE MOST FAMOUS PUB IN THE WORLD

The Hofbräuhaus, 1860

You smell it before you arrive in the small square in front of the long building with the steep roof at Platzl number 9. It's a hot, wet smell: the smell of grain and horses and the pungent smoke of fire and tobacco. A horse and cart carrying sacks of malt and wooden barrels clops and creaks through the arched entranceway to a courtyard where a hundred hard-working Bavarians at the end of their hard day's work sit and drink from great stone mugs.

Men sit and talk; an old woman yells out "Radishes" and "Nuts",[12] hoisting a basket above her head; husbands and wives sit opposite one another taking alternate gulps from a shared lidded mug. Gentlemen and journeymen sit side by side; ladies and sewing girls, officers and soldiers, teachers and students – everyone sits together and everyone drinks the same beer from the same barrel: there's no pride, position or privilege at Munich's Royal Court Brewery.

Step inside the taproom and a hoarse, guttural hum – the Bavarian dialect spoken with tongues thickened by many beers – fills the huge hall, a hall so huge there must be 500 people in here lined up on long, dark benches with no spare seats between the heaving heavy shoulders. Smoke rises up to a dark stained ceiling to blanket the tavern in a brown fug.

The radish seller clatters through the door carrying her basket in the crook of her elbow while gripping a dozen dirty empty steins, which she drops onto a shelf of other used mugs. Men trail behind her, each grabbing a mug and rinsing it in a trough of constantly running water. They take their stein (noting the number pressed into the tin lid) and their seven *kreuzers*, and pass them to a man who pockets the money and passes on the mug to another man who is standing in front of a great wooden barrel. A dull gold tap spills a constant flow of brown beer, each mug filled to the top and foaming over until the lid is snapped shut and the number on top shouted out for its owner to collect it. If there's room, you sit. If not, you stand. You take a deep draw of beer followed by a deep draw on a cigar. People seem to have been here for hours or days or months, but no one seems drunk. As one barrel is emptied, the next is opened with two great hits of a heavy wooden hammer. The beer never stops pouring in the most famous tavern in Munich.

The Royal Court Brewery
In 1589, Duke Wilhelm V needed more beer for himself and his ducal court

---

12 The job of a "radish woman" was to walk around the different taverns carrying baskets of radishes and nuts. They weren't paid by the tavern (or were paid very little), so got all their money from selling their cheap snacks. They did, however, collect up dirty mugs and return them inside, perhaps to gain favour from the tavern owners to allow them to sell their wares. In 1835 the Hofbräuhaus regulars "initiated the legendary race of the radish women", which was a "highpoint of the year for the citizens of Munich". A radish woman from each tavern was selected to participate in the race; the youngest was a sprightly fifty-five, and the oldest, at sixty-eight, was "Nuss-Kathl", or Nut Katie, famous with the Hofbräuhaus drinkers for her "shrill voice" when she was selling her nuts. When the race started the radish women ran through the city with "skirts hitched up, adorned with feathers and ribbons and fired up by the Maibock", a strong and special lager tapped in May. This wasn't just some novelty run: there was a monetary prize plus a garland of Hofbräuhaus sausages for the winner. In the inaugural race, Nuss-Kathl was first and won the wurst.

of staff, some 600 people. Sourcing beer from local monastic brewers for the low-level servants and from more favourable brewers for the higher ranks was proving expensive, so the treasury recommended he construct his own brewery. The "Duke's Brew House" was built in the royal residence at a cost of 1,477½ guilders and took two years. By the end of 1591 a brewmaster named Heimeran Pongraz (formally a brewer in a Benedictine monastery) was ready to make *Braunbier*. In 1605, 2,256 buckets (1,440hl) of *Winterbier* and *Sommerbier* were brewed, most of it drunk by the court staff, with some sent to the royal residences in Straubing, Landshut and Regensburg, and 705 buckets (450hl) sold to the general public.

Duke Wilhelm V's son, Maximilian I, had taken over the running of the royal affairs in 1597, and in 1602 Max inherited the exclusive rights to brew *Weissbier* (wheat beer or white beer, a special Royal privilege that meant they alone could brew with wheat), making it first in the Duke's Brew House, and then building the dedicated Weisses Brauhaus at Platzl 9, running the two breweries parallel to one another: one only made *Braunbier* and had a Braunbierbräumeister; the other only made *Weissbier* and had a Weissbierbräumeister. They brewed like this until 1808, when the original *Braunbier* brewery was closed and all production moved into the *Weissbier* brewery, where they brewed both kinds of beer, and which became known as the Königliches Hofbräuhaus, the King's Royal Court Brewery.

In the early 1800s, as breweries began to open taprooms and beer gardens, the Hofbräuhaus had just one drinking room for brewing assistants plus two small rooms for special guests; it wasn't much like a tavern, but people still visited to drink or to take home jugs of beer. In 1828 the taproom became formally licensed to serve beer and food to the public, and on its first day King Ludwig I (Bavaria was a kingdom by then) was there to toast the thousands of people who attended its opening, and a huge roar of "God save the King" went up. This marked the beginning of the Hofbräuhaus as a great drinking destination.

By the 1850s, the other local brewers and tavern owners were feeling disadvantaged by the Hofbräuhaus, which had become the most popular place to drink (probably because the beer was always sold a little cheaper there than anywhere else). Meanwhile, the Wittelsbachs were losing focus on beer production and wanted to concentrate on their rule, and so in 1852 King Max II transferred ownership of the brewery to the state, making it the Staatliches Hofbräuhaus (the State's Court Brewery). The brewery now effectively belonged to the people of Munich, an emotional connection that many people recognize to this day.

By the 1890s (after off-loading the *Weissbier* to focus on just brewing lager, which they did in the 1870s), the Hofbräuhaus was struggling to make enough beer in the city centre while also running a tavern, taproom and courtyard beer garden that together could serve over 500 people. In 1896, they brewed the final batch of beer at the Platzl brewery, and moved production to a newly-built brewery in Haidhausen, then a suburb of the city. This allowed the former brewery tavern and beer hall to be completely renovated into a "beer palace",[13] which opened in September 1897 and, despite near-total demolition during World War II from which it was subsequently rebuilt, it's remained largely the same for over 120 years, making it a central and important drinking space for many generations of Munich citizens and visitors.

A legendary tavern with infamous guests

There's an angel in the Hofbräuhaus. *Ein Münchner im Himmel* (A Municher in Heaven), written by Ludwig Thoma, has become a real-life legend. It's the story of Alois Hingerl, porter number 172 from Munich's Central Railway Station. When he dies suddenly at work one day he's taken to heaven, but he doesn't like it very much because there's too much worshipping and singing, and because he doesn't like singing he does it angrily and like a hooligan. Alois is so miserable in heaven that God has to get involved, and decides to make Alois an Angelic Messenger, sending him back to Munich a couple of times a week to deliver messages before returning to heaven, where God hopes Alois will then feel happier. When Angel Alois gets his first assignment – to deliver a message to the Bavarian government – he flies back to Munich but doesn't go where he's told, and instead goes straight to the Hofbräuhaus and back to his usual table, where he orders a beer, then another one, and another. Apparently he's still there today, and the joke goes that the government is still awaiting divine intervention.

Franz Mandlinger, the "Lenbach of the Hofbräuhaus", spent up to twelve hours a day painting people for 50 *pfennig* or a mug of beer, eating scraps of left-over food to sustain himself. "Finessing Joseph" or "Postillon d'Amour" would carry love letters from one guest to another for a few *pfennig*.

A regular in and around Munich taverns was a watchmaker named Falk with, as Gaab notes, a "very delicate palate for beer" and a fearsome reputation. Every day he'd test the beer quality in different pubs and post his ratings outside his watch shop. If he drank his beer in three deep gulps, then he liked it, but if

---

13 It was at the end of the nineteenth century that all the major Munich brewers developed their taprooms into beer halls or the grand beer palaces like the Hofbräuhaus and Löwenbräukeller, and around twenty were renovated or built in Munich between 1880 and 1902. The first was called Arzbergerkeller, built in 1881 (but destroyed in World War II) for Spaten on Nymphenburger Straße, and was designed by the famous architect Gabriel von Seidl. It was at this time that the beer hall became a special Bavarian building that changed the social spaces of the city.

he only took one gulp and left the rest it was a very bad sign.

Lenin visited the Hofbräuhaus most Sundays in 1900. The Empress of Austria, Sisi, never left Munich without stopping for a beer (something scandalous for a young lady of her status). John F. Kennedy drank there several times in the 1930s and was caught trying to steal a couple of beer mugs. Mozart drank the beer when he lived opposite in 1780–81, writing a (fairly amateurish) poem about it:

Often sought refreshment in the Duke's brew house
The beer there really pleased me
and the guests never ceased to amuse me
Anyone who's been there would agree with me!

The American writer Thomas Wolfe wrote about it in *The Web and the Rock*, before later visiting Oktoberfest (where he got so drunk he ended up in hospital):

At night he [the protagonist, Monk] walked the streets. He went into the crowded places. He sought the beer-fogged flash and roar, the enormous restaurants. He plunged into the roaring tumult of the Hofbrau Haus [sic], swung to the rhythm of that roaring life, breathed the air, felt the warmth, the surge, the powerful communion of those enormous bodies, gulped down from stone mugs litre after litre of the cold and powerful dark beer. He swung and swayed and roared and sang and shouted in the swaying mass, felt a terrible jubilation, a mad lust . . .

And on 31 July 1888, an escaped elephant from Munich zoo turned up outside the doors of the pub.

The most infamous visitor of all, though, started out in a low-key way. In 1913 an "architectural painter from Vienna" moved to Munich, where he painted postcards and watercolours, including scenes at the Hofbräuhaus, which he'd try to sell in the pub's beer garden. Several years later, on 24 February 1920, now focused on things other than painting, he visited the top floor of the tavern and subsequently wrote these excited words:

I walked through the chief hall of the Hofbräuhaus on the Platz in Munich and my heart was nearly bursting with joy. The great hall – for at that time it seemed very big to me – was filled to overflowing. Nearly 2,000 people were present.

The former painter addressed the people there and, Gaab explains, essentially "complained about all the stuff the average German complained about in their local beer hall": the current political regime, democracy, the Versailles Treaty – only this man did it with great oration and people listened intently (though some also threw tankards at him). His name was Adolf Hitler, and on that night, which he later wrote about in *Mein Kampf*, he set out a 25-Point Programme for the National Socialist German Workers' Party.

From there on, Hitler used the Hofbräuhaus on many occasions for meetings and speeches, often in the Festsaal, the huge festival hall at the top of the tavern, where thousands would listen to him. The Nazi Party was born in the tavern and it grew in them: Hitler routinely visited the Löwenbräukeller, and was almost assassinated in the Bürgerbräukeller, only saved by cutting short his speech in order to catch a train. On 24 February 1944, he made a final address in the Festsaal on the twenty-fourth anniversary of the 25 Points. Just over a year later the Festsaal and the upper floors of the tavern were destroyed, as was much of Europe, though Hitler wouldn't have known, as he'd killed himself a few days before.[14]

All this history and longevity combines to create a pub of unrivalled interest that began as a small brewery making beer for the royal family and grew and changed over 400 years to become the archetype of the German beer hall.

Beer halls and dark lager

There must be over 500 people here already and it's only midday. The brass band has just started. The servers charge around carrying many glasses in each hand – litres of bright golden lager and chestnut-brown lager, and tall curvy vase-like glasses of hazy yellow wheat beer.

Tourists see the Hofbräuhaus first through the screen of their phones, recording their journey in or snapping photos of the ceiling, the band, the beer and the rows and rows of tables in the main hall, known as the *Schwemme*. They look confused, delighted, overwhelmed: it's exactly what they thought it'd be like, only way bigger, way louder, and way more fun.

The Hofbräuhaus is that much-exported ideal of German beer culture: the oompah music, the lederhosen, the litres of lager and the plates of pork. That idea has been taken around the world and appropriated and bastardized

---

14 Hitler didn't drink beer, he didn't smoke or eat meat, making him seemingly the least German (or Austrian) person in Germany, but then it did show a particular kind of dedication to and focus on his regime. One other thing while we're talking about Hitler: he saw alcohol as a poison that might affect learning and the future of the nation, so under him a stern eugenics policy saw alcoholics (as well as others deemed genetically weak) sterilized so as not to pass on negative qualities. Citizens deemed to be deviant but not severe enough to be sterilized were interned in concentration camps, each labelled with a coloured triangle based on their affliction. Alcoholics wore a black triangle.

into the Bavarian-themed pub. Here it's resolutely authentic, with a focus on maintaining its great history and tradition.

Munich's Hofbräuhaus has 3,500 seats, and they average around 4,000 visitors per day, but on the busiest day of their year, which is the day before Oktoberfest begins, they get up to 30,000. The pub has a constant flow of tourists, but also thousands of regular guests; of them, 616 can store their own personal mug in an individual cage they have a padlock and key for, meaning they can always drink from their own mug. Some of these regular guests have their own table, or *Stammtisch*, where they meet with other regulars – look up and you might see colourful signs hanging above different tables. There are around 180 employees, including 100 waiters and waitresses. The beer used to be served from large wooden barrels, but today it's coming from steel tanks with 4,000–6,000 litres in each, refilled regularly; on average, they serve around 3,000 litres of beer a day, and the pale Helles lager is the best-seller. The beers aren't poured by manually opening a tap, but by pushing a button for the volume you want, and somehow it always comes out perfect every single time. In the kitchen: they serve around 1,500 meals a day; there's an on-site butchers and bakery; every year they sell 20 kilometres of *Weisswurst* sausage, over 20,000 potato dumplings, and the most popular item is the *Schweinhaxen* (a huge roast pork knuckle) – on a busy day they might serve 1,000. There are multiple spaces, ranging from the large *Schwemme* downstairs to the beer garden courtyard in the middle, to calmer restaurant spaces on the second floor, and the Festival Hall on the top floor. The pub is run by two brothers, Wolfgang and Michael Sperger, whose parents ran it before them, and, as it's state-owned, they rent the building and every five years need to re-apply for their licence. Somehow the Spergers and their staff make this amazing place work 365 days a year from 9 a.m. until midnight.

I order a litre of the Dunkel dark lager. The distant relative of this beer is *Braunbier*, the original Munich beer style and perhaps the longest-brewed beer style in the world. The beer is a clear coppery brown and, despite looking dark, it's light and fresh with just a little toasted malt flavour. It's a modern beer now, but it has its roots many centuries ago, and it's deeply satisfying to drink: pleasing, warming with its large volume and richness of alcohol while also perfectly refreshing. The best quality of German lagers, indeed all great lagers, is that balance between the flavours and the qualities – the malt, the hops, the alcohol, the body, the carbonation – so that they come together in an uncomplicated and unchallenging way to be beers you want to drink lots of. The success of lager over ale was its cleaner simplicity of taste, but that simplicity makes it no less enjoyable – if anything, it's more enjoyable, especially sitting here now as

I watch the theatre of the beer palace.

I'm in the *Schwemme*, the main room when you walk in the door. This is where the original brewery was situated until the 1890s, and now it's where up to 1,300 people can sit beneath the ornate vaulted (and no longer smoke-stained) ceiling. It's still the heart of the Hofbräuhaus, and some of the tables have been there since 1897. Its name means, literally, "watering hole", which it's thought originates from the trough drinkers used to clean their mugs before getting them filled with beer. That washing station still exists, and around it is a large cage-like rack of beer mugs, all secured with small padlocks. The waiting list can be many years, and once you get your space you have to pay a €3-a-year fee, which allows you to leave your own mug in the Hofbräuhaus, washing it yourself in the fountain.[15]

An old couple dressed in co-ordinated green and white with straw hats take their usual seats at their usual table. She sits while he takes a small key and opens the mug cage behind her. With a warming smile he pulls a half-litre grey stone Hofbräuhaus mug out for her and, opening a second lock, takes a litre mug for himself. His face is childlike in its glow of happiness: a look of comfort, of coming home and sitting in your favourite chair or, better, going to your grandparents' house and getting your favourite treat. The server takes their mugs and returns a minute later with them full of beer. They toast and then they drink, shoulders lifting and lulling with a sigh of pleasure.

Ordering another beer, I watch and listen as the locals mix with the tourists, as the trays of large glasses of gold beer and brown beer and yellow beer pass by, as the air smells heavy with roasted meats, as the lively music plays. From reading old stories, it feels like this place has barely changed (even if there are fewer top hats and cigars nowadays and there are more mobile phones and tourists). The food, the beer, the traditions and the sounds still remain very important in the Höfbräuhaus.

As I finish my second mug of dark lager, the server, carrying a handsome mug of brilliant gold Helles lager, asks if I'd like another. Of course I would, and that golden beer is making me thirsty, but it's time to leave the beer hall and head outside into the beer garden, via some cellars in a forest.

---

15 These cages were put in from the 1970s in response to the number of beer steins being stolen from the pub. Between 1960 and 1980, some 550,000 steins disappeared from the Hofbräuhaus, which is seventy-five a day; during the Munich Olympics of 1972 up to 500 a day were taken. It was also during the Munich Olympics that the pub moved from ceramic to glass mugs, to show the increased numbers of tourists they were getting a full beer.

THE FOREST OF CELLARS

In 1406, the Franconian city of Forchheim, 200km north of Munich and 25km south of Bamberg, built a communal brewhouse for its citizens. In that brewery anyone who had been given the rights to brew, which were typically attached to where they lived, could take their own ingredients and use the shared brewery before transporting unfermented beer back home to ferment it and mature it in their own private cellars.

It was common for towns to have shared breweries or brewing equipment. In Einbeck, a town brewer would take a brewing kettle to people's houses, and the doors there are still wider than normal, to ensure the kettle could fit through. In other cities a central brewery and brewmaster would sell unfermented beer to locals to take home and ferment themselves. Between the early monastery breweries and the shift to larger-scale commercial brewing, it was normal in Bavaria for beer to be brewed this way.[16]

In 1609 Forchheim's town hall had a restaurant and needed more storage space for the food, beer and wine. The town is built at the bottom of a forested hill and brewers ended up walking to the top of the hill (I have no idea why: it seems much more effort than just stopping a short way up) where they dug an underground storage *keller*, or cellar. Between the 1690s and 1750s many other cellars were dug, with two final ones built in 1804 and 1807. Forchheim's brewers were the main users of the *kellers*, making their beer in town and then transporting the barrels up to their *kellers*, where they would leave it to ferment and then "lager" for several months before taking it back to town to drink.

By 1790, Forchheim had sixteen private brewers and two communal brewhouses in which twenty-three people or households had the rights to brew. It's believed that by this time people were already going up to drink the beer fresh in the *Kellerwald*, best translated as "Forest of Cellars" – essentially a collection of large beer gardens in the forest where they were drinking cool beer directly from the cellars.

As industrial and commercial brewing increased through the nineteenth century, as well as the use of ice and artificial refrigeration (more on that later), the cellars were no longer used for storing large volumes of beer. Rather than closing all the *kellers* in the Kellerwald and have them crumble away, Forchheim's brewers and citizens have looked after them, and there are still twenty-three cellars there today. And above those cellars there are still small beer gardens

---

16 You can still find communal breweries today, as we'll see in the next chapter, and one of the world's most famous breweries came out of a city where the locals brewed so much bad beer in the communal breweries that it was decided to build a big commercial brewery for everyone and hire one professional brewmaster. We'll read about that later, too.

in the forest in which you can drink beer. Some open all year round, others just over the summer months, but once a year all twenty-three *kellers* and beer gardens open for the annual Annafest, which started in 1840 and now fills the forest with people and beer. Each year during the eleven days of Annafest around 500,000 people attend and drink in what Forchheimers call the "world's largest beer garden".

****

My best mate Matt and I are breathless as we walk up a steep path through a forest on the edge of town. It doesn't feel much like a beer festival at the moment: just a long, difficult walk in the hot July afternoon. When we finally emerge into a kind of forest courtyard, Annafest reveals itself.

There's a Ferris wheel and many other spinning and dropping fairground rides. Food trucks are lined up and the smoke of grilling sausages catches the sun through the trees. We keep walking up the calf-straining, lung-burning, thirst-developing hill, and turn into a sort of wooded alley lined with a mix of cabins and gardens, the German kind of drinking garden with long tables on the wood-chipped earth. Each garden is cut into the hillside, surrounded by trees, and sits above a cellar. In the cellars there's lots of beer.

Passing under a big banner reading "*Neder Keller*" belonging to Brauerei Neder, one of Forchheim's four breweries, we sit down and order two beers, which are served in one-litre *Steinkrugs*, or stone mugs. The beer is a *Festbier*, like a stronger version of a normal German lager and served, as the name suggests, at a festival, with each brewery making a special *Annafestbier* for the event. This beer is around 6 per cent ABV and it's similar to the beers of this region in that it's maltier and more full-bodied than most regular lagers. It's excellent.

Our view is of the main pathway through the Kellerwald; a unique viewpoint in beer. All up and down this hilly forest street are gardens and bars and benches and it's all sheltered by trees, creating shade on the hot day (when we go back the next day we need those leaves to act as an umbrella from the rain). There's live music in lots of gardens, there's a lot of food all around, and a lot of people drinking from large mugs. It's loud and lively and a lot of fun.

I won't describe the whole festival, and the short version is that we arrived at 5 p.m., we drank a beer, ate some sausages and pretzels, drank more beer, chatted to some locals, drank more beer, watched people singing and dancing as we moved around different *kellers* (each has a different beer and a different atmosphere), drank more beer, went on the Ferris wheel and then that ride that slowly lifts you up and then drops you down to earth really quickly (a dangerous choice after five litres of strong beer), then I think we drank more beer. And then we did the exact same thing again the next day and decided that it's definitely the best beer event we've ever been to. The beer is great, the atmosphere is so friendly and welcoming, and the location is very special.

I then go back again for a third time (in Forchheim there's a saying, *Annafest, alla dooch, Annafest*, which means Annafest, every day, Annafest) because while the above-ground stuff is brilliant, what I really want to see is what's happening underground – not above the cellar, but deep down within it.

* * * *

I'm with Nico Cieslar from the tourist board, and we meet Neder's brewmaster outside a large wooden door that seems somehow sunken: it has a large brass sign, and an old brick wall built around it and the garden above. The opening door drags a cool draught out with it.

It's long and narrow in this first part of the cellar, which is where they would have stored the smaller barrels for serving the beer. Today there are cases of soft drinks, old beer steins and a large machine for washing the ceramic mugs. As we walk down through the damp stone tunnel, rough-cut deep through the hillside, the temperature perceptibly drops with every few metres. This is nature's refrigeration. At the end we get to a larger open space where the big lagering barrels would've been.

Where historically the beer was brewed in town, then carted up here and put into an open wooden vessel to ferment before being transferred into a big, sealed barrel to mature, today the beer is all brewed, fermented and matured in the town brewery, then stored there in large stainless steel tanks at zero degrees. Every night during Annafest, fresh beer is brought up here in a tanker and pumped into a stainless steel serving tank, each one holding 5,000 litres of beer, and from there it's drawn through pipes up to the bar and poured straight into the beer mugs.

No beer is fermented or stored here any more, with a small exception. Nico is a beer lover and homebrewer, and he tells me about his friend Markus Denk, who has an arrangement with one of the *keller* owners who lets him store his beers in the cold cellar. Markus happens to be at Annafest that day, and takes us down into the cellar to where he has a few crates of his own lager in bottles and a couple of small kegs. He pops the flip-cap on a bottle of his *Kellerbier*, an unfiltered beer you'd typically drink straight from the *kellers*. It's nine months old and it's delicious. Nine months would've been about the maximum lagering time in the early nineteenth century, and it's wonderful to taste something that's still very fresh – that's the keeping qualities of well-made lager stored in the cold, and it's great to know that small-scale private brewers can still use these amazing old cellars.

Back outside it's hot and bright, and we're in the middle of the Kellerwald and I have another litre of *Annafestbier* (and then another – the beer is really good). Later that day I leave Forchheim and head back to Munich, because I want to learn more about beer gardens.

BEER GARDENS AND GOLDEN LAGER

In the eighteenth century, Munich's brewers couldn't dig cellars beneath their inner-city brewhouses because there was low ground water and a general limitation on space, so they had to look in the surrounding area. If you were to cut a cross-section through Munich you'd see it as a kind of basin that's flat in the middle, with higher land leading outwards. From the old centre of the city, the land to the east was the closest place with the highest hillside, at around 20m, and since at least 1748 breweries had been buying land around the hill, known now as Nockerberg, and into it they built cellars to store their beer.

The temperature was relatively constant in these cellars, but to ensure it stayed cold year-round brewers would harvest ice from the rivers and lakes during the winter and store it underground. They also planted chestnut trees, which grow fast and have shallow roots and wide leaves, to act as a natural sun shade, and also help maintain a lower temperature.

Being outside the dense, dirty city, these green spaces with leafy trees and stocks of cold, fresh beer were perfect places to drink, especially in the summer. As people began walking east and crossing the river, walking up the steep slopes and arriving in chestnut-tree-covered gardens, the brewers began setting out benches and serving *Sommerbier*, the best-tasting beer of the year, direct from the cellars, and preparing simple food to sell with it. In the warm summer weather going to the beer gardens became the cool thing to do. The beer garden was born.

But by the summer of 1811, Munich's innkeepers were pissed off. The weather was good, the sun was out, and so were plenty of people, but they were all bypassing the hot, dark, smoky, smelly pubs and going to the beer gardens. The tavern owners petitioned King Max I to do something.

On 4 January 1812, the King wrote a decree that was sympathetic to both the large brewers with their gardens and the smaller taverns and brewery tap-rooms. The brewers, he decided, could continue to sell their beer in the gardens in June, July, August and September, but they were not allowed to serve any food beyond bread, but crucially customers could bring their own food. Over 200 years later and, while beer gardens can now serve food, it's still fine to take your own – you just need to sit at a bench without a tablecloth.

There are now around eighty beer gardens in Munich, and I'm going to the Augustiner-Keller, one of my favourite places to drink in Munich and the city's third-largest beer garden, with 5,000 seats.

From the busy garden there's a constant chatter, a clatter of cutlery and the clunking of hefty glasses of golden lager. I can smell grilling fish and roasting meat. The pretzels people carry are as oversized as the *maß* mugs. Kids laugh and run around; adults laugh and run around. Around me, families lay out picnic tables and unpack Tupperware boxes of snacks; old couples sit quietly in the shade of the chestnut trees; groups of twenty-somethings share plates of fries and tall glasses of *Weissbier* and *Radler*, a mix of lager and lemonade. I can barely see the edges of the beer garden – it just goes on and on, beer after beer, table after table, chestnut tree after chestnut tree.

It's here that you see the origin and appeal of the beer garden. There's the spread of land next to the old storage building; the foliage above you that lets the light sparkle through but blocks out the heat of the sun; the pleasant green social space away from the busy grey city.

Cellars have been here since 1807 and the Augustiner brewery, which is Munich's oldest and was first mentioned in 1328 (it started in the Augustinian Monastery in the city), has owned the land here since 1868, buying it to expand out of the city centre. Up until 1891 a "beer ox" attached to ropes and a pulley system had the hefty job of pulling the barrels of *Sommerbier* up and out of the cellar ready for tapping. There's no ox now, but they do still serve the beer from 200-litre barrels.

The wooden barrel is tilted slightly, a server yanks the tap and the beer blasts out into the glass, a yellow spray with loads of white foam. He closes the tap and the liquid whirls around the glass before it's thumped on the counter. A couple of seconds later and the foam has settled into three inches of perfect white head above the bright golden beer. I'm mesmerized as I watch him do it again and again. An aggressive pour, a gush of beer and foam crashing into the glass, and always settling the same. There's nothing delicate about litres of lager. There are also few things more deliciously appealing than a large, full glass of golden lager like this. I pick up the heavy one-litre glass of beer and manage to find one spare seat.

The first gulp – there's no sipping here – is glorious. After the hot walk here and the anticipation of the first beer, this tastes perfect. Cold, gently carbonated, rich with bready malts, a little lemony and fresh, then dry. This is one of the world's great beers, this garden is one of the great beer experiences, and people have been enjoying this in the sunny beer gardens of Munich and beyond for 200 years.

The beer is different now, though. Back in the early 1800s, this beer would've been dark in colour, much sweeter, and maybe a little smoky; today it's brilliant gold, stronger and drier. If Dunkel is the original dark Munich lager, then this is its sister, Helles, a name that means light, bright or pale, and today it's Munich's main beer. It's also the kind of golden lager that took over the world.

I finish the first litre and I want another one. As I'm heading back to the bar, I see a young guy carrying two mugs of beer in each hand, struggling to hold them, his shoulders and back caving under the weight. It's a curious sight – and a funny one. Litres of lager are an iconic image of Bavarian beer-drinking, and all around me people are lifting this unergonomic vessel that's the size of our heads. It's hefty, it's impractical in many ways, and it's something you only see in this part of the world (and in Bavarian beer bars around the world). Why the hell do Germans drink from such big glasses?

Maß is the proper name for this beer, and it means "measure". Most English-speakers colloquially call the litre mug a stein, which actually means "stone" so isn't accurate – typically today the mugs are made of heavy glass – but historically it would've been ceramic and often it came with a lid.

A Bavarian *Maß* once held 1.069 litres of beer, an amount decided in a mandate from 1809 in order to standardize the measure (apparently prior to this there were ninety-three different liquid measurements used). That's an odd volume, and in 1870, after Bavaria joined with Prussia to form the new German Empire, or Deutscher Reich, it was made into exactly one litre (and Bavarians still hate the Prussians for taking away one mouthful of beer from them).

Historically, even back to the *Reinheitsgebot*, you see the price of beer mentioned per *Maß*. It was the basic beer measurement, and it's likely people just drank a litre at a time. Today, the most common places to see the *Maß* mugs are in the beer gardens, beer palaces like the Hofbräuhaus, and at beer festivals, where it makes sense to have staff serve larger glasses less frequently.

I finish my second glass and the sun is just about still flickering through the trees. The iconic Munich social space of the beer garden developed because of the brewers digging deep cellars underground. It's hard to imagine now how the space beneath me once would've had large wooden barrels filled with beer. But it's not hard to see how these places became so popular with the people of Munich, especially when the beer tastes so good.

FROM CELLARS TO SCIENCE AND INDUSTRY

Cold cellars are key to the origins of lager; without them, lager simply wouldn't exist. It was the deliberate action of producing and storing beer underground that produced a beer unique to Bavaria, where a specific lager yeast combined with the cold temperatures, and that yeast evolved over many centuries in the cold environment. We may never know exactly how or where it happened, but it did happen, and the perfect conditions needed to produce what we'd now call lager were in place and being used as early as the fourteenth century. When the purity law of 1516 set a definition for beer, it led Bavarian brewers to make proper use of those conditions and processes that had already been established in the region, but, as we've seen, it was only in Bavaria that this unique combination of yeast, cellars and lagering combined. For now.

Into the 1800s, Bavarian brewing was still a largely empirical process, more luck than science, a rudimentary craft and not yet a technical and fully understood profession. As a result the beers were variable and inconsistent, generally dark and cloudy, sweet and smoky, and sometimes with an edge of acidity. Lager may have been established in Bavaria, but those beers would be largely unrecognizable today.

From the 1830s onwards, the south German brewing industry finally became more established, more formalized, more knowledge-based, and the brewing processes more controllable. Basically, the beer got better. And as it got better, breweries got bigger, and lager was able to move beyond being just a local Bavarian brew, helped in turn by the industrialization and then globalization of the industry.

It's time to meet the Great-Grandfathers of Lager. These are the four breweries who had the greatest impact on the world of lager, making it more like the beer we're so familiar with around the world today.

CHAPTER TWO

THE GREAT-GRANDFATHERS OF LAGER,

OR HOW LAGER BECAME THE DRINK WE KNOW TODAY

FROM MONASTERY TO FACTORY; FROM EMPIRICAL TO TECHNICAL

At the beginning of the nineteenth century, lager was only made in small volumes and only in Bavaria, with perhaps some outliers; by the end of the century, it was brewed and drunk in enormous volumes all around the world.

Here we'll look at the Great-Grandfathers of Lager. This is not the story of four old men: this is the story of four significant breweries, and, while each brewery may have started with one man, they progressed through several generations of the same family (or, in the case of one, the citizens of a whole town), until each was at one time the largest in its own country or indeed the world. These four breweries – Spaten, Klein-Schwechat, Pilsner Urquell and Carlsberg – were helped by a large and extended supporting family of scientists, inventors, industrialists and other brewers, and together they ushered in the modern era of brewing.

This couldn't have happened without new technologies: steam power helped in numerous ways, first around the brewhouse, then inside it, and subsequently by being able to power trains and boats to take the beer further away. Ice and then the invention of artificial refrigeration let lager brewers increase in scale and improve in year-round quality (eliminating the need for the Bavarian brewing seasons). Brewers had to become masters of the finer details, using scientific instruments like the microscope, thermometer and saccharometer to gain greater control of their processes. British malting techniques were adopted in Central Europe, leading to paler beers without any smoky flavours, and scientists finally began to understand yeast and bacteria, developing techniques to purify them and produce better-tasting and more consistent beers (consistency and quality on a large scale represent much of the advances of the nineteenth century).

Then those new pure beers could be put into bottles, now available in mass production, and pasteurized to make sure they tasted good for longer, with those bottles travelling on trains or boats, making lager an international product and enabling it to replace the porters and pale ales of Britain around the world. Then, as it started to be brewed domestically in new markets, brand names became increasingly important.

But we begin back in Bavaria, and there were two brewers – one in Munich and another in Vienna – who would show what was possible for large-scale lager brewing, making the beers of their hometowns famous.

BAVARIAN LAGER AND VIENNA LAGER

"One must have been to England and seen all the masterpieces to be convinced that [we Bavarians] are at least 100 years behind the islanders' development," wrote Joseph von Baader, the Royal Director of Mechanical Engineering and Mining at Munich's Academy of Sciences. In the early nineteenth century Britain was *the* industrial centre of brewing; nowhere else was even comparable, and no one would begin to catch up until the 1850s, when two breweries in particular would lead the way: Munich's Spaten brewery and Vienna's Klein-Schwechat.

Spaten brewery dates back to 1397, when it was founded just beside Munich's Frauenkirche (very close to where the Augustiner monastery brewery was). A Georg Späth would take it over in 1622, and his lasting legacy would be the name Spaten, or "Spade". In 1807, Gabriel Sedlmayr I, who had been a brewer in the Hofbräuhaus, took over Spaten, then one of the smallest of Munich's fifty or so breweries; by 1820 it was the third-largest (behind Hacker and Pschorr, who would later merge); by the late 1860s, Spaten would be the largest brewer in Munich, a position it maintained until towards the end of the century.

Sedlmayr I was a curious, intelligent and practical man who took a scientific approach to his craft, always experimenting, always looking for new technologies and techniques, and even designing his own pressure gauges and thermometer – it's believed he was the first brewer in Munich to use one, which supposedly led to him being mocked: "We *know* how to measure temperature," the other brewers said, "but Sedlmayr needs a thermometer." The quality of his beer, however, was enough for the others to see the benefit.

As Sedlmayr I enlarged his brewery, he built cellars in the Nockherberg capable of holding 1,300hl of beer, while introducing new pumps and an English-style kiln. On the side he pioneered the production of vinegar. In 1821 Spaten were the first Bavarian brewery to install a steam engine designed by Von Baader, who had studied in England and was acquainted with James Watt. This steam engine – bear in mind that this was new technology with many great potential applications in all stages of the brewing process – was used to lift buckets of water. Sure, it could lift 100 buckets an hour up from 12 metres below, but they'd just bought this amazing machine, which every brewery would come to need, and they had it lift buckets. In 1844 they would become the first Bavarian brewery, and possibly the first outside Britain, to use steam power actually for brewing. Between the bucket-lifting steam engine of 1821 and the brewing one of 1844, a lot of interesting things happened at Spaten to change the future of lager brewing, but let's stay on steam for a moment.

Coal was fired in a furnace which heated water which produced steam which drove a piston which created power to turn a wheel or move a machine. Before steam power, it was down to humans, animals, wind or water to create the necessary energy, but the first two were limited by the amount of exertion they could handle and the latter two were location- or weather-dependent.

Steam power had started as a pumping system in mining and progressed to piston-power in mills, able to work continuously and in any location. British textiles were among the first trades to benefit, with the automation of the spinning of wool and cotton in fabric signalling the beginning of the Industrial Revolution. James Watt's improvements of the steam engine from the 1760s onwards saw it move into the brewing industry, at the time one of the most energy-intensive industries of all.

Steam power meant beer could be made anywhere, any time, and in much greater volumes. London's brewers were among the first to make use of it, and it enabled these already large brewers to become enormous.[17]

Initially the steam engines helped with milling,[18] lifting water from wells and moving grain around the malthouse and brewery, but they'd go on to power pumps to move liquid around the brewery, stir the mash vessels, move

---

17 British breweries were the largest in the world at this time, and brewed on a completely different scale to anyone else. London's porter brewers made batch after batch, filling it into enormous wooden tuns where it matured at ambient temperatures for many months. According to a report from 1795, one of the tuns at the Griffin Brewery on Liquorpond Street (now Clerkenwell Road), built by a Mr Meux, was said to be 25 feet high, 95 feet in circumference, and held some 20,000 barrels of beer. That's 7.6m x 29m, which is still kind of hard to comprehend in scale, but when you know it held over *5,000,000* pints of beer you get the idea. And breweries had numerous porter tuns all lined up.

18 In some breweries the mills were on the side of a river – there were some in Munich, including at the Paulaner brewery, where the mill was turned by the flow of water of the Auer Mühlbach. In other places, harnessed horses would walk in a circle, turning a wheel connected to further wheels. The term "horsepower" was devised by James Watt as he sought to work out the strength of a horse and apply it to his new engines; in doing so, he created a practical measure of the relative power of his machines.

casks around the cellar and heat various parts of the brewery, including the brewing vessels. By the end of the eighteenth century there were twenty-six steam engines in London breweries, and dark, long-matured porter became the first true industrial beer.

From the 1830s, steam came to power locomotives, which expanded the railway networks and increased speed: Robert Stephenson's *Rocket* locomotive could travel at a frighteningly fast 45kph between Manchester and Liverpool. As the railways ramified through Britain, Europe[19] and North America, goods like raw ingredients or finished beer could travel faster and further than ever, opening up new sales territories.

****

Gabriel Sedlmayr had two sons – Joseph, the eldest, and Gabriel II – both apprenticed in the brewery, but it was the younger brother who showed the greater application towards the science and technology of brewing, and he's the one who's most important to our story.[20] Gabriel II (hereafter just referred to as Sedlmayr) took a further course in distilling, visited many Bavarian breweries and learned English and French, before undertaking a ten-month study tour of Europe.

In 1833, Sedlmayr travelled to Mannheim, where he took a boat to Cologne, then to Düsseldorf, and then on to Nijmegen in Holland, and at each stop he would visit breweries. Next came a canal boat to Amsterdam, then onwards to Antwerp and Brussels (where he didn't like the sour Belgian beers or the lack of technology). By July, he had reached east London, where he rented a flat with Josef Meindl, a young brewer from Braunau on the Austrian-German border, Georg Lederer from his father's eponymous brewery in Nuremberg (the ones who would first send beer on a German train) and Anton Dreher, from his family's brewery Klein-Schwechat, on the outskirts of Vienna.

---

19 Germany's first commercial railway line, which had approval from King Ludwig I of Bavaria (a Wittelsbach, of course) opened in 1835. The locomotive *Der Adler* (The Eagle) was built by Robert Stephenson and travelled between Nuremberg and Fürth, taking nine minutes to cover the 6km journey (when the engine broke down, and it often did, horses would have to pull the train, and it would take them 25 minutes). In the spring of 1836 two casks of Lederer brewery's beer travelled on the line – said to be the first freight on the railway line.

20 Gabriel Sedlmayr I died in 1839, and his two sons took over the running of the brewery, but that didn't work out, and in 1842 Joseph took over Leistbrauerei, then three years later Gabriel II bought out Joseph's share in Spaten and continued the family business on his own. In 1861, Leistbrauerei took over Munich's Franziskaner brewery. Much later, in 1922, Spaten and Leist-Franziskaner merged to form the *Gabriel-and-Joseph-Sedlmayr-Spaten-Franziskaner-Leistbräu Aktiengesellschaft*. Löwenbräu would also come to join this partnership. In 2003 they would all be bought by Interbrew, which became AB InBev, the world's largest brewer.

Now there were four brewers in London – Sedlmayr, Dreher, Lederer and Meindl[21] – all in their early twenties and keen to learn more about beer, specifically about brewing on a large scale and the new scientific instruments British brewers were making use of.

They wanted to visit Barclay, Perkins & Co., the world's largest brewery at that time, but no one would agree to meet them. Instead, they went on what they called the "tourist tour", taking it over and over again, deeply impressed by the size of the place, the powerful steam engines and the extent to which the brewers could control the brewing process even on such a large scale.

Dreher had brought with him a book called *The Art of Brewing* by David Booth and, along with Sedlmayr, decided to go to Booth's house and see if he was in. He was. And he was delighted to meet them. Booth's book detailed the processes of brewing, and focused on what he knew: the British way. But in front of him now were two German-speaking brewers who were looking to learn from him; Booth could learn from them, too. In 1834, following their meeting and subsequent discussions, Booth published an updated version of his book including a new section titled "The Brewing in Foreign Countries", in which he is "indebted to the manuscript and oral communications of two German brewers (from Vienna and Munich), who have been, and now are, visiting the principal towns of Europe, for the laudable purpose of acquiring information concerning their business".

In his updated book, Booth tells us that "*Unter-gährung*" fermentation – that is under-fermentation as opposed to the upper-fermentation of ale – "is almost universal throughout Bavaria, where the beer is most famed; but it is scarcely known in any other quarter".

Booth taught the travelling brewers about malting techniques, brewing processes and getting better control over their fermentation, including the use of the saccharometer. He notes that the German brewers have "hitherto had no saccharometers".

A saccharometer is a hydrometer specifically used for measuring the amount of solid matter dissolved in a solution; for beer, it's primarily measuring how many malt sugars are dissolved into water. They had been available to British breweries since around the 1770s (though had already been in use for many years in British distilleries). Saccharometers are fundamentally important in

---

21 Sedlmayr and Dreher would remain friends for life. Lederer kept contact with Sedlmayr and Dreher, and there's a wonderful photo taken in 1839 of the three of them all wearing top hats and overcoats, each with a thick moustache, and all holding hands (it's worth taking a moment for an online search for that image, to imagine them all walking together through the streets of Georgian London). In 1848, wanted for being part of the Committee of the Peoples' Assembly, Lederer was exiled to France. Upon his return in 1851 he installed the first steam engine in a Nuremberg brewery and was the first to use a saccharometer. The Lederer brewery still exists today. Nothing more is known about Meindl or his brewery.

breweries because they enable brewers to measure sweetness, which in turn allows them to work out how much sugar they started with before fermentation, and how much they finished up with after it was done, leading to a calculation that could give a measure of the alcohol content. Previously this was done by the unreliable method of tasting the liquid; the saccharometer made it a scientific reading, which helped brewers to achieve more consistency. At some point on their travels, Sedlmayr and Dreher acquired their own saccharometers, and they were among the first non-British brewers to use them.

Alongside the saccharometer, the thermometer was now an important instrument in breweries (we've seen that Spaten was one of the first Bavarian breweries to use one). The difference of a few degrees at numerous stages of the production can impact flavours, so thermometers helped brewers understand and control their processes.[22]

The first brewer to write about using a thermometer is believed to be a Michael Combrune of a brewery in Hampstead, London, in an *Essay on Brewing* in 1758. It's thought thermometers were first marketed to breweries years earlier, but it took time for them to gain wider acceptance (as with the saccharometer, brewers didn't see why they needed one when they seemed to have managed all right without). By the 1780s, the thermometer was in wider use by commercial British brewers, especially the bigger ones, for whom spoiled beer could be very costly, and by the turn of the nineteenth century it had been generally adopted. There are reports of thermometers in use in Bavaria from the late 1810s onwards, and they became more common through the late 1830s.

The German brewers left Booth carrying a letter of recommendation to show to any breweries they visited. The letter worked, and between July and September 1833 they viewed twenty breweries, though they didn't manage to spend an extended period working in any of them, denying them the full insight into the processes or recipes they were hoping for.

In October, Lederer and Meindl returned to Germany, while Sedlmayr and Dreher headed north from London with the ultimate destination of Edinburgh. Their journey took them on the *Rocket* train from Manchester to Liverpool (Dreher was excited about travelling at 43kph), before a steamship to Glasgow and then across to Edinburgh, which Sedlmayr described as "the brewing capital of the north of Britain".

---

22 The term "rule of thumb" perhaps apocryphally links to brewing before the thermometer, where brewers would assess the heat of their liquid by putting their thumb in it. They may also have used their elbow, but no one says "rule of elbow", do they?

In Edinburgh they spent a month living and working with John Muir, an Edinburgh brewer, where they got his attention by talking about lager beer production and discussing the long shelf-life of the beer, which impressed Muir. "Finally," Sedlmayr wrote home, "we were allowed to monitor the fermentation process," and see some entries in the brewing book, a book so important to Muir he had two locks on it. Sedlmayr was able to copy down a small amount of information, but what they really wanted was to be able to analyze the beers themselves, using some of their new scientific instruments. So they came up with a plan.

To his father Sedlmayr wrote about his "thoughts of a thief and beautiful theft", and explained how they had been able to take away samples of beer to analyze back at their hotel, a subterfuge that involved modifying some walking sticks. These were made of "sheet metal, lacquered, below a valve, so that when you dig the cane in [the beer], it fills up, the valve closes when you take it out, and we have beer in the stick so we can steal safer". They would go around the brewery, dip their walking sticks into the tanks and draw samples out. They lived in "perpetual fear of discovery and beatings".

Sedlmayr filled a notebook with everything he learned from Muir's brewery and sent the information back to his father. Both Sedlmayrs thought it ought to be possible to brew British-style ales in Munich, and were later to attempt it, though ultimately without success. Muir, meanwhile, was encouraged to try brewing with bottom-fermenting yeast, and in 1835 Sedlmayr sent some of his yeast to the Edinburgh brewer, who made the first known lager in Britain. This was "a great novelty", said Muir, "because we had neither seen nor heard anything of a similar kind." The beer brewed was "so transparent that we had never seen anything like it, and all our customers were quite delighted, but the yeast lost quality after repeated use and the breeding failed". Lager wouldn't be brewed again in Britain for another forty years, and it'd be 120 years before it became a prominent drink there, making Britain one of the final countries to embrace it. Had Muir's experiment worked out better, the whole modern history of British brewing could've been very different.

After Edinburgh, Sedlmayr and Dreher travelled south to Burton-on-Trent, where they met Michael Bass, the third generation of his family's eponymous brewery, which would one day become the world's largest. They spent a week in Burton, but didn't get to see much brewing, as Bass kept them entertained by taking them fox hunting and generally lording around, though it has been reported that it was he who gifted the brewers their saccharometers.

They left Burton-on-Trent on New Year's Eve of 1833 and spent three more weeks in London before heading to Paris. Dreher returned to Vienna, while Sedlmayr stayed on until his father suspected he was now just on a jolly and suggested it was time he came home. Sedlmayr went via Strasbourg, where he interned at Hatt brewery, which would be at the forefront of lager brewing through the nineteenth century – Hatt later became known as Kronenbourg.

Sedlmayr got back to Munich at the end of March 1834 and implemented some changes almost immediately. His new saccharometer was "like the light of the rising sun", so eye-opening were its insights, and led him to pioneer the use of ice to control the fermentation temperature. No one else in Bavaria was using such techniques.

It took Dreher a little longer to make an impact. His father's old brewery was run-down and in debt, and he needed to find some money to rejuvenate it. He managed to get that money from a distant cousin, and by 1836 was leasing the brewery from his mother and making 600hl. In 1839 he bought the brewery outright. He started by brewing a top-fermented "*Kaiser Bier*", and then produced what he called a "Bavarian-style *Kräusenbier*".

A significant development was both brewers' adoption of British-style malting, which meant using a slower germination time, slower kiln drying and indirect heat using coke instead of wood, giving malts that were paler in colour than before, contained more potential fermentable sugars and didn't have the smell or taste of smoke – it was around this time that any flavour of smoke disappeared from most beers altogether.[23]

The new paler malts gave more fermentable sugars than dark grain (think about the difference in sweetness between a golden slice of toasted bread and a slice of almost-burnt toast). Each brewer produced a slightly different type of malt, which became known after their home city: Munich malt and Vienna malt. These new malts were a great leap towards the flavour profile we know of lager today, eradicating the harsher, darker, more acrid taste in favour of more toasty, bready flavours.

In March 1837, Spaten brewed a special beer using the Munich malt and stored it right through the summer, releasing it as one of the final *Sommerbiers* of the year. It was called *Märzenbier* (meaning March beer) and described as "*Helles*" or "pale", though that paleness is likely to have been relative to the much darker brews of the time (brewing with just Munich malt today would give you a deep amber-brown beer). Almost all Spaten's and Munich's beers back then were still dark, and it's here we see a shift from the generic *Braunbier* to a

---

23 It's difficult to say just how smoky beers were because there are almost no mentions of the specific tastes of beer centuries ago. Some might not have been smoky at all, given how they were made with air-dried malts, while others would've been more pungent. We can make a reasonable assumption that smoke was a prevalent characteristic of beer but also that as the technology and technique to produce a non-smoky beer became available, it was universally adopted. This was partly for taste but also for efficiency: the indirectly fired grains typically had more fermentable sugars.

more consistent Bavarian lager, which developed as its own distinct beer style.

In 1841, Klein-Schwechat produced a beer using Vienna malt. It was probably an amber colour, fermented with a bottom-fermenting yeast and stored in the cold brewery cellars. Dreher called it a *Lagerbier*, giving us one of the first mentions of the word lager in relation to a beer's name. This paler beer would become the archetype of Vienna lager.

By combining British-malting techniques with bottom-fermenting yeast, ice-cold cellars and long maturation, utilizing new scientific instruments like the thermometer and saccharometer to gain greater control of their brewing, Sedlmayr and Dreher had created two new kinds of beer.

Now they could control their brewing, they could start to grow, employing steam power to move towards industrial-scale production. Spaten installed steam engines in 1844, and then in 1851, constrained by space in the inner-city location, Sedlmayr built a large new steam-powered brewery on Marstrasse with a spacious network of cellars. The brewery is still in the same location, including much of the old cellar network (Löwenbräu is across the block – a bridge now connects the breweries. They once had similar cellars, but many were demolished to build the U-bahn).

Klein-Schwechat installed a steam engine in 1848 – said to be Austria's first – and that, combined with additional cellars and storage barrels, saw them expand rapidly through the Austro-Hungarian Empire, where they took over other breweries: in 1859 they bought Michelob, near Saaz in Bohemia; in 1862 Steinbruch in Budapest; in 1869 a brewery in Trieste. They were the first Central European brewery to pioneer production of the same beers across multiple facilities, something most major brewers would come to do.

Dreher died unexpectedly in 1863 at the age of fifty-three, but not before seeing his brewery become the largest in continental Europe.[24] Around the time of his death, the Klein-Schwechat brewery had 1,240 fermentation vats and over 4,300 lager barrels of between 28 and 113hl; their cellars covered 15,000m^2 and could store over 234,000hl of beer next to 8,600m^2 of ice pits, storing "up to 800,000 Zollcentners" of ice (about 40,000 tons). The brewery had its own railway running through it, 350 people worked as brewers and brewing assistants, while there were an additional 250 drays and labourers.

---

24 In 1865, Klein-Schwechat brewed 230,995hl of beer. This is big, but British beer was on a far larger scale: in 1865 London's largest brewer, Truman's, made 879,142hl, and in 1877 Burton's Bass Brewery became the largest in the world and was the first to pass one million barrels, or 1.6m hectolitres. In comparison, Spaten brewed 190,107hl in 1863–64, and all of what we'd call the Big Six Munich brewers were in the top 10 at that time: Löwenbräu was the largest (260,550hl), Spaten was second, Joseph Sedlmayr's Leist-Franziskaner third, Hacker and Pschorr fourth and fifth, Zacherl (which became Paulaner) and Augustiner sixth and seventh, two now-closed breweries, Singlspieler and Mader, eighth and ninth, with the Hofbräuhaus tenth, brewing 29,358hl that year.

In 1867 Spaten became the largest brewery in Munich. Sedlmayr's sons, Johann, Carl and Anton, took over the running of the company in 1874, and they remained Munich's largest until the 1890s when overtaken by Löwenbräu.

Dreher's son Anton Jr, who was only fourteen when his father died, would take over the running of the company in 1870 after apprenticing for three years at Barclay, Perkins & Co. Dreher Jr would increase the size of the Vienna brewery to eventually earn himself the nickname "*Weiner Braukaiser*" – the Vienna Beer King.

In the 1870s, sales of bottom-fermented lager in Germany surpassed top-fermented ale production, thanks mostly to the breweries in the north of the country moving into lagers.[25] Even in the country where lager originated, it took some time for it to overtake the more common (and easier to produce) ales. But now lager was ascendant, triumphantly growing, and Spaten and Klein-Schwechat were at the forefront of an industry about to hit a growth spurt. For that expansion to happen, however, breweries needed a more reliable way of staying cold.

****

Whenever a lager brewery wanted to get bigger it would have to buy more lagering barrels, and more barrels meant more underground cellars. But the bigger the cellars got, and the more activity that took place down there, the harder it was to maintain a low temperature, especially as fermentation is exothermic.

"Ice is absolutely necessary for the production of our modern beer; the safety of the business is increased by extensive use of it," wrote the brewing professor Julius Thausing in 1882, "and an uninterrupted carrying on of the brewery is made possible by it." Harvesting ice had previously been the only way to keep beer cold, especially during the summer months, and it required cutting huge chunks of ice from lakes and ponds.

Using North America as a reference, ice needed to be 18 inches thick to harvest it, and large-scale harvesting required 100 men and 30–40 horses. It was typically cut at night, when it was at its thickest, and once any snow had been scraped off. The further the ice had to travel, the larger the block. The blocks were floated to shore, caught with ice hooks and put into pinewood ice houses stuffed with sawdust. From those ice houses they went on wagons, then ships, then on to a brewery, where they would be stored in special ice pits or

---

25 Outside of Bavaria and the south, top-fermented beer accounted for 43 per cent of German beer in 1873, when around 8.4m hl of top-fermented beer was brewed. By 1890, the ale volume was still about the same, but bottom-fermented beer had more than doubled from 11.2 million to almost 24 million hl, which jumped to 40 million hl by 1905 when top-fermented beer had dropped to 6.2 million hl.

caves within the cellars, hopefully to stay frozen through to the following year.[26]

Ice stores meant the Bavarian summer brewing prohibition was removed, because by 1850 breweries could maintain a more constantly cool temperature in their cellars, but as the breweries grew this became more difficult, even with vast reserves of ice. In 1868–69 Spaten used 16,800 tons of ice (imagine, if you can, the Eiffel Tower with about 1,000 elephants on it and you're close to the total weight), which worked out at 72kg of ice per 100 litres of beer brewed. Klein-Schwechat could store more than double that, and in the "ice-free" winter of 1872 had to import 100,000 tons of ice from Poland. That's a *lot* of ice, and it had to go into cellars already filled with thousands of wooden barrels. There simply wasn't the space for this to continue and beer could no longer remain reliant on an unreliable natural resource.

Artificial refrigeration had been around since the mid-1700s, but had not been a commercial success. By the late 1850s, ice-making machines still weren't a commercial proposition, but if only someone could make the technology work on a large scale . . .

The science-minded Sedlmayr read a paper written by a Carl Linde, Professor at the Technical University of Munich, on improving techniques of refrigeration. Sedlmayr and Dreher Jr contacted Linde and effectively financed his research. It was an ideal partnership: wealthy technical brewers looking to grow their businesses, and an inventor and engineer who needed the money to create an industry-changing new technology.

In 1873, the first (and still experimental) Linde cooler was built in Augsburg, and the 4-ton machine was transported to Spaten's brewery. For a refrigerant it initially used dimethyl-ether in a vapour-compression system, this being replaced in 1875 with the more efficient ammonia. Now Spaten's cellars could be artificially cooled all year round. Dreher installed a Linde cooler at his Trieste brewery, and then added one to the Vienna brewery. Joseph Sedlmayr bought one for his Leist-Franziskaner brewery. Heineken bought an ice machine in 1877, and Carlsberg installed one the following year.

By 1878, Linde had sold twenty machines, and decided to quit his professorship and found *Gesellschaft für Linde's Eismaschinen* (Linde's Ice Machine Company), with Carl Sedlmayr as a shareholder and board member. By 1890 Linde had sold 747 machines and equipped 445 breweries (a warm winter in 1883–84 helped convince brewers), and by 1929 over 2,000 breweries had Linde cooling machines. Linde also built ice factories capable of manufacturing ice throughout the year.

---

26 Ice could be very profitable. By around 1828 there was an ice shop on the Strand in London, while in 1833 ice was shipped from Boston all the way to India, a 16,000-mile journey that took four months: 180 tons left the US, and 100 tons arrived. In today's money it sold at a profit of $283,000.

Artificial refrigeration made year-round lager brewing possible, which meant breweries could make more beer, which then meant they needed to look further away to sell it, and from the 1860s we start to see Vienna and Bavarian lagers on sale (and brewed) outside of their own areas.

A key moment came in 1867, when both Spaten and Dreher won gold medals at the World's Fair in Paris. Dreher's beer was served in a Viennese beer hall and widely celebrated, increasing its exports and seeing it become the first lager style regularly sold in Britain. A report from 1869 in the *Journal of the Society of the Arts* describes Vienna beer as

> tolerably bright, and had a thick persistent foam on the surface. The taste ... is sweeter and more luscious than that of English beer ... and there is a peculiar flavour of barley. The hop flavour is distinct ... and the bitterness more perceptible, a minute or so, after drinking.

In the *Cornhill Magazine* a writer described Vienna beer as

> less bitter, less *capiteux* [heady or intoxicating], and more ethereal in flavour than Bass and Allsopp [sic], weaker in alcohol, and more neutral in taste than other German beers – above all, that, when poured into a glass fresh from a cask just brought up from the ice-cellar, it glows like fluid amber, and is crowned with a delicate beading of bubbles of the air.

The beer is marked out as different from British ale: Dreher's beer and one from Liesing have "no counterpart among the different varieties of English beer, and supplies what has long been recognized as a want – a light, pure, clear drink, of good flavour, but weak alcoholic strength". The price was a problem, however: Vienna beer was three times more expensive than a standard English ale.

Yet we wouldn't necessarily call these beers commercially popular, as they were only sold in small volumes and mostly to Germans and Austrians in London. The importance is that lager was beginning to reach into established beer-drinking nations.

The amber Vienna lagers were soon joined by dark Bavarian lagers, and by 1868 there were several Bavarian and Austrian beer halls in London, with lager also on sale in Manchester and Glasgow by the following year (more on this later). It's from this time that Bavarian became the more prominent lager type, one synonymous with quality, and the main style of lager brewed around the world through the second half of the nineteenth century.

"There can be no doubt that, amongst all Continental towns, Munich produces the finest and most wholesome Lager Beer. By the unrivalled excellence of its brews and by its enormous output, the fame of Munich beer has spread throughout the whole world," asserted the Spaten brewery, who by the 1890s had five establishments in England. By the turn of the twentieth century, lager was being brewed around the world, and from Singapore to St Louis or São Paulo, it was almost always a Bavarian-style lager – that is, a dark lager. But tastes were beginning to change.

The emergence of amber Vienna lager was a brief flirtation in Victorian London and its popularity waned as a new kind of lager grew in popularity: Pilsner. (Even Dreher's breweries were making Pilsner beer by now.) These pale, bitter, bright lagers were commonly seen next to the dark Bavarian lagers on the bar, with a general shift occurring towards lighter lagers. A shift that was happening even in the embedded traditions of Munich's brewers.

The first Bavarian "*Helles Lagerbier*" is debated: some say Spaten brewed it; others that it was a now-closed brewery called Thomasbräu. Some documents from the 1820s talk of the majority of Munich beers being "wine yellow", we've already seen that Spaten made a *Märzenbier* described as "*Helles*" back in 1837, and *Helles Lagerbier* would be used as a way to describe a pale moderately strong lager in Austro-Hungary, but it's generally accepted that the modern version of a Munich Helles lager was released in 1894. That's when Spaten put on the market a bright and pale lager, ostensibly to compete with the spread of Pilsner (it looked similar but was less bitter than the Bohemian beer).

They first sold the Helles in the north of Germany as a trial market, where they considered many different brand names for it, including *Edelbitter* (Noble Bitter), *Herren-Bier* (Men's Beer), *Nektar-Bier* and *Walhalla-Bier*, before settling on just *Helles Lagerbier*. It was a success in the north, and first sold in Munich in June 1895.

Some brewers reacted quickly to release their own lighter Bavarian lagers: it's said Thomasbräu was eleven days after Spaten, while Löwenbräu's came in September 1895. But not everyone thought it was a good idea. One of the most vocal was Joseph Wagner of Augustiner-Brauerei, who thought it a fad and believed the pale beers damaged the reputation of Munich's *Braunbier* and were nothing more than "an unnecessary advertisement for Pilsner beers" (he'd brew one within three years, though). Other brewers were concerned about the lack of capacity to add an entirely new kind of beer. But lighter beers were what the drinkers wanted.

Sedlmayr and Dreher professionalized lager brewing techniques and were among the pioneers of industrial-scale lager brewing, leading with their hometown lager styles, which would come to be brewed around the world. But dark Bavarian lager and amber Vienna lager were not ultimately the styles that took over the world. That was the lager first brewed in Pilsen.

Before we see how light Pilsner beer emerged from the dark cellars, we're going to drink a communally brewed lager called *Zoigl*.

ZOIGL: A COMMUNITY OF BREWING

As Reinhard Fütterer looks at the 400-year-old farmhouse, at the dozens of people sitting in his pretty garden, at the glasses of his *Zoiglbier* they're all drinking, he has the deeply contented smile of someone who knows he is doing something worthwhile.

Zoigl is an anomaly of a beer. It's a hazy amber lager that's unique to the north-east of Bavaria, in the Upper Palatinate, near the Czech border – where it's thought bottom-fermented beer was first brewed, possibly as early as the fourteenth century. And there are only five breweries in which this beer is made.

The name *Zoigl* derives from the word *zeichen* or "star". A six-pointed star has been used as an emblem of brewing for many centuries, the significance of the six points being that it overlaps the elements of brewing (earth, fire and air) with the ingredients of beer (water, malt and hops). In illiterate times the star became the sign that a house had beer for sale. It's a symbol still used by the *Zoigl* brewers today.

Zoigl is brewed in a communal brewery, and can only be made by some-one with historic "*bierrechtler*" (beer rights). There used to be over a hundred communal breweries in the area, with many towns and villages having their own shared brewery and certain local properties having the right to use the communal kit. As commercial breweries grew and the state funding that sup-ported the communal brewers was discontinued (in 1805), "most people who brewed for themselves realized that they couldn't do it as well as a professional brewhouse," says Fütterer, so the breweries closed. But not *all* of them. "It's funny," he says: "there are several thousand people still with the rights to brew communal beer, but they don't have a brewery."

I'm in Neuhaus, which received the rights to have a communal brewery in 1415. There are twenty-five properties in Neuhaus that still have brewing rights: six brew commercially, nine brew for themselves and the other ten don't exercise their rights at all. In Windischeschenbach, the town next to Neuhaus and a fifteen-minute walk over a river and up or down a very steep hill, there's a communal brewery too, as well as six brewers. The small towns of Mitterteich (three brewers), Falkenberg (two brewers) and Eslarn (just one) also each have their own shared brewery. And these are the only ones that remain.

Fütterer leads us from his farmhouse restaurant and up the central Marktplatz in Neuhaus, where most of the brewing-rights houses are. The shared brewery is at the top of the street. He pulls open big wooden doors on what looks like a barn to reveal beautiful old copper brewing vessels. Under one of them there's a wood fire – I've never seen that in a brewery before: even in breweries that still use a direct flame, they've replaced the wood with a more reliable and constant heat source. To the side of the small, clean brewhouse there's a kind of garage space where you might normally see fermenters, but here there's a small tanker trailer parked. To the back there's a small taproom where the brewers will meet to drink some beers.

The brewing process is old and traditional, barely touched by any notion that maybe a better or more efficient way exists. All the ingredients are local, and recipes are conceived almost empirically rather than informed by science, with the result that there'll naturally be variation between batches; if it sounds like something from the nineteenth century then that's basically because it is.

Fütterer brews 2,500 litres at a time, around ten times a year; he can brew all year round, but won't make beer if it's especially hot and humid, as it's more likely to go sour (even today the brewing seasons affect the beers). After a twelve-hour brewday, the hot, bitter-sweet hopped wort (what we call the liquid before fermentation) is pumped to the floor above the brewery and into a large, flat tray where it's left overnight to cool down – not many breweries do this any more for fear contact with the air will lead to contamination with wild yeast. First thing next morning the brewer returns, fills the small tanker trailer with the liquid and takes it back to his house. This is another key thing with *Zoiglbier*: it's brewed in the communal brewhouse, but the brewer always takes the liquid home to ferment and then mature in his own cellar: there are no fermenters in the brewery.

Those cellars were once underneath the houses, and the beer would've been stored in wooden vats and barrels. Fütterer takes us to see the old cellar in his farmhouse, leading us down a dark, damp, stony corridor cut into a rocky hillock. They used to store beer, potatoes and sauerkraut down there, but now they have a modern cold room. This new "cellar" is like any in a modern brewery or bar, and it's in a barn on the side of the house. It has horizontal lagering tanks stacked up, and an open stainless steel fermenter in the corner. The beer will ferment for ten to fourteen days before being transferred into one of the lagering tanks until it's ready, which might be anywhere from four to twelve weeks depending on how quickly the beer is drunk – it's served direct from the horizontal tanks.

All the beer is served on site: another special thing about *Zoigl* is that each brewer has a *Zoiglstube* (a "*Zoigl* living room"). Historically it would've literally been a living room, and people who made their own beer and had some left over would let their neighbours know they could go round for a drink by displaying a star symbol. Over time, some started to charge a nominal fee for the beer and the *Zoiglstuben* became a more commercial undertaking, with small snacks being served. These days most *Zoiglstuben* are still part of the family home and they only serve simple snacks like bread, cheese, sausage and cake. They don't open every day and a calendar or "*Zoigltermine*" records when each *Zoiglstuben* is pouring beer, which is typically one long weekend a month, and that's done to ensure there's always at least one beer available and somewhere to drink it (there is one *Zoiglstube* in Windischeschenbach that opens all year round).

Fütterer's beer and *Zoiglstube* is known as Schafferhof, and he spent many years renovating an old sky-blue farmhouse to turn it into a large restaurant and beer garden. "This was an old, messed-up place," he says. "We bought it in 1999, and people said we were crazy. But then everybody started to come. There were no beer gardens here, and now it's the most famous thing in the area." Since then others have opened larger and more comfortable spaces, moving away from the literal living room. The tradition of *Zoigl* may be centuries old, but Fütterer and others are slowly, gently, keeping it relevant. "We want to protect this tradition. It doesn't exist anywhere else," he says. "It's very special for our region. When you hear about the Upper Palatinate, that's what we're famous for." And keeping it small and local is important too: "You can't fill this tradition in a bottle and sell it somewhere else." If you want to drink *Zoigl*, you'll need to check the *Zoigl* calendar and go to one of the breweries.

Because the *Zoiglstuben* only open once a month, all the brewers have other jobs: *Zoigl* brewing is a kind of inherited hobby. Among the Neuhaus *Zoigl* brewers there's a butcher, a farmer, an engineer, one who works with glass and another in the cemetery. Fütterer is a chimney sweep. "We didn't learn it as a profession. I didn't study," he says. Instead he learned from previous brewers.

Fütterer passes me a mug of hazy amber-orange beer. It's delicious: toasty and smooth, a little sweet, a little bitter, and somehow unlike any kind of other lager I've had before. It's one of the closest things you can get to what lager might have been like a century or more ago. I want to know how it tastes to *him*, though. He laughs: "I never thought about it! I've drunk so much beer that I can say if it's good or not, but I can't say specifically about its taste." He adds: "I am selfish. I have to like it, and everyone else has to like it, too!"

His beer is excellent, and so was some of the other *Zoiglbier* I drank, but some were not so good. One was tart, another had an odd aroma of wild yeast and one had an overwhelmingly buttery flavour. It leaves me wondering: what if the beer was *really* bad? What if a couple of the communal brewers got greedy and tried to put the price up? And what if people started to revolt against the revolting beer?

Because that's what happened in 1838, in the communal breweries in a town 100km east of here, and the result was the most famous style of beer in the world.

PILSNER: BEER STRIKES GOLD

Pilsner Urquell is, in a way, the child of both Bohemia and Bohemianism, for it is a product of people who rejected the established, went against the grain of convention and in doing so created something of true originality . . . the beer that took brewing out of the dark ages, in the golden era, the beer seen by many today, as the way beer is meant to taste.
The Beer That Changed the Way the World Sees Beer, Pilsner Urquell Brewery publication

The greatest place in the whole world to drink lager is not in the beer halls or beer gardens; it's not on the beach, in the bath, the rooftop bar or on your sofa. The greatest place to drink lager is in the cold cellars of the brewery, direct from the vessel where it's been lagered for many weeks, catching the beer at its purest, freshest, ripest moment.

There's one cellar that's greater than any other, where you'll be many metres below ground, where your breath forever condenses, whether it's January or July, where the walls around you were hand-dug over many decades and are scratched and storied. Those walls have seen 180 years of human activity, and the production of millions and millions of glasses of golden lager beer. Today those cellars lead nowhere, but you could walk for many kilometres in the darkness, past where thousands of barrels were once stored. And while they lead nowhere now, look back in time and they take us to the beginning of the world's most famous beer style: Pilsner.

This underground world was a city beneath the city of Pilsen (known as Plzeň in Czech), in what was once that evocatively named area of Bohemia in the Austro-Hungarian Empire. At one time, tens of thousands of large wooden barrels would've been lining vast underground cellars, with hundreds of men down there working. Those great barrels held 3,000 to 4,000 litres of beer each. They're taller than you and I and wider than our arm span. Men built those huge barrels above ground and rolled them underground. The brewers made their beer above ground and then transferred it into the cellars, first into open-topped wooden vats where the liquid's sweetness turned into alcohol, and then into bigger lagering barrels to mature in the cold for three more months, all cooled by huge amounts of ice. I can't even imagine how it all might've smelt: the cold mineral air, the sweet musk of old oak barrels, the fruitiness of fermentation, the smell of hard labour from the men employed to spend their long working hours in the unbroken darkness. I can't imagine a brewery where almost everything took place underground. Spaten was like this. Klein-Schwechat was like this. Carlsberg would've been like this. All large lager breweries would've been like this. Barrel after barrel slumbering in the deep, cold cellars.

The first beers made underground in Pilsen in 1842 were unlike any beer at that time. Those dark cellars produced a bright golden lager, ostensibly the world's first, and it would become a sensation. Pilsner is the local beer of Pilsen, which became the local beer of the world.

****

Pilsen's first malthouse and brewery was recorded in 1307, with a brewer named Wolfram Zwynillinger, but it's likely there was brewing happening before that, as the current city had been there since 1295, when King Wenceslas II ordered that a new Pilsen be founded a few miles from its original location. This city was designed by the royal architect, who drew a central square with a cathedral and surrounded by a rectangular network of fifteen streets.

In Pilsen, certain houses on and surrounding that central square were given brewing rights, which were hereditarily passed on, so if you lived in a house with brewing rights, you were allowed to make beer; if you didn't, then you couldn't make it yourself, and had to buy beer from the brewing-rights citizens or the commercial breweries.

Beer was central to the city, but not everyone liked Pilsen's beer. In 1467, the then-head of the Catholic church in Bohemia, Hilarius of Litoměřice, said in a public sermon that the town "brews a venomous and acrid beverage which develops stone and crushes the kidneys". Then in the sixteenth century, a writer called Ondřej Bakalář Klatovský said: "Citizens of Plzeň, your beer, pour some up a swine's arse and the poor beast won't stop squealing for a fortnight."

In the eighteenth century, brewing-rights citizens were no longer allowed to brew it in their own homes because of the risk of fire, so the local beer was produced in one of four communal breweries. They brewed for personal consumption and sold any excess beers to individuals or taverns. Pilsen also had three private breweries: the Municipal Brewery, the Manorial Brewery and the Privileged Church Brewery.

The normal beer of the time in nearby Prague was made in a similar way to that from Munich: brown, malty and sweet, perhaps a little smoky, and it underwent three mash decoctions.[27] It differed from Munich because it was top-fermented, and then typically didn't get stored or matured at the brewery but was transferred straight to inns, where it went into their cellars or vaults. Each underground vault was "covered with a deep mass of ice, which never melts; and upon this mass the beer is placed, when received from the brewer". Then "after it has lain from four to six weeks on its icy bed, it is fit for drinking, and is served out to the customers in that chilly State". So it was a dark ale, brewed and fermented in a brewery and matured in an icy pub cellar, then served cold. (These quotes are from David Booth, who likely learned this from the well-travelled Sedlmayr and Dreher.)

We don't know how similar Pilsen's beer was to this, but we do know it wasn't all delicious, and the old habits and rudimentary equipment produced inconsistent beer. Indeed, according to a plaque in Pilsen's Brewery Museum beer was "brewed by thoroughly incompetent individuals", whether from inferior wort or through not being able to ferment and mature the beer in their own cellars, while others hoarded the best ingredients, and others still tried to charge too much money (when prices were supposed to be fixed). When a combination of these failings made the beer slow to sell, it turned sour – which was spoiling the city's beer reputation.

Neighbouring Bavaria, meanwhile, had a growing reputation for quality beer, and it was beginning to be seen and drunk in Pilsen's taverns, and at nine crowns a glass, it was two crowns cheaper than a glass of Pilsen beer. A number of brewing-rights citizens, including Václav Mirwald, František Brettschneider, Josef Jan Klotz, Václav Starý and Jakub Michl, some of whom were innkeepers, undersigned a letter of complaint to Mayor Martin Kopecký.

The response they got might not have been what they wanted, but it would catalyze what happened next, because Kopecký replied that any innkeeper could choose the beer they wished to sell, even foreign beers, but he recommended that the citizens with brewing rights build their own brewery, "because only wholesome and tasty beer may win in the competition and bring profit to Plzeň".

---

27 A "decoction mash" was common for Bavarian and Bohemian brewing at this time, and continues today. It involves mixing the malt and hot water in a wooden mash tun, then a portion of that liquid and grain was drawn off and boiled separately in another vessel, before returning it to the overall mix (a double decoction does this twice, while a triple does it three times). The purpose was to create additional sugars from the malt, while it also gave the brewers some control over the temperature increase. Decoction has the impact of creating a fuller mouthfeel and a caramelized flavour. Most Czech breweries still do this today, and so do some German brewers, while smaller craft brewers are also rediscovering this old technique.

Those citizens began to talk, often led by Václav Mirwald, innkeeper at U Zlatěho orla, the Golden Eagle. "We, citizens of Plzeň, need one thing," Mirwald is said to have declared frequently: "good and cheap beer!" It would later be claimed in the town chronicle of 1883 that "the greatest credit for the founding of the [Pilsner Urquell] brewery should go to Václav Mirwald."

As in every good story, the city of Pilsen needed an inciting incident to force change. With the unrest of the innkeepers, the poor-quality local beer, a reluctance or inability to do something new, and the emergence of Bavarian beer, the moment came in early February 1838.

The tale of Pilsen's "Beer Disaster" has been repeated like liquid lore; a dark moment that led to the birth of a bright golden legend. The local council had the rights to demand a brewer pour away any beer deemed detrimental for health and unfit for consumption, and on a cold February day in 1838 they enforced that power when thirty-six barrels of beer were poured out, the foul and dark ale soiling the dirty street in front of the Town Hall. Supposedly bystanders cheered at the spectacle.

By the end of 1838, the idea had developed of building their own town brewery, one owned by all the brewing-rights citizens. It would be a large brewery and malthouse with a shared goal of great beer, instead of many separate individual enterprises of competing or varying qualities. Their plans were expedited when it was discovered that a Bavarian brewery had built a storehouse outside Pilsen to deliver beer to the city.

On 2 January 1839, almost exactly one year after the Beer Disaster, twelve men, all tavern owners and important townsfolk, gathered to present a document entitled the "Request of the Burghers with Brewing Rights for the Construction of Their Own Malt- and Brew-house", which contained their plans for the *Měšťanský pivovar* or *Bürgerliches Brauhaus* (they still spoke and wrote both Czech and German back then – in English it translates as the Citizens' Brewery). Together, they believed, they could increase overall production, as well as achieving other advantages, including:

a) there would be savings on rent for the malthouse and brewery;
b) all overproduction would be prevented;
c) mature, unspoiled malt would be produced, and thus
d) the best quality of beer;
e) a burgher, who would himself brew, would not have to entrust his barley and malt to foreign hands, his capital would not be threatened by fire, etc., and finally

f) the quality of the beer could be improved by moving to produce bottom-fermented beers and lagers, and in so doing the market for Pilsner beer could be expanded even outside the territory of Pilsen.[28]

This new malting house and brewery, they declared, would be "their own permanent property and an honourable memorial to their descendants".

They found a location a short walk from the town square on the bank of the Radbuza River, close to a good source of pure soft water (uniquely so, and very important for producing a clean, smooth, pale lager) and above soft sandstone, perfect for digging cellars. It was an elementally unique location.

An architect named Martin Stelzer was hired, a 24-year-old local who had never built a brewery before but would become an expert – he would also become the unofficial city builder, responsible for over 200 buildings in Pilsen.

The city's existing commercial brewers challenged the building permit, but Stelzer's men began digging the foundations anyway, a job that would continue for fifty years as the brewery constantly grew: eventually they would total more than 9km in overall length, and cover 32,000m². Stelzer had travelled to Bavaria, and the influence was certainly evident in his brewery's construction, with the malthouse, the cellars, and indeed the beer that ended up being made in Pilsen.[29]

In spring 1842 a brewmaster was hired: not a local man, but a Bavarian, Josef Groll from Vilshofen, almost equidistant between Munich and Pilsen. The stern-looking, jowl-jawed, double-chinned, large-nosed, beady-eyed Groll would come to be known as the "inventor" of Pilsner beer, the Father of Pilsner, and yet we don't know much about him apart from that his father owned a brewery in Vilshofen, that he was offered a three-year contract,[30] and that records from the time describe "a common man of simple manners whom his own father mockingly dubbed the grossest Bavarian in the [whole of] Bavaria". I've read the word "grossest" also translated as rudest and coarsest, but you get the idea.

---

28 Credit to Evan Rail for his great research and translations of Pilsner Urquell's history.

29 This is hopeful speculation based on timing and location, but Stelzer was in Munich at the end of 1839 and Spaten, then the city's third-largest brewery and one of the most open in terms of sharing information, would have been worth visiting at that time. It certainly seems plausible that Stelzer could have visited Spaten and learned new techniques and processes there.

30 When Groll's contract expired he applied for his own job but didn't get it, and a fellow Bavarian named Šebestian Baumgärtner was hired instead. Pilsner's supposed inventor disappeared from everything apart from the beer history books, although there's now a small bust of his ugly head in his hometown of Vilshofen, though not many there know or care much about him. And why should they? He left their city to go and brew somewhere else, where he's credited with making the most famous beer style in the world, and then he did nothing else of note for the next forty years of his life. He died in Vilshofen in 1887, and it's often misreported that he was sitting in a tavern in town when he expired, but he actually died in bed of a heart attack.

The brewery talks of Groll as the legendary brewmaster who created Pilsner, but he arrived three years after they'd already decided to brew Bavarian beer, when the building work was mostly complete, and with almost everything in place to make beer – he just needed to brew it. Whatever the truth,[31] Groll, Stelzer and the brewery's committee combined to create the right conditions for producing lager. Next came the process of making that brown Bavarian beer into a golden Bohemian one.

To begin with, they had to wait. They followed the Bavarian brewing season, which meant they couldn't make beer until the end of September. Moreover, that year's barley and hops had yet to be harvested, so the important job of malting had still to be done. This was something that would change the history of beer, and again we have no idea *why*.

What is generally believed is that the malt made in Pilsen from Moravian barley was fired indirectly in the same manner as in British maltings, using the techniques Sedlmayr and Dreher brought back to Central Europe. The indirect heat eliminated the smell and taste of smoke, while also giving more control over the exact colour of the malt. It was a new technique for Bohemians, and some suggest that producing such a pale beer was actually a mistake. What certainly happened is that they created a paler malt, one capable of producing a paler beer, and the new malt would take the name of the city that produced it: Pilsner malt.

By early October the malt was made. Fragrant Bohemian hops had arrived fresh from their harvest; the cellars were dug and lined with wooden barrels built by a team of coopers; there was the pure, soft water and, to complete everything, the brewery had purchased yeast from Bavaria.[32] Groll lit the fire under his brewing vessels and started to make the first batch of beer in the new Citizens' Brewery. He did three decoctions on his pale malt and filled a large copper tun, made by Josef Schallander, a local kettle-smith, with over 3,000 litres of sweet, golden wort, which boiled with the aromatic and bitter Czech hops. Later that day the golden liquid ran down into the open wooden fermentation vats in the cellars, where it would have sat for a week while the yeast gradually turned the malt sugars into alcohol. From there it moved into the larger enclosed barrels, deeper in the cellars, where it would be stored for four weeks.

---

31 The brewery's archivist, Anna Perinova, explained that a lot of the early history of the brewery was lost because they used many books from the early nineteenth century to line, strengthen and insulate the roof of the old Town Hall. Maybe one day the full story will be discovered.

---

32 This yeast is known as the "H" yeast, and it's believed the initial refers to Munich's Hacker Brewery (now Hacker-Pschorr), then the fourth-largest in the city. There is a myth that the yeast was smuggled to the brewery by a monk, but that's not true. The Citizens' Brewery once also had several strains of yeast, using different ones in different areas of the cellars. They later decided on the "H" as the best one for them.

Martin Hruška, the then-archivist of Pilsen, visited the brewery in its early years:

> The spacious building, in a plain, yet graceful style, has excellent cellars, mostly hewn in rock, which can accommodate some 12,000 tubs [around 6,800hl], it has beautifully equipped copper rooms, two extremely large vats from which soaked barley grain falls onto a magnificent germinating floor. The water piping with a pump brings water from the brewery's well to all rooms, except the granary, and the brewery boasts all that belongs to such a huge brewing plant. Let me mention the English kiln heated by heat transferred from the boiling room, and the iron crusher made to an American design. It is linked to a water-lifting tackle (made of iron in the Metternich Foundry in Plasy) and propelled by a horse mill.

The beer was to be first served at the St Martin's Fair on 11 November 1842, and three inns sold the city's new beer on that day: U Bílé růže (The White Rose), U Hanesů (named after innkeeper Josef Hannes) and Vaclav Mirwald's U Zlatého orla.

"The public awaited this new lager with anticipation," wrote a chronicler of the brewery's history, and years later

> eyewitnesses of this event reminisced about the ceremonial moment when the lager of a sparkling colour and delicious taste was first tapped ... Exclamations of awe were heard when its golden hue shone underneath the snow-white cap of froth; then the drinkers cheered its crispy, delicious taste, the likes of which they had never tasted before.

This was the first ever taste of the beer that came to be known as Pilsner Urquell, and it was the world's first golden lager. Supposedly.

In July 1829 the *Wöchentlicher Anzeiger für Biertrinker* (Weekly Indicator for Beer Drinkers) published an investigation into Munich's beers, with the results showing that there were fifty-one Munich breweries, and twenty-eight of their beers were classified as "wine yellow", twenty-two were light brown and one beer was dark brown. What colour was "wine yellow" in 1829? Who knows, but it sounds like pale lagers, doesn't it? (In the following years something changed, and by the middle of the 1830s, the main lagers in Munich were all brown, and they'd remain that way until 1895.) There's also speculation that Sepp Pschorr, who had been running the Pschorr brewery since the early 1790s, was the originator of Munich Helles, a consequence of instructing his maltsters to save wood and roast the malt for less time. In 1837 Spaten had released a special pale *Märzenbier*. In Vienna Klein-Schwechat were making amber-ish lagers. So was this new Pilsner beer *really* the first golden lager?

Pilsner Urquell claim to have been the first to produce a golden lager and no brewery has made a counter-claim, so there is insufficient evidence to give a definitive answer. But it was certainly the beer that gave birth to the style of Pilsner.

This new pale lager beer came at a time when Bohemian brewing was rapidly changing: In 1841 only around 10 per cent of Bohemian breweries were making lagers; in 1860, lager accounted for 30 per cent of Bohemian beer, but then by 1870, 831 of the 849 Bohemian breweries – an astonishing 98 per cent – were brewing lagers.

The daily routine of brewing continued for Groll and the Citizens' Brewery, and production in the first year was around 6,300 tubs, or 3,580hl, and there were at least two types of beer made, following the Bavaria tradition: a 10° or 11° short-lagered beer (the beer first drunk on 11 November had been brewed thirty-seven days earlier, just into the new brewing season, so was what the Bavarians would call a *Winterbier*); and a stronger 12° long-lagered beer (in Bavaria's *Sommerbier* or lager tradition – this was lagered for three to four months). In the first brewing year, around two thirds of their output was the 10°. The 10° no longer exists, and it's the 12° beer that we now call Pilsner Urquell.[33]

The Citizens' Brewery was soon expanding and upgrading. This report from Jan Neruda in *Hlas* (Voice) magazine in 1863 gives us a wonderful feeling for what it was like at the time.

> I have seen it, so I can die! I have seen the patch of land surrounded by tall walls and concealing deep cellars, a place which Prague talks of more often than Žižka Field near Přibyslav or the ash spilled in Konstanz. Should the Plzeň brewery committee decide no longer to export beer to Prague, Prague's wives would carry their husbands to Plzeň on their backs, for otherwise they could not stand them. Should the committee require a guilder for a pint of beer, Prague's pawn shops would be full overnight. Those 250 Plzeň holders of the brewing right comprise an oligarchy and Czech history records their names in letters of gold and loves them more than the Greeks love their 300 but one oligarchs. You

---

33 When you see 10° or 12° in Czech it's a measure of the original gravity using the Plato scale. The original gravity is a measure of the concentration of sweetness extracted from the malt into the wort. Using the most drinker-friendly explanation, this is like telling us the expected level of alcohol – the more sugar in there, the greater the potential alcohol content will be. A 10° beer is going to be your standard-strength lager, around 4 per cent ABV, while a 12° will be around 5 per cent ABV (and a 14° will be 6 per cent and so on). Pilsner Urquell is technically a 12° beer (because of its higher original gravity and more premium status), though it has a lower attenuation rate than other lagers, meaning there's more residual sweetness, and the alcohol content is only 4.4 per cent ABV. The best-selling lagers in the Czech Republic are 10°.

will certainly forgive me that I am being so sentimental that I feel elated by the mere thought of the brewery, however, I may be the first columnist to visit the Plzeň brewery and anyway – I too cherish a secret love!

The Plzeň brewery is genuinely magnificent. Its premises span from the right shoulder of the Radbuza River, far across the road and other plots are still being purchased. Its mighty buildings, enclosed by a tall wall, are like a small town. Everything is controlled in an industrial way, yet despite the use of machines, the brewery employs 250 people who brew 90,000 tubs [some 50,000hl] every year; this is another similarity to industrial plants, owing to the sudden transitions from the heat of boilers to the chill of ice rooms the people working here do not live long. Yet I must add that I was moved to tears while walking in the endless cellars hewn in the living rock. Holding lanterns, like miners, we descended in shafts of liquid gold. First we plodded through the old narrow corridors with barrels only along one wall, but then we strolled round the endless new, broad and high vaults. In a quiet slumber 35,000 tubs of lager like the Army of Blaník awaits the moment of direst need when they march out and liberate the dear homeland. The flickering light of our three lanterns gave those grave sixty-tub barrels a peculiar impression. Long, long do they rest in pensive solitude only occasionally disturbed by mortal aliens, and it is hardly surprising that having amassed so many thoughts they sometimes instil wit in people and make good friends out of foes.

A single long cellar contained 150 such barrels. Our guide, an elderly Bavarian gentleman, turned to me and said: "*Das ist die schönste gallerie.*" I have seen copious famous galleries, but had to agree with him.

In 1885, Pilsen's other famous export, E. Škoda engineering works, installed an artificial cooling system in the cellars that "would maintain a stable temperature of 3°C (37°F) in all weather, no matter whether the rooms were empty or full of fermenting beer", while an additional ice machine was capable of producing 1,000kg of ice an hour. In 1889, Škoda installed a steam engine in the brewery, which by now had also installed a bottling line and added new 100hl brewing kettles, allowing them to make 1,800hl a day.[34] A couple of years later they had

---

34 Emil Škoda was born in Pilsen in November 1839 – his father was one of the 12 men to undersign the founding document of the Citizens' Brewery. He studied engineering in Prague before returning to his hometown to work, where in 1866 he became chief engineer of Ernst Fürst von Waldstein-Wartenberg, a manufacturer specializing in "machinery and equipment for sugar mills, breweries, mines, steam engines, boilers, iron bridge structures, and railway facilities". Škoda bought the company and began to expand it – by the outbreak of World War I it was the largest arms manufacturer in Austro-Hungary, and in 1917 employed 35,000 people in Pilsen. In 1925, looking to produce more than just guns (and they made a lot of guns), Škoda took over the car manufacturers Laurin & Klement, and it's cars they're most famous for today.

seventy different sections in their cellars, holding 6,000 oak barrels ranging from 50–80hl each. There were 52 ice rooms for 60,000m³ of ice. They had 175,000 transport barrels and 80 railroad freight cars, as well as a railway line running right through the middle of the brewery. There were 200 brewers and brewing assistants, 100 people employed in the malthouse, 145 coopers and 140 general workers. And around one fifth of their beer was being exported.

Export became, and would continue to be, important for Pilsner Urquell – and many other lager breweries. If we look back to the founding document, the citizens had the foresight to consider export by writing that if they made quality beer then a "market for Pilsner beer could be gained even outside the territory of Pilsen". By the end of 1842, Pilsner beer had already got to Prague. U Pinkasů claims it was the first tavern to sell it in the city, but it was actually U Modré Štiky, which no longer exists, that received the first barrels (U Pinkasů is still serving the beer today). In 1856 Pilsner was first sold in Vienna. In 1862 it left the Austro-Hungarian Empire for the first time when it was sold in Paris. By 1873 "a number of major cities and towns had established "Pilsner Restaurants" serving Měšťanský pivovar's beer: e.g. Brno, Bratislava, Linz, Salzburg, Graz, Krakow, Lviv, Trieste, Budapest, Berlin, Dresden, Frankfurt, Cologne, Leipzig, London, Mainz, Munich, Vienna, Paris, Strasbourg and many more" (Kejha et al., *Plzeňský Prazdroj: A Story That Continues to Inspire*). In that same year, the beer was first sold in the United States in the town of Racine, Wisconsin. By the 1890s, almost 20 per cent of overall production was exported around the world, and by the time of Prohibition Pilsner Urquell was the best-selling imported beer in the United States. All around the world, people were drinking Pilsner beer.

The brewery had made sure to trademark "Pilsner Bier" back in 1859, and in 1898 they also trademarked "Plzeňský Prazdroj" and "Pilsner Urquell" – the name translates as "Original Source of Pilsner". Anyone could use the name Pilsner, but the brewery officially had the trademark on the original name.

****

The Citizens' Brewery wasn't the only brewery in Pilsen: there was the Prior Brewery, Svetovar, and the Erste Pilsner Aktien-Brauerei (First Joint-Stock Brewer). The latter was founded in 1869–70 next to the Citizens' Brewery, led by a committee of twenty entrepreneurs (including Emil Škoda) and designed and built by Stelzer. In 1919 the brewery's name changed to Gambrinus, and later it was taken over by the Citizens' Brewery to help try to settle "the fierce rivalry and price wars" between the two neighbouring breweries. Gambrinus, it was decided, would make 10° pale beer and a dark beer, while the Citizens'

Brewery would focus on the 12° Pilsner Urquell. That decision worked out well for both companies: Pilsner Urquell is seen by many as the best premium lager, while Gambrinus is the best-selling beer in the Czech Republic, accounting for something like one in four of the beers sold in the country.

In 1913, Pilsner Urquell produced one million hectolitres for the first time. That's 176 million British pints. But as in much of Europe and beyond as the continent became consumed by war, the next few decades of the twentieth century were not good for business. Barley rations were implemented, and for an additional income soda water was produced. Brewing equipment was requisitioned for munitions factories. At various times between 1918 and 1935 the domestic beer was 7° or 9° (around 2.5–3.5 per cent ABV, though it was still brewed at full strength for export). And then during World War II it went down to as low as 3.5° (barely 2 per cent ABV). By that time a central agency in Prague was determining which breweries could remain open, which would be closed, what each remaining brewery could make and where they could sell it.

In 1944 and 1945 the Citizens' Brewery was heavily damaged in air raids, with more than 150 bombs landing on or near the brewery in three separate attacks. Production understandably dropped, but 325,000hl of 4° beer was still produced in 1945, and it was that 4° beer that American troops drank to celebrate the liberation of Pilsen on 6 May 1945 before they went on to Prague. The end of the war was nearby, but a new reality was coming.

In May 1945, all big breweries were nationalized, and brewing-rights payments stopped. The Citizens' Brewery no longer belonged to the people of Pilsen: it belonged to the Communist government.

Between 1946 and 1948 the beer varied between 6° and 8°. Through the 1950s, strength increased from 8° to 10°, and finally in 1956 the 12° overtook everything. By 1957, Pilsner Urquell was being exported to 57 countries. It took until 1965 to get back to one million hectolitres, and by then 95 per cent of that was the 12° Pilsner Urquell.[35]

From the late 1930s transport barrels were increasingly made of aluminium (and supplied to the brewery by Škoda). The wooden lager barrels in the cellars were joined by over 100 steel tanks by the end of the 1950s. In 1962 they commissioned 128 steel fermenting vessels, followed by another 120 lagering tanks and an additional cooling system in the cellar. After steel came conical tanks in which they could ferment and then lager the beer all in one vessel, and with the increase in steel came a reduction in lagering times: in the early 1980s

---

35 The 8° disappeared completely in 1971, though it returned for a few years in the 1980s when it was made exclusively for the canteens of the Škoda factory. They were still brewing a 10° beer in 1989 and made 143,000hl. Today there is only one Pilsner Urquell and it's 12°.

they were still lagering the beer for three months, but by the early 1990s that had decreased to around five weeks – the same time it took Josef Groll in 1842.

In 1989 the Velvet Revolution ended the control of the one-party Communist government. The brewery was privatized, and then in 1999, on the symbolic date of 5 October, Pilsner Urquell was incorporated into South African Breweries. SAB later took over Milwaukee's Miller Brewing to become SABMiller, then in October 2016 a $107 billion dollar merger between SABMiller and Anheuser-Busch InBev created Anheuser-Busch InBev SA/NV, the world's largest beer company, and several European brands were then taken over by the Japanese brewing giant Asahi, including Peroni, Grolsch, Gambrinus and Pilsner Urquell. The brewery started by a few hundred citizens of Pilsen, which gave the world a golden lager, a beer born in revolution – or revulsion – against bad brown beer and created what became the most popular beer style in the world, was now part of a global Japanese company.

Pilsner's 176th birthday

At the St Martin's Day Fair there's a discordant mix of church bells and piped music, a chiming echo with a tinny orchestral undertone that reminds me of a Christopher Nolan soundtrack.

We're in Pilsen's busy central square surrounded by a mix of pretty pastel-coloured buildings and some bleak Communist blocks, with the dark and impressive old town hall on the north side – it was in front of this town hall that in 1838 the thirty-six barrels of bad beer were spilled into the streets. In the middle of the square, the huge cathedral towers into the sunny sky over the people browsing the market stalls, eating snacks and drinking hot wine or cold beer.

But on this cold November afternoon the sound and sun feel oddly ominous. It's the scene in a movie where people look happy one minute and then a flutter of pigeons disturbs the fragile peace and BOOM! – something forces the hero into action.

Maybe this is what it was like 176 years ago to the day in this very square, because that's when the new beer from the Citizens' Brewery was first served. The people of Pilsen had waited almost four years for the new brewery to open. Were they excited, were they anxious – were they just really thirsty to finally drink the new beer?

None of the three inns that sold the beer on that day still exists. Vaclav Mirwald's the Golden Eagle was the most important and was located directly on the town square. Today if you look up at the old buildings on the square's western side it's not where the pretty pink one is, nor the charming yellow one, nor the handsome pale green one. Instead, look for the ugliest building on the square, the Communist-era Central Hotel: that's where Mirwald's pub used to be. I'm not going to drink a beer there. There's only one place where I really want to drink the beer, and that's in the brewery cellars, where they still make a small amount of Pilsner Urquell in the old way, and serve it direct from the lagering barrel.

When the brewery was transitioning out of wood and into steel – something that every large old brewery did – it started a process called "parallel brewing": brewing in both kinds of vessels and then matching the flavour from the steel to that in the wood. Unlike every other brewery, here they decided to keep on brewing a small amount of beer down in the cellars to continue that old lagering tradition.

I'm on the public brewery tour, and we pass the old copper brewhouse on the way to the modern stainless steel one; we see the large packaging lines; we see what the brewery say is the original copper used by Josef Groll in 1842; there's some interactive bits where they show movies and let you smell hops. We learn how the brewery still uses some important old brewing techniques like triple-decoction and a direct-fired copper (it's just not wood-fired any more), and employs a workshop of coopers to build and maintain the wooden barrels, and that sometimes you'll find one of those barrels in a pub for a special event and it'll be filled with unfiltered beer. All very interesting, but I'm getting thirsty.

The cellars are wide like big railway arches as they lead down into the cold. We stop at a map of the whole underground complex: it's huge, although now only a small amount is accessible.[36] As we pass through a small door, there are several open wooden barrels lined up along the wall, scratched with chalk to measure the gravity of the beer and the temperature – as the gravity goes down, the natural exothermic generation of heat from the yeast goes up. Just sixty years ago there would still have been more than a thousand of these open fermenters in this part of the cellar.

Straight ahead is a cathedral-like corridor, dark and with spotlights hanging in the air, shining onto the large wooden barrels. They're double-stacked on either side, capable of holding around 4,000 litres of beer in each, with some over 100 years old, and there must be more than 30 of them – there used to be 6,000.

You pick up a glass, a man opens a tap in the barrel and a hazy golden beer pours out, filling to the top with a thick white foam. All around it's cold, the floor is wet, the wooden barrels are imposingly large and old. The beer is bitter-sweet, fragrant with hops, full-bodied by being unfiltered (meaning there's still yeast in it), and it's smooth and deeply delicious. This is the original Pilsner, and as

---

36 I once got to explore a little off the tourist route, and it's bloody scary. It's so dark, it's damp, it's eerily quiet, and it's just row after row of abandoned and icy cellars. It still amazes me that if you worked in the brewery this was where you spent your time; deep underground, all year round, always dark and always cold.

close as we can get to how the beer might've tasted in 1842. Pilsner might have inspired countless beers around the world, but not many taste quite like the one you get to drink straight from the lagering barrel.

CARLSBERG AND PURE YEAST

The life of the brewer
Jacob Christian Jacobsen, who went by JC, was born in 1811. As a young man his father had found work in Copenhagen in the King's Brewhouse, one of the city's largest breweries, and later (certainly by 1811) moved to become a tenant brewer, meaning he rented a brewery. In 1826 he'd buy it, and on his death in 1835 JC reluctantly took over – reluctantly because although he'd been working in the brewery for many years, he still hadn't completed his formal education. But family loyalty saw him devote himself to the brewing business – something that would come back to bite him later.

Though he continued to brew as his father had done – likely to have been a wheat beer – in 1836 he visited a Copenhagen wine merchant who was selling Bavarian beer, and, according to historian Kristof Glamann, "pronounced it to be a remarkable type of beer which invited further investigation". He travelled to Germany to learn more, and on his return made some experiments in his mother's cellar using her wash copper and a couple of small malt vats, initially using his regular top-fermenting yeast. After several brews he bought a bottom-fermenting yeast to do further trials.

"This venture has worried me for some time," he wrote, "not for its importance in a pecuniary sense, but because I regarded it as a touchstone of my competence, of which I have not entertained the highest opinion since my unsuccessful effort last year." In April 1838, JC had advertisements for Bavarian beer in the local newspapers, and by 1844 he was committed enough to bottom-fermented beer to apply for permission to build cellars in the fortress ramparts on the edge of the city, where he would have two vaults capable of holding 700 barrels to store his "*lagerøl*."

While he was awaiting approval, he spent the summer travelling through central Europe. He went to Dresden, Prague, Vienna and Munich, staying in the Bavarian city for a week, where he met Gabriel Sedlmayr and visited the Spaten brewery – it would be the beginning of a lifelong friendship. In 1845 he went to Munich and to Spaten again, this time wanting something specific: yeast. On the stagecoach home he carefully carried a tin holding around two litres of Spaten's lager yeast hidden inside a hat box, and at every stop on the long journey he rushed to cool it in water to keep the yeast alive.

That winter he brewed 300 barrels of *lagerøl* with Sedlmayr's yeast and by the following April various beer merchants were advertising a Bavarian beer from "Brewer Jacobsen's cellar under the ramparts".

JC looked for a new location for a brewery. Fresh air, a good source of clean water and lots of space to dig extensive underground cellars (by the 1880s he'd have 10km of cellars and tunnels dug beneath his brewery) were difficult to find in the compact, crowded city, especially the water, because Copenhagen at that time was quite literally shitty: the population in 1847 was 126,000, plus 1,500 cows and 3,000 horses, and in that year 24,000 cartloads of crap (or "night-soil" as it was more euphemistically called) were removed.

He found the right location on Valby Hill, half a mile from the city fortress, where good water had been discovered by workers constructing a railroad. In April 1846 JC wrote to the King for "permission to construct and operate a Bavarian beer brewery", stressing the importance of the "Bavarian *Lagerkjeller*", which "can not be lowered when the brewery is located inside a city, between tall houses, where the air is always more degrees warmer than outside".

He named the new brewery after his only son Carl and the Danish word for hill, *bjerg*. JC brewed the first Carlsberg beer in November 1847, and in the first full year he made 94 batches. By the early 1850s he reached the brewery's initial capacity of 5,000 barrels. Dark Bavarian lager (all Danish lager then was still dark and Bavarian-style) accounted for just 6 per cent of Copenhagen's beer output, but in modern terms it was the premium beer of the day.

Carlsberg was a permanent building site, always expanding or modernizing, above ground and below. By January 1856 JC was brewing twice a day and using mechanical mashing instead of wooden paddles, which helped to save brewing time. In 1857 he added a closed copper vessel and then another two years later, meaning he could brew four batches a day. By the early 1860s he was brewing 25,000 barrels a year and would soon be using steam power, enabling further expansion.

JC was a driven man who worked tirelessly.[37] He was forever seeking new technologies to improve his beer, travelling every summer during the months when no brewing took place at Carlsberg to learn more, and challenging current or perceived truths. He was rarely the first to use a new technology, but was

---

37 As did his staff: a normal work day in 1860 was 6 a.m. until 7 p.m., though they might drink up to 4.5 litres of beer during that time. That might seem a lot, but it's nothing compared to a story in the *Coventry Evening Telegraph* in 1954, which called Carlsberg "Europe's largest brewery" and claimed their 4,000 employees got six free beers a day but could, in effect, drink what they liked. Some employees who "have worked in the hotter parts of the brewery for thirty years or so can, *and do*, drink as many as fifty bottles a day. And that is twenty-nine pints! Not every day, of course, but just when they are thirstier than usual."

always looking to understand new developments – and to try to improve them. He was constantly striving for perfection.

In 1865, JC wrote a letter to his son Carl, now 23-years old and on his way to becoming a brewer himself, which reveals the brewer's mindset.

> I appropriated the experience of [the Bavarians] and applied it in Denmark at just the right moment, and luckily I had acquired sufficient knowledge and sufficient insight to understand tolerably well what it all meant, at any rate better than most brewers in Germany and better than all of them in Denmark. But the world does not stand still, knowledge broadens and insight increases everywhere. Many of the fundamental conclusions handed down by the Bavarians are disputed; it is certain that their correctness is not unqualified; the metamorphoses during malting, mashing and fermenting are demonstrably not as simple as was previously supposed; there now appear to be different substances and different changes of substance which we had not dreamt of before but which we must now know about if we are to explain the phenomena we see and if we wish to direct the progress of our operations with a clear awareness, not stumbling forward in the dark like crude empiricists until we happen to hit the right path.

JC concluded with a pointed comment presumably aimed at inspiring his son: "He who possesses the most thorough knowledge of chemistry and its auxiliary sciences along with the necessary practical proficiency and insight will be Europe's leading brewer of the coming generation." That year was a critical one in the relationship between father and son. JC was a controlling father and Carl frequently resisted, even if he tolerated and abided by his father – for now, anyway. JC expected greatness from his son because one day he wanted him to take over the family brewery, but, he wrote:

> If you think to be my successor at Carlsberg, you must make yourself worthy of that position.
>
> Only a proficient and energetic brewer, with the ability and the will to continue what I have begun, and who wants to be ever at the forefront of progress in brewing in Denmark and Scandinavia, shall come into possession of this place after me, which is dedicated to this undertaking. God forbid that it should be anyone but my son.

In the summer of 1865, while JC was on one of his trips through Europe, Carl secretly got engaged to his cousin, Emilie. When JC found out he wasn't happy, partly because he didn't approve of Emilie, but also because he thought his son lacked worldly experience; marriage wasn't yet part of JC's plan for Carl.

So in 1866 JC cut short Carl's academic education and sent him to get a practical education as a brewer. Carl wouldn't return home until 1870.

In Strasbourg Carl met several brewers, including Louis Hatt, then he travelled on to Marseilles, Munich and Vienna, where he spent time respectively at the Spaten and Klein-Schwechat breweries, then Budapest (probably to visit Dreher's brewery), before re-joining Hatt to travel through Bohemia, Silesia and Prussia. During the whole period JC's correspondence was directing Carl to ask the right questions.

After two years in Central Europe, Carl was sent to Britain. "The main task of your study", wrote his father, was

to learn to brew beer for Export, especially to distant countries but also for shorter journeys, with the same quality and the same Taste, Appearance and Composition, as the best English Ale and Porter, who are rightly famous and famous all over the world, except where in the place or in immediate proximity can be a good Bavarian beer. (Bavarian Beer is not suitable for shipping quite far).

Carl worked at Younger's brewery in Edinburgh, where he learned about porter brewing, then travelled to Burton-on-Trent and London, although he repeatedly asked if he could go back to Edinburgh, most likely because there he'd met his future wife.

On Carl's twenty-eighth birthday his father wrote:

You are now as fully equipped for the fulfilment of your task as almost any young, or even older, brewer in Europe can be, and with an interest in your calling which warrants the highest hopes. And what higher hope can there be for me than to see the goal which has seemed to be before me since my earliest youth, realized through you?

It was a rosy-eyed but veiled hope, because by the time of Carl's return, JC had begun work on a second brewery, to be known as the Annexe Brewery. Carl wouldn't be taking over at Carlsberg just yet: he would have to prove himself at the Annexe, where he would be the tenant brewer in a word-of-mouth agreement between father and son.

JC had also decided that Carl would brew British-style ales, because he didn't think there was room in Copenhagen for more dark Bavarian-style beer. In this

JC was proved to be wrong, as within three years Carl was hardly brewing any ale and making Bavarian beer in a similar way to his father. Between 1871 and 1881 Bavarian beer production in the city would increase from 71,000 barrels to 330,000, much of that made by Carlsberg.[38]

JC believed the storage of the beer was the key to his success, and was leaving his beer to lager for between six and nine months, and still only brewing in the winter season. Carl, however, with his education in year-round porter production, thought differently, and didn't think six months was necessary for his Bavarian beer. Where JC had storage for 40,000 barrels, enabling him to produce 80,000 to 90,000 barrels of beer a year, Carl's Annexe Brewery had storage for only 14,000, yet he was selling almost as much as his father, meaning it was aged for far less time. Meanwhile, in Strasbourg Louis Hatt had developed "lighter short-storage types of lager beer", which Carl admired but JC saw as only "half-stored".

Their relationship was strained, and Carl was about to make it a lot worse: he started calling his beer Ny Carlsberg, or New Carlsberg. It was JC's belief that Carl's beer wasn't of a high enough quality, and that consumers would be confused as to who made Carlsberg beer, potentially ruining the reputation he'd spent more than thirty years building up. He started looking for a way to secure the future of this brewery – a future that didn't necessarily involve Carl.

In 1876 JC set up a Carlsberg Foundation, and wrote down his "Golden Words", which would direct the future of Carlsberg:

> In working the brewery it should be a constant purpose, regardless of immediate gain, to develop the art of making beer to the greatest possible degree of perfection so that this brewery as well as its products may ever stand out as a model and, through their example, assist in keeping beer brewing in this country at a high and honourable level.

The Foundation was to oversee and manage the brewery without JC – he'd effectively gifted his brewery to it. To Carl it must've seemed he couldn't be trusted to run Carlsberg and was being disinherited – and in many ways he was.

The relationship deteriorated. Carl wanted to grow his brewery to be able to make more beer, but as the landlord of the brewery JC had the final say, and wouldn't agree. JC also thought it was time to sign a formal business contract

---

38   Bavarian lager was 95 per cent of the Danish market in 1893. But the shift to Pilsner was coming. As early as 1881, the Tuborg brewery had made Denmark's first Pilsner-style lager, and Carlsberg introduced their Pilsner in 1904 – this is the ancestor of the beer we know simply as "Carlsberg" today. By 1912, pale lager was two thirds of the market and Denmark was on its way to becoming a Pilsner monoculture.

on Carl's tenancy of the Annexe Brewery, and offered a full or part sale to Carl. The brewery was effectively Carl's already and now he could own it outright. But the offer came with conditions: he had to store his beer for longer, limit output to 40,000 barrels a year and stop using Ny Carlsberg as the name. Carl didn't agree to any of that.

So now JC proposed that Carl build a new brewery on land adjacent to Carlsberg, while still leasing the Annexe Brewery. The Annexe would be renamed as "Albertina", Carl's new brewery would be called Valby Brewery and Carlsberg would remain as it was. In November 1879 Carl accepted, and began work on his new brewery, but he defied his father by continuing to use the Ny Carlsberg name for the Annexe beers. That was too much for JC, and in July 1880 he gave his son notice of eviction from the Annexe Brewery, offering a generous year to allow time for Carl's Valby Brewery to be finished.

"If he does [call his brewery Valby]", JC wrote to a friend in November 1881, "we could live as peaceful neighbours. If, however, he does not do that, there will be a continuing war between us, which must be continued even after my death, for 2 breweries with the same name next to each other, driven in opposing spirits, must always be in war on life and death." Carl even tried to officially change his own name to Carl Jacobsen Ny Carlsberg, so that even if he called his new business the Valby Brewery it would be owned by Carl Jacobsen of New Carlsberg, giving him the right to call his brewery after his own name.

Eventually he got formal approval to use the name Ny Carlsberg, leaving JC no option but to change the name of his brewery. He altered it to Gamle Carlsberg, or Old Carlsberg.

Through all this father and son were brewing side by side as neighbours and competitors. There's a report of JC nailing shut the blinds in his dining room so he didn't have to look at Carl's brewery at mealtimes, and Carl barricading the gate between Gamle and Ny Carlsberg, forcing his parents to drive by a different route; the two brewers even called the road between them different names. "The two crazy people put up signs, each successively bigger than the other," JC's laboratory director wrote in his diary, "because each is trying to conceal the other's signpost. They have thereby made themselves targets of ridicule for the workers, and news of the scandal has reached many newspapers."

Late in 1881 the separation was made complete when Carl was given a patrimony payment of one third of JC's fortune in return for renouncing any future legacy from his father.

The brewery names became official in October 1882 and Ny Carlsberg would start brewing in 1883, while JC undertook significant investment to combine the Annexe Brewery with Gamle Carlsberg, increasing his output:

in 1881 Gamle Carlsberg sold 123,440hl of beer, which jumped to 192,040hl in 1882, and then 282,459hl four years later. But that growth made quality – a particular concern of JC's – an even greater challenge, and if 1881 and 1882 had been rough years personally for him ("I live in a constant turmoil," he wrote), then 1883 was about to get even worse.

The beer of national revenge

All beer will eventually turn sour, and the challenge for any brewer was to make it taste good for as long as possible. With an imperfect understanding of the science, brewers had limited actual control: hops are anti-bacterial, so they helped; keeping the beer cold helped, and storing it for longer in the cold seemed to extend the shelf-life as well; but despite that you could almost guarantee that beer contained bacteria or wild yeast that would one day make it taste bad. Not until the 1860s and 1870s, when it was already being brewed in huge volumes, was beer properly understood on a microbiological level, and its pioneer was Louis Pasteur.

By the 1870s, Pasteur was a very famous and acclaimed research scientist who had developed many of the basic techniques of microbiology. He was a French national hero for his work in vaccinations, immunology, fermentation, and his development of a technique to prevent wine, beer, milk and other drinks from bacterial contamination. He spent his life dedicated to understanding and preventing diseases, with remarkable success.

Before Pasteur, even pre-eminent brewing scientists didn't fully understand fermentation. First, Pasteur looked at bacteria and proved they were definitely living things, and didn't come from "spontaneous generation", as others believed (i.e. that fermentation began spontaneously in a dead substance, producing bacteria from within). Then he looked at wine and showed that yeast cells were present in the air or on the grape skins, and that they were the things causing a physiological reaction and starting the fermentation (others had argued for centuries that yeast was created in a chemical reaction from inside the grape juice as a kind of inactive waste by-product). Pasteur revealed that it was yeasts that were consuming the sugars in the grape juice and converting them into alcohol and carbon dioxide. Barley or grape sugars had been turned into alcohol for thousands of years without anyone *really* understanding how until now.

Then the yeast and the bacteria came together. In 1863, Emperor Napoleon III requested that Pasteur investigated the cause of "disease" in wine. When Pasteur looked at bad wine under his microscope he saw not only round yeast micro-organisms, but also elongated bacteria micro-organisms, and it was these, he theorized, that were making the wine go bad: get rid of them, or somehow kill them, and he could get better fermentation and cure the disease.

He developed a method of heating filled bottles to 50–60°C (122–140°F) for a short time, which killed any microbes or bacteria within the wine without affecting the taste too much. The process came to be called pasteurization[39].

Pasteur published his *Études sur le vin* in 1866, but didn't advocate the heating process for beer. That didn't stop brewers trying out the technique, and by the 1870s it was common practice – Carlsberg were using it as early as 1874, initially using hot air, which was then superseded by putting the bottles in a large hot-water bath. When Pasteur did turn to beer it was with a new motivation: revenge.

The Franco-Prussian War of 1870–1871 was a humiliating defeat for the French, and had a personal impact on Pasteur when his only son was forced to enlist and construction on his own laboratory was interrupted. Now that more German beers were entering the French market without many French beers going the other way, Pasteur wanted to make the French brewing industry better and more competitive. Pasteur called this pasteurized beer the *"Bière de la revanche nationale"* ("The Beer of National Revenge"), and didn't want his *Études sur la bière* translated into German. He even called his new science "microbiology" instead of "bacteriology" because to him the latter sounded Teutonic.

Because pasteurization only has the ability to make finished beer bacteria-free Pasteur went back to look at the fundamentals of fermentation, and found that beer could contain other impurities in the form of "vinegar and lactic acid bacteria, different mould and mould fungus, the green *penicillium* and diverse species of wild yeast" (Glamann & Glamann), and if the wrong micro-organisms got into the beer then it could turn the liquid sour. He developed a purifying process that effectively "cleaned" the yeast while killing the bacteria. This was a revolution, but an incomplete one, and Pasteur still didn't realize there could be multiple strains of yeast present in a beer, and that some of these "impure" yeast cultures could be responsible for the "beer sickness".

The cure for beer sickness

By autumn 1883, JC Jacobsen had been brewing for almost fifty years (and would have less than four years left before he died) and in that time had proved to always be at the forefront of the ever-evolving industry. His real focus was on quality beer. In 1876 he had decided to do something quite unusual, and built

---

39 Pasteurization is better known as a process used on milk, but it was wine and beer that were pasteurized years before dairy – in Europe that'd happen in the 1880s while in the US it wasn't until the early 1900s that milk was pasteurized.

a privately managed laboratory to study the finished beer, from its taste to its longevity, as well as the question of *ølsygen* – "beer sickness".

Emil Christian Hansen was hired as the lab's director in 1879 and he would unlock one of the most important mysteries in the history of brewing.

Hansen didn't start his working life as a scientist, instead apprenticing under his artist father and becoming a journeyman painter around Denmark before realizing that maybe that wasn't for him. He returned to Copenhagen where he studied to be a teacher and then moved into academia and focused on botany and zoology. He came to work with several of the board of Carlsberg's laboratory, which led him to study fermentation and eventually write his doctoral thesis on organisms in beer and wort. Through his connections he worked for a while in Carl's brewery before applying for the director's role in JC's laboratory.

Hansen found a peer in JC. The men had similar social backgrounds and had worked their way into prominent positions. Now as director of the laboratory, Hansen was the man charged with understanding Carlsberg's yeast. And he was about to face a career-changing challenge.

In 1881–82, the brewery was struggling to keep up with orders despite the additional capacity of the Annexe Brewery. JC had to choose between cutting his lagering time or brewing in the summer months, something he considered dangerous despite the artificial refrigeration he'd installed in 1878. Regardless of the risks, he started brewing through summer.

In the middle of 1882, Carlsberg's local rival Tuborg suffered the beer sickness, leading to many complaints. JC visited Tuborg and made suggestions for how they could improve the situation, which involved pouring away all the beer and starting from scratch. He also gave them fresh yeast with which to brew, and took some of their bad yeast back to the lab for Hansen to analyze.

Then, in early autumn 1883, the Gamle Carlsberg beer itself developed a bitter taste and an unpleasant smell. Wild yeast, Hansen discovered, had infected the beer. Carlsberg had caught the beer sickness.

It was a matter of great pride to JC that'd he'd been using the same yeast he'd carried in a hat box from Munich in 1845. Sure, his beer would've varied from batch to batch just like everyone else's, but there was always good yeast in his brewery, and that yeast could ultimately be traced back to Spaten. Almost immediately, the brewery's director was ordered to go to Spaten and bring back a fresh batch of yeast.

Back in the lab Hansen studied the wild yeast, and had a new idea: to try to separate the good yeast from the bad yeast, isolating the healthy ones. Pasteur's purification method didn't work, so Hansen's new technique would be to find a single healthy yeast cell and grow more cultures from that. Only by doing this could he be certain that just the one kind of yeast was present.

He took a small slurry of yeast and diluted it with water, before shaking it vigorously to evenly distribute it. Then he dripped a little of this yeast sample on a glass plate to look at under his microscope. He then further diluted the solution until he could isolate single cells, which he added to sterilized wort. When it grew as a single spot in the wort Hansen knew he had successfully isolated the yeast.

In the process, Hansen discovered that Carlsberg's yeast actually contained two different types of lager yeast, as well as wild yeast. The two good yeasts, which he named *Unterhefe No. 1* and *No. 2*, both made fine beer, but No.1 was better overall and had better keeping qualities. Hansen then developed a method and the machinery for propagating the single healthy cell into a full batch to be used in the brewery, which became known as the Hansen–Kühle as it was developed with Søren van der Aa Kühle, the brewery manager.

The beer sickness had struck in the September, and by November Carlsberg were brewing with pure yeast. The following year, they made 200,000hl of beer with just that pure yeast: they were the first brewery in the world to certifiably be fermenting with a pure single strain of yeast.

Early in May 1884, JC sent his pure yeast to Spaten, explaining that the only change in their method of brewing with Spaten's original 1845 yeast had been the recent move to brewing without a summer break: "I am now convinced that the yeast in all breweries is more or less infected with wild yeast species, because now one is boiling almost everywhere in the dangerous summer months, and the infinite change of yeast therefore does no good."

Fermenting with a pure strain of yeast gave a much higher chance of good-tasting beer. Hansen had cured beer sickness: the single greatest revolution in brewing science.

Hansen's yeast propagator became an important piece of machinery for many large breweries, especially large lager breweries, and by 1892 over 130 breweries were using the Hansen–Kühle equipment, including many famous names: Pabst, Schlitz, Anheuser-Busch, Fosters in Melbourne, the Osaka Brewing Company (now Asahi), Klein-Schwechat, Amstel, Heineken, Tuborg and Weihenstephan (who sent an academic to Hansen's lab to study the technique before returning to teach it to aspiring brewers and make it part of the brewing curriculum). It was sold to breweries in Russia, Sweden, Chile, Argentina, Uruguay, Bolivia and Brazil. And if breweries weren't isolating and propagating their own pure yeast (still a difficult thing to do), many were now ordering pure yeast from special laboratories. Eventually almost every brewery in the world would be using pure yeast.

From Great-Grandfathers to Beer Barons

No other brewery can claim to be as important in the development of lager brewing as Carlsberg. Not Pilsner Urquell, not Spaten or Klein-Schwechat, nor Anheuser-Busch or Miller or Coors or Heineken (we'll look at all those breweries soon). In fact, it's not just lager that Carlsberg had a profound effect on: it was *all beer, in all the world*. Before 1883, there was the perpetual risk of sourness or simply just fluctuating quality. With a pure yeast strain the potential for sourness didn't disappear, but it did allow the good yeast to thrive on their own, less burdened by bad yeast and bacteria, and that did ultimately lead to improved quality.

Pure yeast came at the same time as we see artificial refrigeration becoming more widespread and the additional use of pasteurization to ensure more stability. It was also the period when we see greater transit in beer, meaning more beer was being drunk outside of the town it was made in as brewers continued to expand and export. Meanwhile, breweries were starting to open in more remote or hotter climates, like South America and Asia, able to do so because of the new technologies and scientific advances. And now the old ales of Britain were less favoured than the cold-brewed, cold-drunk lagers of Germany, Austria, the Czech Republic, Denmark, the Netherlands and, increasingly, North America.

Within fifty years, the Great-Grandfathers of Lager were able to change the beer that people drank – globally. They transformed beer from small-scale and variable, to large-scale and consistent. Ultimately it was pale Pilsner that would be established as the most widely drunk beer in the twentieth century, yet there's a strong argument that it was in North America that lager was really able to develop and grow into the standardized product we know now.

The Great-Grandfathers gave birth to the next generation of brewers, many of whom became known as the Beer Barons.

****

In 1886 Carl and JC were reconciled, less than a year before the old man died. In 1887, JC and his wife travelled to Rome, where he met Carl and his wife before they continued on to Greece – Carl would become one of the great donators of art, even giving Copenhagen its famous Little Mermaid statue. In Rome, JC got sick. Carl was called to return and, despite JC drinking half a bottle of Spaten beer every day to aid his recovery, he died there.

Gamle Carlsberg was managed by the Carlsberg Foundation, with Carl continuing to run Ny Carlsberg as a totally separate enterprise. Then in 1902 Carl donated his brewery to the Carlsberg Foundation, while creating a Ny

Carlsberg Foundation to make money available for art alongside his father's donations to science. When the manager of Old Carlsberg died in 1906, Carl took over all three breweries, eventually closing the Old and the Annexe breweries and merging them all into one. Carl died in 1914, but the future of the Carlsberg brewery was assured, and it would continue to be one of the world's leading brewers – indeed, probably the best of all, as well as the most important historically and, as we'll see later, for the future of lager.

CHAPTER THREE

HOW AMERICA
SUPER-SIZED LAGER
AND TURNED IT FROM DARK TO LITE

A SPECTACULAR BINGE

Alcohol was pervasive in American society; it crossed regional, sexual, racial, and class lines. Americans drank at home and abroad, alone and together, at work and at play, in fun and in earnest. They drank from the crack of dawn to the crack of dawn. At nights taverns were filled with boisterous, mirth-making tipplers. Americans drank before meals, with meals, and after meals. They drank while working in the fields and while travelling across half a continent. They drank in their youth, and, if they lived long enough, in their old age. From sophisticated Andover to frontier Illinois, from Ohio to Georgia, in lumber camps and on satin settees, in log taverns and at fashionable New York hotels . . . Early nineteenth-century America may not have been "a nation of drunkards", but Americans were certainly enjoying a spectacular binge.
W.J. Rorabaugh, *The Alcoholic Republic: An American Tradition*

Only they weren't drinking beer.

There was "unrestrained consumption" of liquors in America in the early 1800s. At least half the population drank more than 6oz of liquor daily, while one eighth of the population, considered "confirmed drunkards", averaged 24oz of hard liquor *a day*. They drank rum, gin and brandy, but mostly they drank lots and lots of whiskey, often diluted with water to make it more refreshing. A low-salary working man might earn a dollar a day, and with that money he could, if he wished, get *two gallons* of whiskey – that's 7.5 litres – and still have money left to eat.

Four fifths of adults were farmers, and they pretty much all farmed corn, which was the fuel of pre-Civil War America. Most people ate corn with most of their meals, and if they didn't directly eat corn – as corn meal, corn bread, corn mush, corn pudding, corn cakes – then they ate a hog fed on corn. In the early 1800s, the average American ate one pound of corn and one pound of pork a day, mostly as salt pork or smoked hams, typically fried in pork lard. Any corn not eaten, fed to pigs or sold to other people to eat or feed to their pigs was distilled into whiskey.

There was beer in the early nineteenth century, and there had been beer in the US since before the Pilgrims and the *Mayflower*, but it was heavy, dark, bitter-sweet English-style ale of variable quality, brewed in small amounts. In the early 1800s there were under 130 breweries, and per capita beer consumption was around 3 litres (that's less than a tablespoon's worth a day per person).[40] By contrast, there were 20,000 distilleries in 1830, with per capita consumption of spirits 36 litres per person fifteen and over. Through the nineteenth century beer consumption rose to almost 60 litres, while distilled liquor would fall to just 3 litres per capita. But for that to happen, beer had to develop into a new industry.

America in the nineteenth century was a land of promise and possibility, and a place to build a new life. For a lot of Europeans, suffering political problems, wars and famine, America provided hope – maybe the hope of amassing a fortune, maybe just the hope of survival. In the 1840s and 1850s, 4.2 million immigrants arrived into America, mostly from Central Europe, the United Kingdom and Ireland, including almost 1.4 million Germans. It's probably not a coincidence that between 1840 and 1860, per capita beer consumption in America trebled. Before the end of the century another three million Germans would arrive and beer consumption would quadruple.

The mid-century immigrants arrived in a changing American landscape. Where just fifty years earlier most adults were farmers, now a capitalist marketplace had developed. Work moved from farm to factory, handmade to machine-made, small-scale to industrial; cotton was the product of the south while the urbanizing north-east had industry. Cities were forming and growing: in 1790 there were just eight places in America with a population of over 5,000 people, but by 1830 that had increased to forty-five, including non-coastal cities and new cities that hadn't existed forty years earlier, many around the Great Lakes, which became accessible with the opening of the Erie Canal.

By the 1850s there were significant German populations in several rapidly expanding cities, including New York, Philadelphia and what became known as the "German Triangle" of Milwaukee, Cincinnati and St Louis. The Germans

---

40 For comparison: In England in 1831 there were over 40,000 breweries and the largest made more than all the American breweries combined.

brought skills, a strong work ethic and sometimes some money, and they assimilated by bringing cultures from home: the food, the music, the customs and the drink. Brewing beer created an economic niche for themselves using the skills they knew, employing their countrymen and primarily selling it to their fellow Germans.

The first lager brewed in America was probably made in 1840 by a man named John Wagner, who brewed in a "miserable shanty on the outskirts of Philadelphia", as Carl Miller puts it in *The Rise of the Beer Barons*. It's thought he brought the yeast with him from a brewery in Bavaria where he'd worked, but if Wagner was the first to make lager then it was just for his local community.

From 1840 there are increasing references to German brewers making lager in America: Engel & Wolf in Philadelphia came soon after Wagner; Adam Lemp brewed St Louis's first lager around 1842 (though there are some claims that it might have been as early as 1838); Milwaukee's first lager was brewed by Herman Reutelschöfer in 1841, by which time a third of the city's population were German; Cincinnati had lager by 1844; New York had its first lager in 1844, brewed by a George Gillig; John Roessle brewed lager in Boston in 1846; John A. Huck and John Schneider made lager in Chicago in 1847.

The Germanization of the American brewing industry had begun, and with it America became one of the first places in the world to brew lagers outside Bavaria, the Austro-Hungarian Empire and its fluid borders. They had to create it and develop it themselves, which meant innovating in a way that wasn't happening in Bavaria – the German brewers in America had to create new techniques to make lager work in new brewing conditions, and they were able to do this because they had no rules to follow and no rules to break. A pioneering entrepreneurialism and a progressive can-do approach become a central feature of this new hybridized German-American industry.

THE SALOON, THE BEER GARDEN AND EXTREMELY UNFASHIONABLE LAGER

In the colonial days at the turn of the nineteenth century there were two forms of drinking: to sip watered-down whiskey throughout the day as a kind of constant unintoxicated refreshment; or to get absolutely wasted at communal binges. There wasn't an occasion that didn't warrant a binge; just having three or more men together in the same place, for example, was a good enough reason to get hammered. As the 1800s progressed, the day-long lapping of liquor decreased as more people just drank hard all the time.

Colonial taverns were simple places. You rode up, parked your horse outside and entered into a small room with tables to sit at; there were bed chambers if you wanted to stay the night; spirits were served from a kind of cage and mixed into punches, cobblers and smashes; and there might have been food out, including ham, pork, pies, potatoes (there were no vegetables, and fruit was either fermented or distilled).[41] It was as much of an inn and a place to rest as it was a social space for leisurely drinking.

The saloon developed from the 1820s, and was more established by the 1850s. These were places for proper drinking. They had long wooden bar tops with brass rails by your feet. A large mirror was behind the bar, and in front of that were bottles of spirits. There might've been a barrel of beer beneath the bar, but most people drank liquor. There were spittoons on the ground surrounded by sawdust and wayward gobs. A moustache towel hung from a rail. There might be a billiard table and sometimes, in rougher saloons, the occasional boxing match. Some people played dice, while the camaraderie of the card table was a universal language at a time of growing immigrant numbers. They were smoky, dark, male-orientated places. There were pictures on the wall of prize fighters and pretty women, and that's the closest a female got to the main bar-room of a saloon, though some places had ladies' entrances where they might come in and get a pail, or "growler", of beer to take away.

The spit-sodden and salubrious saloon was a place of refuge for many working men. Work in the cities was hard, hours were long, conditions were often either too hot or too cold, dusty or damp, and generally uncomfortable. Salaries were below subsistence levels and, especially for a single man, there was no leisure time or activities apart from drinking. The saloon provided more luxuries than a working-class man might find at home: warmth in winter, light at night, hot food,[42] cold beer, hard and cheap liquor, a toilet, chairs, billiard tables and companionship. The saloon had other functions, too: a place to find a job, the post office, the bank, somewhere to cash your paycheck (and spend most of it), somewhere for politicians to poll, a place for unions and clubs to meet and a source of the latest news, which also made it a place where un-educated men could learn.

---

41 Hard cider was one of the most-drunk drinks of this time, with per capita consumption being over 110 litres. This hard cider was much harder than we know today, often 10 per cent in alcohol, and fortified with spirit to keep it longer.

---

42 The "free lunch" was an institution where for the price of one beer – just five cents – customers could help themselves to the buffet of food on offer, and soon this became the principal sustenance during the day for a lot of working-class America. The food varied according to the tavern and the nationality of the person who ran it. It wasn't always good, but it was cheap and reliable.

Saloons were the centre of the urban working man's life and, as beer drinking increased through the century, so the number of saloons in America grew, from 150,000 in 1880 to 300,000 in 1900. In the early 1880s, Milwaukee had a saloon for every 130 people. In 1899, the Chicago police department estimated that half the population entered at least one saloon at least once a day. In 1883, a New York map of four blocks by eight blocks between Bowery, Broome, Norfolk and East Houston marked up 242 lager saloons and 61 liquor saloons. In that area on the Bowery, says Christine Sismondo in *America Walks into a Bar*, "some bars did away with the nicety of glasses and, instead, allowed customers to suck alcohol from the barrel through a rubber tube. For three cents, patrons could drink until they had to come up for air."

Beer consumption steadily increased through the nineteenth century (not just via hoses but regular ways of drinking, too), but to many Americans Germans and their lager remained a curiosity, something the *New York Herald* addressed in 1867:

> But a few years since, the quiet German, alone in his halo of tobacco smoke, blown from big-bowled pipes – articles that they prize dearer than their babies – entrenched behind barricades of squirming pretzels, and secure from invasion by reason of the penetrating odors of redolent *Sweitzer* and *Limburger Käse*, could while the silent hours away, quaffing in semi-somnolent happiness the then almost unknown and extremely unfashionable lager.

But that view was changing. "That season of stupidity is past," the article continued. "The aggressive American has stormed and captured the abdominous offshoot of Faderland in his very vat and taken him prisoner. Lager is now the American hot weather beverage."

In June 1856 the *New York Herald* writes about the German population "in a state of great excitement yesterday, growing out of the annual return of the Festival of the Sangerbund". This Sangerbund is an association of choral clubs "who cultivate music and *lagerbier* throughout the year" and annually hold a "grand demonstration . . . to show their proficiency in both accomplishments". At this festival, or "monster picnic", which *30,000* people attended, the groups sat on grassy banks overlooking the East River (in what's now ironically known as Bellevue Sobriety Garden) and "ate, laughed, sang, flirted, or lay gazing at the flashing water beneath them". It was jovial, social, happy, wholesome: young couples could walk together and families could sit together. And lager was everywhere:

> It was rye bread and *lager bier*, cheese and *lager bier*, sausages and *lager bier*, dancing and *lager bier*, flirting and *lager bier*, music and *lager bier*, talking and *lager bier*; inside the garden was *lager bier*, outside in the road was *lager bier*; *lager bier* in barrels, kegs, cups and glasses; old and young drank it, and children sipped it, until everything in the celebration and about it was intimately associated with this fascinating beverage.

Germans brought yet more influence from home as beer gardens opened around the country, moving beer into public, social spaces. The gardens ranged from small yards beside breweries, to indoor beer halls decorated with pastoral murals, to huge pleasure grounds, and always everyone was welcome, women and children included. The gardens hosted concerts, orchestras, singing, theatres and dances; there were breads, cakes, ice creams, cheeses and sausages; some had aquariums, fountains and zoos. Instead of sawdust and sticky floorboards there were gravel paths and flower beds; people bowled instead of boxed; they gambolled instead of gambled; and the gardens were the American embodiment of German *Gemütlichkeit*, the untranslatable but universally knowable feeling of contentment and belonging.

In Milwaukee, Schlitz Brewery ran Schlitz Park, "a virtual entertainment Mecca", in Carl Miller's words, featuring an octagonal concert pavilion with 5,000 seats and space for a 25-piece orchestra. It had a three-storey pagoda with panoramic views of the city; there was a dance hall, four bowling alleys, refreshment parlours and a restaurant, a carousel, grass for the children to run around on; there were tightrope walkers and circus entertainers; in winter there was ice skating. Pabst had a 15,000-foot-long roller coaster and a "Katzenjammer palace" fun house in their garden.

Americans who attended the beer gardens often commented on how the Germans drank lager all day long but were never seen to be intoxicated. Had it been the Americans or the Irish there'd be "broken heads, bloody noses, and the wayside strewn with the wrecks of humanity in beastly intoxication", according to F.W. Salem's 1880 *Beer: Its History as a National Beverage*. Visitors to the Sangerbund of 1856 were "exuberantly joyous" but "not a single disorderly person was to be seen". The Germans drank beer slowly and they socialized, and were caricatured as portly, jolly and capable of drinking dozens of mugs of smooth, full-bodied, malty lager in a sitting.[43] But the Americans didn't drink like the Germans, they drank harder and faster, and by the 1870s, as they began to drink more and more lager, they came to want something lighter.

FROM THE DEUTSCHER'S DELIGHT
TO AN AMERICAN PLEASURE

Americans, hearing the praises of the new beverage and seeing their Teutonic friends roll their eyes and smack their lips in ecstatic contemplation and enjoyment of it, used to make bold essays at its consumptions, with the almost universal result of being intensely disgusted by its novel bitter taste. With many contemptuous ejaculations, wry faces, and much sputtering and rinsing of their mouths with the more familiar whiskey, they would revile and condemn the Deutscher's delight.

"The Million's Beverage", *New York Times*, 20 May 1877

From the beginning, lager brewed in America was made in similar ways to the traditional German beers and, despite a lack of engineering, infrastructure and local heritage, the processes in the 1850s and 1860s sound just like those in Bavaria. A typical lager would be amber to brown in colour, full-bodied and malty, relatively sweet and nourishing, a little bitter, pleasingly carbonated and around 4 per cent in alcohol. The brewers would use just the four classic ingredients of the *Reinheitsgebot* and roughly follow the brewing season of September to April. They dug underground cellars and matured their beer in wooden barrels in the cold, typically for three to eight months. The beer was mostly sold locally and mostly on draught, and to begin with it mostly appealed to Germans.

There were some differences, though: the hops that grew in America were stronger and rougher than the delicate European ones, which were expensive to import, and the barley was a different variety, but otherwise these were German-style lagers brewed in America. It would be the domestic ingredients that would come to change then define the developing German-American lagers.

American barley was a variety known as "six-row" for its star-shaped appearance of kernels. Six-row has a higher protein content, fewer fermentable sugars and a more grainy flavour than the "two-row" barley grown in Europe (but six-row was cheaper and gave better yields). The significance for brewers was that more protein in the beer gave more body, more sweetness, potentially more foam, but it could also leave a cloudier beer and lead to instability and a shorter shelf-life.

---

43 Brewery workers were notorious heavy drinkers. Most started work between 2 a.m. and 4 a.m., and in some breweries they were allowed to drink as much as they wanted before 7 a.m., while others let their workers drink all day. It would be usual for someone to drink forty glasses of beer a day, and breweries would all have their prized drinkers, those men who could drink 100 glasses or more, and were championed as a matter of pride. As a counter to those who think this sounds like a good work environment, they usually worked six 14–18-hour days a week plus a half day on Sunday, mostly either underground in the cold and dark or in the hot, dusty, steamy brewery or malthouse, neither of which was good for one's health.

It tasted good, but that fuller flavour and mouthfeel didn't suit the fast, heavy-volume gulping of Americans (even if it was fine for the steady-sipping Germans), while glasses of cloudy beer weren't as appealing as clear ones, so in the early 1860s brewers had begun experimenting, brewing with corn, which was cheap, abundant, low in protein and high in starches, which could be converted into fermentable sugars. Unfortunately, corn's high oil content killed any foam and could leave a rancid flavour.

In 1868, the Bohemian brewer Anton Schwarz arrived in America as a 29-year-old brewing expert. He got a job writing for *American Brewer*, the first trade journal in the country, and as an advocate for better, clearer beer he championed the possibilities of brewing with "adjunct" grains like corn and also rice. Some corn, he discovered, had less oil, so was a better malt substitute, and by adding corn to a beer he was able to stretch and dilute the heavy six-row malted barley while still giving fermentable sugars (barley contains some enzymes that are particularly good at converting corn's starches to sugar, so they also had a symbiotic relationship). Overall this gave a drier, lighter and less hazy beer. Schwarz then experimented with other adjuncts, like corn grits, corn meal, corn flakes, corn sugar, rice, sugar, glucose and grape sugar, to see which could be viable to produce lighter-tasting and lighter-bodied beers, while also using different mashing techniques in the brewhouse and moving away from the old decoction process used in Germany.[44]

Brewers didn't necessarily adopt these adjuncts immediately. The largest brewery in America in the late 1870s, George Ehret's Hell Gate Brewery on the Upper East Side, was always and only all-malt. The second-largest brewery in the country, Best Brewing Co (which we now know as Pabst), was all-malt until 1877, then for one year used rice as 6 per cent of the overall grain bill, switching to corn in the same percentage the following year. By 1879 they were using 9 per cent corn, but by 1893 their grain bill for a typical lager was 30 per cent corn – a percentage consistent with most brewers then and now. Throughout these years a general lightening of beer was taking place.

Corn was the more common adjunct, but in St Louis they preferred rice, an ingredient that was more expensive and harder to brew with but gave better brilliance, stability and foam.

****

---

44 There are also reports of bicarbonate of soda being added to kegs of fresh tap beer to sweeten its flavour and allow younger beer to be sold. Bicarbonate of soda also gave the beer a thick, full foam, which was prized at the time.

In 1852 a German migrant called George Schneider built a brewery in St Louis. His "Bavarian Brewery" was capable of brewing only 500bbls a year, and though there was high demand for beer in the German-dominant city of St Louis there wasn't demand for the Bavarian Brewery's beer, and by 1860 it had been declared bankrupt. Two of the brewery's creditors assumed ownership, with full control given to one of them, a wealthy candle and soap manufacturer named Eberhard Anheuser. In 1864, Anheuser's son-in-law, Adolphus Busch, a co-owner of a wholesale supply business specializing in malt and hops, bought out the other partner. Busch became one of the most progressive and innovative people in the history of brewing.

Busch, as we'll see, instigated some pioneering decisions and processes in his brewery and in the early 1870s introduced a new beer called St Louis Lager, a Bohemian-style beer lighter than most of his other dozen or so lagers, and it would go on to be the brewery's best-selling beer into the twentieth century. Then in 1876 Anheuser-Busch created another Bohemian-style lager, this time with his good friend, a local wine and liquor importer and dealer called Carl Conrad, who had the sole rights to sell the beer. The new recipe was 5 per cent rice and the rest a mix of American six-row malt and Bohemian two-row malt, plus some Bohemian Saaz hops. The beer was called C. Conrad & Co.'s Original Budweiser, after the city of Budweis in the south of what's now the Czech Republic. There aren't reports of either Conrad or Busch travelling specifically to Budweis and it's believed they were simply inspired by the beers of that area and used the name to denote a *style* of beer, with Budweis becoming Budweiser in that same way as Pilsen became Pilsner. It was a "very fine and elegant" beer, said Conrad, adding: "It has a very pretty flavour, it sparkles better [than other lagers] & [is] not so heavy."

Conrad sold 250,000 bottles of Budweiser in the first year, and between March 1876 and December 1882 he sold some 20 *million* bottles of the beer. But Conrad was an inept businessman, and in 1883 filed for bankruptcy, owing $94,000 to the brewery. As compensation Anheuser-Busch agreed to take the Budweiser trademark, and by 1886, Busch had increased the production of Budweiser to be able to sell 14 million bottles in one year.

By the end of the nineteenth century, most American breweries were using some kind of adjunct – corn, rice, sugar – as standard, creating a uniquely new kind of beer: the American lager. These beers came to be defined by a general mildness of flavour, but it took more than just using corn or rice to modernize lager in America.

THE FIRST ERA OF BREWING TECHNOLOGY

American brewers were quick to utilize steam, initially to power pumps and hoists, then machines like the ones that mixed the mash and cleaned barrels, then to replace fire in heating the copper kettle, and finally to power ice machines for artificial refrigeration. We've seen how steam and ice changed brewing in Bavaria but it arguably had an even greater impact in the New World.

Underground lagering cellars were standard for a German-American brewery. New York's brewers dug several storeys below the city and spread out miles and miles of subterranean halls of wooden barrels. St Louis had natural cave systems beneath the city: Lemp, the city's first lager brewer, even had an underground saloon where people could go and drink beer. But the trouble in St Louis and elsewhere was that, even in the deepest cellars, it sometimes got too warm.

Natural ice, harvested from the lakes in winter, became a key commodity in lager breweries, and by the early 1870s American breweries were building above-ground storehouses and ice houses in which to mature their beer – a revolutionary change (and one that made the job of the cellar master a little more pleasant than spending twelve hours a day underground in the dark). But natural ice was expensive and took a lot of manpower, plus it relied on the inherent unreliability of a natural resource.

Commercial-scale mechanically-produced ice started to become available from the 1870s. Machines were able to produce many tons of ice a day, which could be used to fill ice houses and cellars. Then came machines capable of refrigerating large spaces with cold air. As early as 1882 Anheuser-Busch were one of the first breweries to go fully ice-free, by installing the world's then-largest-capacity mechanical refrigeration plant, which artificially cooled entire cellars or stores with cold air. The ability to control temperature year-round, and to cool above-ground spaces, allowed brewers to make more consistent beer and to make greater volumes of it, unrestricted by space or seasonal weather changes.

With more volume came more need for efficiency, while maintaining quality, and here we arrive at two more industry advances pioneered by American brewers: filtration and forced carbonation.

Drinkers were now demanding clear beer, not beer that was cloudy with residual yeast. The old Bavarian method of clarification was simply leaving the yeast to naturally settle out, but that was too slow for these growing American brewers. Some used "chip casks", in which matured beer is moved into a vessel filled with wooden chips, often beech wood, along with a fining agent and then krausened with fermenting beer.[45] But a better and quicker option was soon devised: a filter. Finished beer was passed through a filtration device that captured the yeast, letting the beer pass out the other side perfectly clear.

Then came carbonation. In the old days, matured beer went into a serving barrel, was krausened, and a bung sealed the barrel tightly. The fresh beer started re-fermenting, creating carbon dioxide, which was then absorbed in the beer, making it fizzy. But that took a few days, so a way of force-carbonating the beer was developed. This collected carbon dioxide from the original fermentation process, removed any impurities, and then injected the gas into the finished beer. It was a uniquely American innovation. Thanks to the growing demand for brilliant and sparkling lager, by the 1890s filtration and forced carbonation were common.

Almost all beer was still being made and sold locally and on draught at this time, so to make *and* sell more beer, breweries in lager-saturated cities like St Louis and Milwaukee had to look to new, even faraway markets. There was no advantage for a brewery like Anheuser-Busch to look to the brewery-dense north and east, so instead they looked south and west, and made use of the growing network of railroads: in the early 1850s there were 9,000 miles of railroad in America; by the end of the century there were 190,000, peaking at 254,000 in 1920, just as trucks and cars became more available. Putting lots of barrels of beer on a train was impractical, but no-one was filling bottles on a large scale yet. To start with, in the early 1870s there were only three types of bottle that could even withstand the pressures of the carbonated beer inside, and there weren't many manufacturers capable of supplying them in the volume brewers like Busch and Pabst wanted. So the challenge was the mass-production of bottled beer.

Huge bottling halls were built, with brewing becoming one of the first industries to use assembly-line production. Busch's first major bottling plant needed 80 staff to fill 42,000 bottles a day; by 1877 they were filling 100,000 bottles a day. By the early 1890s, up in Milwaukee, Pabst were employing 900 people in their bottling department.

As it travelled far away the bottled beer needed to look good *and* taste good. The looking-good part evolved with the use of adjunct grains and filtration, while for stability brewers began to pasteurize their beer, the first being Anheuser-Busch in 1872 (four years before Pasteur even published *Études sur la bière*). Pasteurization alone didn't guarantee a good-tasting beer (remember this

---

45 Finings are clarification agents that, in simple terms, will attach to the yeast and allow it to settle out in the bottom of the barrel. Krausening means adding fermenting beer to almost-finished beer, with the fresh stuff able to awaken any residual yeast and re-start fermentation, which was often done to create carbonation and to reinvigorate a beer that had been in cold cellars for an extended length of lagering time. Wood chips were used as they are able to draw the yeast out of suspension.

was still a full decade before Hansen's pure yeast), and it sped up oxidization, so keeping the beer cold was also important.

At the Centennial Exhibition in Philadelphia in 1876 the refrigerated railway car debuted, cooled by ice, and by the following year Anheuser-Busch owned forty of them. Two years later Busch co-founded the St Louis Refrigerator Car Company, which by 1888 had a fleet of 850 cars (the meat industry also became heavy users of these). Across the ever-expanding rail networks, Busch built ice houses to top up the refrigerated cars along the way. When the beer arrived in new cities there were more cold stores and depots, and local salesmen to distribute it to bars.

Now light, bright, pasteurized, cold bottles of lager were spreading across America, with a small number of "shipping brewers" – names like Anheuser-Busch, Pabst, Schlitz, Blatz, Lemp and Moerlein of Cincinnati – becoming nationally available.[46] As a result, branding and advertising had to be as much a focus as the actual beer. One of Pabst's methods of standing out was to hand-tie a silk blue ribbon around the neck of every bottle. They started in 1882, and ten years later were using 170 miles of ribbon a year. In 1898 they officially renamed their beer Pabst Blue Ribbon.

American brewing was the first true modern brewing industry and by the turn of the twentieth century it had become one of the largest industries in the country. Fire was replaced by steam. Machines made ice and cold air. Huge aboveground rooms could be made cold (something that would ultimately be standard in every brewery in the world). Trains could take beer 1,000 miles away. Adjuncts, filtration, forced carbonation, pasteurization and mass assembly-line production all led to a new national consistency to lager, and that led to a new national taste for lager, with per capita consumption continuing to rise into the early 1900s. The men who led their breweries became known as the Beer Barons and they created new products, new processes and new ways to sell beer, and they faced new challenges and overcame them in a way that would've been unimaginable to the founding German-American brewers of the generation before.

The yellow American lager the Beer Barons made was the next variation in the changing shades of lager from Bavaria's brown to Vienna's amber to Pilsner's gold. It became one of the most important types of lager, and arguably the flavour the world came to know of as simply "beer". We can say that lager came from Bavaria, but it might be more true to say that the lagers we know today came from America.

---

46 Almost none of the New York brewers shipped significant amounts of beer. Their local market was so big – the population of New York City alone grew from 1.2 million to 5.6 million between 1880 and 1920 – that all their sales could be done in state. This was fine to begin with but, as the country grew and the industry progressed, they'd come to be left behind.

****

And then it all disappeared.

A lot changed between 1920 and 1933, the years in which Prohibition left America dry of legal alcohol.[47] There is no simple precis of what happened in the lead-up to Prohibition, and it took a long time for temperance campaigners to dry out the whole country, aided in the final years by wartime rationing, but the simple fact is that all the incredible growth of the brewing industry during the previous fifty years finished on 17 January 1920.

A lot of breweries closed for good in 1920 – or earlier, as even by 1916 twenty-three of the forty-eight states were dry – but many survived. They did so in numerous different ways, including making "near beer" (at 0.5 per cent ABV or less).[48] Some made malt extract and yeast (which enterprising people could mix together with warm water and leave for a few days to create their own beer – Gussie Busch, Adolphus's grandson, called making and drinking homebrew the great indoor sport of the 1920s); others diversified into dairy, ice cream, ice or soda, or they relied on the money they'd invested in property or other businesses.

In 1914, the last normal year before Prohibition, there were around 1,300 breweries making 66 million barrels of beer. When alcohol returned on 7 April 1933, beer initially poured into 19 states, made by 31 breweries; by 1934 there were 756 breweries producing 37 million barrels. The beer was only allowed to be 3.2 per cent alcohol by weight (4 per cent ABV), but beer was back.

Only it had never really left. Neither had hard liquor, and it's estimated that Americans spent $36 *billion* on bootleg and smuggled spirits during Prohibition, and instead of alcohol being one of the government's main sources of tax income, it became a huge source of untaxed income for bootleggers around the country. Many of these were controlled by gangs run by notorious figures like Al Capone, who ran numerous breweries and supplied a demand that never ceased.

Speakeasies opened in big cities – New York had some 32,000 drinking establishments in 1929, way more than before 1920. The Jazz Age came; it was the decade that roared, the years of aeroplanes, cars, radios, music and movies (there was even "Booze Porn" and a genre of movies that showed people getting drunk). Men and women, rich and poor, came together to drink socially like they'd never done before.

---

47 There was no legal alcohol, but they were absolutely sozzled on the illegal stuff – you could probably argue that the greatest years of American drinking were during Prohibition.

48 To make "near beer" the breweries made proper beer and then took the alcohol out, so you had huge breweries with tanks filled with actual beer... There were definitely a lot of people helping themselves to those great vessels of lager. Even Gussie Busch, then in charge of Anheusuer-Busch, was known to fill jugs of beer to take home.

The real story with Prohibition is not that it happened, or why it happened or what breweries did during the dry years: the story is how beer became relevant again afterwards, and adapted to a changing society with new kinds of consumers.

CARS, FRIDGES AND TVS

By the mid-1950s Anheuser-Busch were second in overall volume behind Schlitz, who had been the number-one brewery in the US (or close by) since the turn of the twentieth century.

Schlitz started in 1849 when a Milwaukee saloon and restaurant owner called August Krug added a brewery to his business. He died in 1856 when he fell down an open hatch, and the brewery's book-keeper, Joseph Schlitz, offered his savings to Krug's widow in return for a partnership in the company. He clearly offered more than just cash, and in 1858 married her, then named the business after himself. Schlitz would run the brewery with Krug's nephew, August Uihlein, and it would continue in the Uihlein family's management for over a century. The brewery would remain in the top two until the 1970s, when they made some catastrophic mistakes.

The Joseph Schlitz Brewing Company made one beer called, simply, Schlitz. Anheuser-Busch had a few beers, but by the 1950s Budweiser was their number one, with an all-malt, draught-only brand called Michelob also popular. Pabst was in the top five overall, and Blue Ribbon was their flagship beer. The beers themselves were, ostensibly, very similar. Because they were so alike, so well known, and also sold as being more expensive, these few national lagers came to define what good beer tasted like to American consumers.

Outside beer, the 1950s was the decade of Wonder Bread, instant coffee, canned soup, processed cheese and TV dinners. There was a general standardizing and simplifying of flavour that saw products sold in new kinds of packaging and be promoted in new ways, changing buying habits. Take oats, for example: they used to be sold out of large containers with the shopper scooping out what they wanted and putting it in a bag. Simple and cheap, and as a way of purchasing oats it didn't seem like it needed fixing. Then Quaker Oats decided to put oatmeal in a branded package, they spent money to advertise it, and consumers swapped the self-serve bins for pre-filled boxes – and they paid more for them. Consumers were now happy to spend more for convenience and for well-known brands.

For beer, the first big post-Prohibition shift was the increased sales of bottled and canned beers over draught beer. The first canned beers were released in

1935, a year when draught still accounted for two thirds of American beer sales, but by 1960 80 per cent of beer was sold packaged in bottles and cans. Partly this was due to the familiarity people now had with drinking soft drinks and fruit juice from a can (per capita soda consumption in 1941 was 133 bottles), partly to the technological advances in the packaging industries during the years of Prohibition, and partly it came as people spent less time in bars and more time at home. And here the home becomes important, because domestic changes like car ownership, home refrigeration and television had a big impact on the beer industry.

Take refrigeration: in 1925, of all the American homes wired with electricity only 1 per cent had a refrigerator; five years later 12.8 per cent did. It passed 50 per cent in 1938, and reached 72 per cent in 1940 (by contrast, the UK wasn't even at 1 per cent of refrigerator ownership in 1940, and didn't get past 50 per cent until 1968). American shopping habits changed during the middle of the century, shifting from independent downtown grocery stores to regional shopping centres and chain retailers. Between 1939 and 1944 the number of supermarkets grew from 3,900 to 16,000, and by the early 1990s there were almost 39,000 shopping centres, including almost 2,000 regional malls. Instead of going to the butchers, then the grocers, then the hardware store, you could now buy everything in one place. And to get to these supermarkets and shopping centres, people drove: already by the 1930s over 40 per cent of American households had a car; in 1960 it was over 80 per cent.

The spread of large supermarkets and the many items they stocked gave an illusion of choice, but the reality was a lack of actual variety: everyone could buy the same stuff everywhere – and not just beer: food, clothes, washing powder and everything else a modern home needed in the 1950s. It made the familiar and reliable (and heavily advertised) even more important than the new: we bought what we knew and trusted. A number of large brands were able to become widespread in households all around the country: Heinz, Colgate, Kellogg's, Coca-Cola, Kraft, Campbell's. People started buying specific brands, and competing brands had to act like the market leaders to compete with them (if you wanted to sell ketchup then it'd better look and taste like Heinz).

Then came television, and a whole new medium for the national brands to advertise their products and shine their names and images into living rooms. Even if you didn't have Colgate or Kellogg's in your cupboards, they still made their way into your personal space.

In 1948, just 8,000 American households had a television, but owning one became an imperative regardless of income, and as early as 1955 over 75 per cent of households had a black-and-white TV. By 1960, 45.7 million homes

(80 per cent of households) had a television set. No new technology had been adopted so quickly. Colour TV came out in 1961 and ten years later was in 75 per cent of homes.

Television enabled a hegemonic conformity as it created unified ideas and ideals: it taught us how to shop, eat, drink and think. It's from here that the standardizing of products increased, and there was something about that era that led people to buy less flavoursome, less natural, and more processed products, perceiving them to be better quality.

Beer advertising in the 1950s was wholesome and domestic (albeit often sexist, another reflection of that era): it was illustrated with food to elevate its status on the tables of dinner parties. Smartly dressed people share nice golden glasses of lager. Men who hold bowling balls or who are about to play tennis tell of their love for beer. It was "Miller Time"; "Where there's life . . . there's Bud"; "If you like beer you'll love Schlitz"; "Pabst . . . Makes it Perfect". By the early 1970s, however, beer advertising and sponsorship had shifted to live sport, and it was a surging brewery from Milwaukee that made the biggest move.

Philip Best, who started what eventually became Pabst Brewing Co., had emigrated from Germany to America with two brothers, Jacob and Frederick, who was known as Carl. Carl Best started out by making vinegar, a common side-line for brewers and wine makers (back home in Mettenheim, the Best family made wine). In 1849 Carl sold the vinegar business and decided to build a brewery on what was then the main track in and out of the town, known as the Plank Road for the wooden rails that the horses and carts ran along. Best dug cellars and filled them with lagering barrels, but by 1855 he was bankrupt and sold the Plank Road Brewery to a wealthy Bavarian brewmaster called Frederick Miller. Miller named the company after himself, developed the brewery, dug more cellars, opened a pleasant beer garden and brewed in the traditional manner that he knew from home. It was a reasonably sized regional brewery through the 19th and 20th centuries, but that changed in 1970 when Philip Morris, the mega-rich cigarette and tobacco company behind Marlboro, bought the brewery.

Philip Morris applied their expertise of selling cigarettes to selling lager, and transformed the business. One of their earliest decisions was to focus on sponsoring major sporting events like the World Series, Monday Night Football, Indiana 500, and more.

Anheuser-Busch, the number-one brewer, retaliated hard, sponsoring any game or event that they could. They went for big sports and small ones, niche ones, college ones, professional and amateur ones; if there was a chance to put their logo on something near a sports arena, they did, and if there was a commercial break during a sporting event, they were going to be advertised during it (one executive would even speak, perhaps apocryphally, but I hope it's true, of flicking through TV stations one day to see a duck race – literally ducks waddling in a race – and the finishing line had a Budweiser logo on it). In 1976, Anheuser-Busch sponsored a quarter of 28 NFL teams, half of MLB teams, 23 out of 24 NBA teams, 13 of 14 NHL teams, 300 colleges, and even arranged a deal to be the exclusive beer advertiser on ESPN. If you watched sport, you saw the name Budweiser. If you watched TV, you saw Budweiser. If you just looked out the window you probably saw something with Budweiser on it. Or Miller. Or some other brewery, because now hundreds of millions of dollars were being spent on advertising beer.

By the end of the 1970s the American beer industry was dominated by a few large and ubiquitous breweries. The biggest were able to stay ahead by spending more money and having low profit margins, while to try to keep up the challengers were faced with more difficult decisions, many of them about the beer itself, which was becoming less important than the way it was advertised and how much of it was sold.

THE SECOND ERA OF BREWING TECHNOLOGY

"Beer is an amber, aqueous solution that contains gas (CO_2), ethyl alcohol, several inorganic salts, and about 800 organic compounds." That, in the 1995 *Handbook of Brewing*, is one of the least romantic descriptions of beer you'll ever read, but by the 1970s much of the old romance of brewing had been engineered and optimized out.

We get a good insight into the North American brewing industry in 1947 from the visit of a group of British brewery workers from Mitchells and Butlers, in the West Midlands, who travelled around America and Canada and documented what they found. They talk about how lagering was down to three weeks, "curtailed under pressure of demand"; six-row malt was still being used in beers, some of which had an adjunct content of 40 per cent; hops were sometimes only a cursory addition at the end of the boil, as pasteurization had relegated the anti-bacterial properties of hops; one-piece, glass-lined fermentation tanks were universally popular; it was standard to filter and force-carbonate; Anheuser-Busch (who the Brits were particularly impressed by) fermented their beer in large, open, square vats built in concrete, and instead of "quick chill and carbonate", like other brewers, they still kraüsened their beer and left it on wood chips.

As the century continued, however, there were to be lots of changes as breweries became automated, computer-controlled factories. Most beer came to be made in large stainless steel conical tanks, in which it fermented and then matured. In the past, beer was fermented in one vessel in one part of the brewery, which was cooled to around 8°C (46°F), then the beer was moved into another vessel in a colder part close to 0°C (32°F). Now each tank could be individually temperature-controlled from within by a coolant like glycol, and the temperature changed inside based on the stage of production, meaning there could be a tank of fermenting beer (held at 8°C/46°F) next to one near the end of its maturation (at 0°C/32°F). The beer could now stay in one tank from the day it was brewed until the day it was packaged. But the number of days it stayed there was decreasing.

Accelerated fermentation, done in pressurized tanks, was one method of speeding up the process. Schlitz introduced this in the 1970s and cut their fermentation time from twelve days to four, and their overall production time to two weeks. At a time when Budweiser took up to forty days, it meant Schlitz could potentially brew twice as much their rivals with the same tank capacity. Schlitz would boast about being the most efficient brewery in the world, but that came at a future cost.

One of the main new processes adopted during the 1970s and 1980s was "high-gravity brewing". Do you think American lager tastes like it's watered down? Well that's because almost all of it *is*.

In high-gravity brewing, a beer will be made stronger than the "sales percentage" (the strength the beer is sold at, say 4 per cent ABV), and then when it's about to be packaged the brewery will blend in de-oxygenated water to get the desired and correct alcohol content (de-oxygenated water is important because any oxygen in the beer will speed up the staling process). For example, a beer might be brewed to be 8 per cent ABV in a vessel that can hold 50,000 litres. If another 50,000 litres of water are blended in (or "liquored back" as brewers say) before it's packaged, then the final beer will be 4 per cent ABV, and the brewery can sell 100,000 litres out of a tank capable of brewing only 50,000 litres. High-gravity brewing has the benefits of "better plant utilization" (in other words, same tank space, more beer), and the water dilutes any errant flavours, improving consistency – or standardization.

From the late 1940s we see the increase in multi-plant brewing, something pioneered much earlier by Anton Dreher and then later by Heineken. Breweries took over or built additional facilities to be able to brew the same brands in multiple locations, increasing overall capacity and reducing shipping costs. In 1951, Anheuser-Busch built a new plant in Newark, and then in 1954 one in

Los Angeles; by the 1990s they had thirteen breweries. In the 1960s, all of the top ten breweries but one (New York's Ballantine's) had multiple sites.

Around all of this developed "processing aids". There are antioxidants and flavour stabilizers. There are enzymes to prevent something called chill-haze, which can occur if a beer is warmed up and then cooled down again. Other enzymes can be used to help break down malt sugars, something done in light, dry or low-carbohydrate beers, making the sugars more fermentable to the yeast, to leave a drier beer with a lower sugar content. There are ingredients to help maintain a beer's foam. Almost all brewers adjust their water by adding different minerals. Most use "kettle finings" to help clarify the wort and remove proteins before fermentation. Some add nutrients for their yeast.

Should this be worrying to drinkers? No, not really – no more than with any other processed product. Almost all breweries use some processing aids, though beer brewed properly, using great ingredients, and left to mature for a reasonable amount of time won't need many things at all, and in that sense is much less processed. These additions are symptomatic of the desire for breweries to produce lighter beer, make more of it and sell it faster. But all beer is still brewed, it's still raw ingredients combined in different tanks, using different process, taking a few hours to brew, a few days to ferment and then a few more days or weeks to mature. No one is (yet, anyway) brewing a beer like they would make a soda.

With these new processes and processing aids, the taste of the beer has definitely changed. Just before Prohibition, the average barrel of American lager used 45.6lbs of malt, 13lbs of corn and/or rice and 0.68lbs of hops (in 1900 the hops were 1lb per barrel). By 1980 it was 26.7lbs of malt, 12.3lbs of corn and/or rice and just 0.22lbs of hops. The malt content, as we can see, has dropped significantly (while the adjunct percentage has increased), creating much lighter beers (in body and probably colour, too), which in turn use far fewer hops. Clearly American drinkers wanted beers that were lighter and lighter (or Lite-r).

EVERYTHING YOU ALWAYS WANTED IN A BEER, AND LESS

A biochemist called Joseph Owades transformed the American beer industry when he discovered an enzyme that was able to break down more of the sugars in malt and produce a more fermentable beer, giving something drier, lighter and with less sweetness, carbs and calories.

Owades was working with Rhinegold Brewery in Brooklyn, and they produced a new beer called Gablinger's Diet Beer with the tagline "It doesn't fill you up." It wasn't a success. No one wanted diet beer, while the picture of a doctor on the can wasn't especially appealing. Then Owades shared the brewing technique with Chicago's Meister Brau, who released a beer called Lite. The brewery was making a million barrels a year and was a favourite local producer, but when bad business moves left them bankrupt, Miller bought the Lite brand.

With more people associating beer with big bellies and taking an interest in dieting, Miller saw the potential for a new kind of beer, and after trialling Miller Lite in several blue-collar test markets, they started proper sales in 1975 and applied the Philip Morris approach to mass-marketing and hard selling.

Miller Lite wasn't a diet beer. It was "Everything you always wanted in a beer. And less." The adverts were fun. They showed ex-pro sports stars drinking it. They used the line "Tastes Great, Less Filling", and they managed to get into some deeper psyche of modernizing America: a beer you could feel good about drinking, a beer that was better for you, a beer that was even more refreshing.

The advertising budgets helped, of course, and they spent $10 million in the first year and then $15 million the following year, and it was a near-instant success: between 1974 and 1978 Miller more than tripled their sales, and jumped into second place behind the perpetual leaders in St Louis.

In 1978, the American industry had consolidated to under fifty brewing companies. Anheuser-Busch and Miller had 44 per cent of the market between them. Schlitz and Pabst were number three and four respectively, but now even they were fighting to keep up, and beneath them were many other national breweries just trying to find ways to sell more beer. With most breweries struggling, however, one brewery in Colorado thought they might have a chance to catch the others.

Adolph Kohrs (or Kors, as his father had misspelt his surname on his birth certificate) was born in the city of Barmen, east of Düsseldorf. He lived opposite the Wenker Brewery and apprenticed there as a teenager. In 1868 he stowed away on a ship sailing to Baltimore. He arrived in America with no papers, no money and no prospects (when he could afford it, he returned to pay for his fare as soon as he could and it was supposedly a lifelong shame to have made the journey illegally). He Americanized his name to Coors and went west, eventually working at the Stenger Brewery in Naperville, Illinois, where, the story goes, the brewery owner, who had three daughters but no son, offered Coors whichever daughter he liked and the promise that one day the brewery would be his.

Not much is known about the daughters, but Coors didn't hang around and by 1872 he was a partner in a bottling company in Denver. There, Coors met Jacob Schueler, who owned a confectionery and ice cream parlour in the city, and together they opened a brewery next to Clear Creek in Golden, which Coors had chosen because of the quality of water (there's a clue in the name, isn't there). Coors was a good businessman and brewer. He built a malting facility, a bottling plant, stone cellars, a large ice store, a lake to cut ice from, and by 1880 he'd saved enough money to buy the brewery outright from Schueler, renaming it the Adolph Coors Golden Brewery.

Almost a century later, Coors Banquet had become a cult beer, the kind people drove hours to buy a case of, mostly thanks to it only being sold in sixteen states, and only west of the Mississippi. The beer was all still made in Golden, Colorado, at an enormous brewing facility (at one time the largest single-site brewery in the world), it was sterile filtered instead of pasteurized (Coors hated the idea of "cooking" his beer) and there was lots of demand, so they decided to invest in more tanks, brew more beer, distribute in more states and brew a new beer, Coors Light, which was released in 1978. By 1991 Coors were the third-placed brewery in the country and everyone else around them – at least the ones below – were falling further behind.

Back at the top Miller Lite was still surging. Anheuser-Busch had to react. They tried with Natural Light and Michelob Light in the late 1970s before deciding to extend the line on their main brand and make Budweiser Light (it later lost the "-weiser"). It was released in 1982 (the same year as Diet Coke was introduced), became an even more astonishing success than Miller Lite and saw Anheuser-Busch's total market share grow from under 30 per cent to almost 50 per cent by the end of the 1980s (helped by spending hundreds of millions of dollars on advertising).

In 1988 light beer took a quarter of the market. In the 2000s it would be half the market. Bud Light did so well that in 2001 its sales overtook Budweiser, and the top three breweries were then accounting for 80 per cent of American beer, with imports 11 per cent. Then in 2017, for the first time the three best-selling beers in America were all light: Bud Light, Coors Light and Miller Lite, with Budweiser slipping to fourth (its sales had been declining for numerous years, and in 2019 it would drop to fifth place, with Michelob Ultra, the lightest of the light and low-carb beers, overtaking it). Light lager was – and is – definitely America's beer.

But the birth of Lite beer was the death of many once-great brewing companies, as light beer scythed through the industry. The marketing budgets and national dominance of Budweiser, Coors and Miller left the top three breweries in an insurmountable position, and causing a series of consolidations, closures and takeovers, including some names that had seemed untouchable.

At first, to try to keep up, breweries implemented changes and "efficiencies" (in other words, made more beer and made it quicker and cheaper). Schlitz, once the best-selling beer in the country, cut fermentation time, poured in corn syrup, replaced hop pellets with extract and added stabilizers, which turned out to affect the beer's appearance and leave gloopy lumps in suspension. They had to recall ten million bottles, and the brand was terminally tainted.

In 1988 Schlitz were bought by Detroit's Stroh's, making Stroh's the third-largest in America, with seven brewing facilities. It was a last-chance move to compete with the pre-Coors duopoly, but they didn't have the same marketing budgets as Anheuser-Busch or Miller and their main products were heavier lagers at a time when all the other beers were getting lighter. Stroh's lowered prices, becoming a commodity brand, which just made things worse. Coors overtook them in 1989 and moved into third place. Stroh's closed in 1999, and their brands were bought by Miller and Pabst.

Pabst had been one of the great breweries for over a century when, in 1985, they sold to Paul Kalmanovitz, a California investor, and by 1996 their mega Milwaukee brewery had been shuttered. The brand was sold on in 2014, but continues to be brewed (much of it by Miller in Milwaukee), with PBR gaining a cool cultish profile. What they have done, however, is become a kind of collector of old American beer brands, amassing them from closures over the last decades, and contract-brewing numerous heritage brands like Schlitz, Stroh's, Old Style, Blatz and Old Milwaukee. The old breweries might not be there any more, but some of the famous old names still are.

Light lager, a beer that was part malt, part adjunct, and low in calories, carbohydrates and character, became a distinctly American-tasting drink. But not everyone wanted these mild lagers: some people wanted beer with *flavour*.

IMPORTS AND CRAFT BEER

The growth of the American beer market made it lucrative to some of Europe's bigger breweries, who were shipping beer there as early as the 1870s. As Prohibition was called, the most-imported beer into America was Pilsner Urquell; with repeal, it was Heineken who would become the largest.

Heineken's success story in the US is almost solely the responsibility of Leo van Munching, a brilliant and charismatic beer salesman. He started selling the beer at the end of 1933 – Heineken, as we'll see in the next chapter, was the first legally imported beer in America after Prohibition – and while there were several struggles in the first few years (high import duty, the return of local beers after the dry years, a maximum alcohol of 4 per cent ABV when Heineken was 5 per cent), by 1936 it was on sale in around a hundred venues in New York City, eventually competing with other main export breweries like Beck's, Löwenbräu and Amstel.

In the late 1950s, Van Munching & Co. had become Heineken's biggest single customer. Van Munching was in such a powerful position, selling huge amounts of beer in the world's largest beer market, that in 1959 he negotiated an extraordinary deal whereby he would be the sole importer of Heineken in the US for his lifetime *and* the lifetime of his son, Leo Jr.

In 1960 they sold one million cases of Heineken, and in 1976 that had grown to 12 million. America accounted for more than half of Heineken's exports out of the Netherlands, and Heineken over one third of the total US import market, making it the number-one import beer. Van Munching had developed a network of over 300 agents for distribution and sales, with the beer arriving at eleven US ports. With that volume of beer and the logistical challenges it made sense for Heineken to build a brewery in America, or at least have it brewed domestically, but van Munching fought vociferously against this. For him, the specialness of the Heineken beer was simple: the neck label that said "Imported". For consumers, this had a premium appeal and a sense of something more special and more flavoursome at a time when the local beers were becoming perceived as weak and watery.

Heineken's dominance didn't last forever. In the 1980s, with Leo van Munching Jr now running the company, more European breweries were trying to sell in America: Kronenbourg spent millions of dollars on US advertising with their slogan "Europeans like Heineken but they love Kronenbourg," and Stella Artois also became a prominent import lager. But ultimately it wasn't fuller-flavoured European lagers that took over the American import market, it was lighter Mexican lagers.

In 1982 Corona sold around 11,350hl in the US, which exploded to around 443,000hl just three years later. Corona had its early success in California and the south-west, and soon spread east, taking an astonishing 17 per cent of the import market within five years of its introduction. In the late 1990s Corona overtook Heineken in the US as the number-one imported beer, by which time Leo Sr had died and Leo Jr had decided to let Heineken manage their own sales in the US.

Corona's great success wasn't that it tasted delicious but that it encapsulated the feeling of being on the beach. Its ice-cold refreshment evokes the white sand, yellow sun and blue sea and sky – even the bottle somehow looks like the beach. Where Heineken sold the ideal of a quality, flavoursome, expensive imported beer at a time of cheap, bland lagers, Corona sold sunshine in a bottle. As of 2018, Constellation Brands, who have the brewing and distribution rights in the US for Corona and other Mexican lagers like Modelo, were the third-placed brewer in the US (after Anheuser-Busch in first and MillerCoors in second – they merged and we'll get to that). Heineken were fourth and Pabst were fifth, despite not having a brewery.

And then came the microbreweries.

Craft beer emerged in earnest in the first years of the 1980s, right at the time when there were fewer breweries in America than at any time in documented history. The big breweries were now *so* big and the market was so used to just light-tasting beer that starting a small brewery was a stupid thing to do. How could someone making a few hundred litres a day compete with a brewery making a million bottles a day? But somehow they could, and, as in the early days of Germans brewing in America, a handful of plucky, brave, resilient, determined brewers were able to create a whole new side of the industry.

The earliest craft brewery didn't really start out as "craft". In San Francisco, the Steam Beer Brewing Company had been making beer since 1896. Steam Beer was a uniquely Californian style originating as the population spread and ended up all the way on the west coast, lured by the golden sunshine, golden beaches, and the gold in the hills. From around the 1850s brewers developed a method of brewing with lager yeast in the warm conditions, a necessity given the difficulties of getting ice and the non-existent refrigeration at that time. These beers were fermented warm with a lager yeast and then, instead of going into cold cellars to mature, were put straight into small serving barrels. The barrels were stored for a few days, by which time the re-fermenting beer had built up a large amount of pressure and carbonation, so when the beer was tapped a blast of steam emerged and it poured with a lively foam. It was a kind of lager, but one that didn't get lagered, and wasn't produced in the cold (and was probably pretty rough to drink). It was one of the first indigenous American beer styles (cold-brewed lagers did eventually get to California in the 1880s with the advent of mechanical ice-making and refrigeration).

In 1965 the Steam Brewing Company were struggling. The machinery was old, the beer wasn't very good, they didn't make much of it, and what they did make contained food colouring and sugar, but something convinced 27-year-old Fritz Maytag, heir to the Maytag home-appliance company, to buy a 51 per cent stake, which he increased to 100 per cent a few years later. He now owned the smallest (and probably shittiest) brewery in America. He gradually improved the beers and the processes and refined this special kind of lager, which was an oddity of a beer: a handmade outlier at a time when only large brewing companies and imported beer existed. Maytag persisted, and Anchor Steam remains a classic beer today.

Maytag didn't kickstart an immediate revolution. Homebrewing was illegal until 1979, and there were many other barriers, principally that it was an industry that effectively had to be created from nothing. But from 1980 things did start to happen. A brewery here. A brewpub there. Then a few more. And a few more after that. Most started with similar aspirations to one another: to brew something tasty to drink; and inspiration typically came from Britain and Belgium, with pale ales, amber ales, brown ales, stouts, porters and wheat beers all common in the early years. But very few tried to make lager; that was what Big Beer did.

One of the first to introduce – or reintroduce – a flavoursome lager to America was Jim Koch. His great-great-great-grandfather had emigrated from Germany and settled in St Louis, founding the Louis Koch Brewery. Most of Koch's family had been in the beer industry, and that convinced Jim that he *didn't* want to do the same, so he went to Harvard and then law school and then got a job in a management consulting firm, which ultimately convinced him that he *did* actually want to work in beer. He found old family recipes of pre-Prohibition lagers, and did a deal to contract-brew out of Pittsburgh Brewery, selling his first batches of Boston Beer Company's Samuel Adams Boston Lager in 1985. The malt-flavoured amber lager with a bitter finish was nothing like a Bud Light, yet within a decade and through tenacity and hard work (while mass-consolidation and closures rained brewhouse debris all around him), Koch was selling 700,000bbls (820,000hl) of lager a year and was the tenth biggest brewer in America.

The largest craft brewery in America is also the oldest: D. G. Yuengling & Son. In 1829 David Jüngling arrived into Pottsville, Pennsylvania, from Württemberg, and established the Eagle Brewery. Yuengling initially brewed ales and porter, but it's thought he was making lagers by the 1840s. With the repeal of Prohibition, the Yuengling brewery sold a lager inspired by the brews of their founder, but it came to be replaced by lighter Pilsner-style lagers. Then in 1987, when the brewery was unable to compete with the large brands, they introduced Yuengling Traditional Lager, an amber beer inspired by the pre-Prohibition recipes and using corn and American hops. The unlightened, old-style American lager had more flavour than a light beer, but not so much flavour that it alienated "normal" drinkers, and in 2018, D. G. Yuengling & Son was the sixth-largest brewery in America and it's still run by the Yuengling family, meaning at least one true German-American brewing family has managed to succeed and not concede or accede to multinational companies.

There were others – many others – as craft beer grew to take over 13 per cent of the beer market in volume and over 24 per cent in dollar value (and that's of an industry worth over $114 billion). In 2015, the 142-year-old historic high of 4,131 breweries was surpassed, and as of early 2019 there were close to 7,500 breweries in America (and in the last chapter of this book I'll look at a few of those who are making lagers, whether with traditional Bavarian-style brewing techniques or innovating with new styles).

Back to Big Beer, and 2008 was a big year: Miller[49] and Coors merged to solidify second place behind Anheuser-Busch, who in the same year were taken over by Interbrew, a Belgian-Brazilian company, to become AB-InBev – and for the first time since 1880 there wasn't a Busch as president of the brewery. Now brewing was getting even bigger and spreading to new markets all around the world, combining companies and using broad portfolios of local, national and international beer to increase overall sales.

The MillerCoors merger saw changes to the Coors beers. For the first time in its history, Coors was brewed outside Golden, utilizing the Miller breweries around the country (Coors Banquet is still only brewed in Golden, Colorado, though, where they now also brew Miller Lite, with Coors Light made in Milwaukee and in the other Miller breweries). The Coors recipes changed, too, going from rice to corn syrup and introducing pasteurization instead of sterile filtration. But as we've seen, the one consistent aspect of the American beer industry is that it's always changing.

THE BREWERY

"The 10.10 Bud Light Tour starts in five minutes. Dilly Dilly," calls an announcement as I'm looking at the blinding embodiment of Americana: everything is red, white and blue. There is neon everywhere. In the gift shop there is almost nothing they haven't attempted to put a Budweiser logo on.

I've been to the Anheuser-Busch brewery in St Louis before, and was amazed the first time; I'm still amazed the second time. It's a grand old red-brick campus that sprawls over many city blocks. The main brewhouse building, from 1892,

---

49 In 2002 Morris sold Miller to South African Breweries to create SABMiller (they basically had no hope of catching Anheuser-Busch so passed it on to someone else to try). In 2005, Canada's Molson merged with Coors to create MolsonCoors. Then SABMiller and MolsonCoors combined their American operations to become MillerCoors, with SABMiller remaining for the rest of the world (all these mergers and acquisitions get complicated: a warning for what's to come later).

has a huge clock tower with the A and Eagle logo at its base. This is a building from a time of unrivalled grandeur in the brewing industry, built by a company that wanted to be the biggest and the best in America. It's opulent, enormous, stately, and they still make the beer in the same place – albeit with modern tanks in the historic old structure.

The brewhouse is one of the most beautiful working breweries I've seen anywhere in the world. There are tiled floors and they are immaculate. There are gilded columns. Ornate railings and staircases going up and down the many floors. There's a large mural at the end of the brewing hall. There are even chandeliers. I've never once been to a craft brewery with chandeliers.[50]

Brewing today is not like it was when this place was built. The brewers are not here on the brewhouse floor, and they're sitting in front of multiple computer screens. Everything can be managed remotely, and they're dealing with dozens of processes simultaneously, which is itself an astonishing thing – like a really difficult computer game based around fast-moving numbers with terrible consequences if you fail. The only person I see on the brewery floor is someone measuring hops and putting them into the hop doser.

I wish I could've seen this place over a hundred years ago when it was at a peak of pre-Prohibition production and filled with men working amid noise, steam and heat. I wish I could've experienced the cold cellars, too, when they were underground and filled with huge wooden barrels and blocks of ice. Now it's remarkable in a new way. The tanks are great silver units of a scale that defies useful explanation: I stand beneath one and it's like being at the front door of a three-storey town house. We see one section of the cellars, but I bet there are dozens of them, stacked up, spread all around the site. Some of these vessels can hold 6,000bbls, or two million regular beer bottles. When Eberhard Anheuser took over the Bavarian Brewery in 1860 they made 3,200bbls in one year – now they could make that in a morning.

They still follow old processes here in a way others have long forgotten. They use beechwood chips (more for tradition than taste now), it takes around 25 days to produce a batch of Bud, they use hop pellets and a mix of malt and rice. They do brew it high-gravity, and it's been engineered, optimized and stabilized, but that's part of the marvel of modern mass-produced beer.

---

50 By contrast, the Coors brewery in Golden is one of the ugliest brewery buildings I've ever seen. It's an enormous utilitarian unit of concrete on the outside, and a tired, packed brewhouse inside. While the brewery buildings might be a big slab of charmless rock, you barely notice it as the backdrop is the full cliché of snow-capped mountains and big blue sky, and somehow the gargantuan grey blocks sympathetically blend in with the landscape as a kind of camouflaged optical illusion. In Milwaukee, the Miller Brewery is very impressive, taking up multiple blocks on the edge of town and still with a good-looking old brewhouse, plus a replica of the original Plank Road Brewery. If you're ever in St Louis, Golden (or Denver as it's nearby) or Milwaukee, then do the brewery tours.

I order a Budweiser in the bar after the tour. Whether you like this beer or not, it's a remarkable brand with a great history. Sure, they've bullied, bought and fought their way to where they are, but the beer itself is very good in the simplest of ways – crisp, refreshing, brightly carbonated, light, but balanced and unchallenging (and definitely better – for me, anyway – than the frankly bland Bud Light). The earliest Anheuser-Busch beers were nothing like this: they would've been dark, malty, full-bodied and bitter. The first Conrad Budweiser was nothing like the beer we know as Budweiser today, either, but by the time Bud became the brewery's main brand it had evolved into this kind of lighter and more refreshing lager, and the changing tastes of American consumers had made this an appealing beer, one mass-made, standardized, always available, always affordable and always the same. It came with a familiar reliability that consumers understood, trusted and enjoyed.

There's a perception that America ruined lager or that they made it something overly bland and watery – you've probably heard the joke about sex in a canoe and Budweiser both being fucking close to water – but that's a simplified misconception that doesn't account for what the drinkers actually wanted, and in reality the engineered – in terms of beer and science – developments of lager brewing in the second half of the twentieth century became the archetype of what modern lager is.

Germans transformed American drinking habits. It took a couple of decades, but from the 1870s America became a nation of beer drinkers – of lager drinkers. Those old émigré brewers in cities like St Louis, Milwaukee, Cincinnati, Chicago, New York and Philadelphia created a new industry based on old German traditions, and transformed it into one of the great American industries. Lager became America's beer, and they would define new tastes and processes of lager brewing. But it wasn't the Americans who ultimately got the whole world drinking lagers in the first place. It also wasn't the Bavarians or the Bohemians or the Viennese or the Danish. It was the Dutch.

CHAPTER FOUR

HOW LAGER BECAME THE WORLD'S LOCAL DRINK

HEINEKEN: THE BREWERY THAT TAUGHT THE WORLD TO DRINK LAGER

Heineken is the world's second-largest brewing company. It sells beer in over 190 countries and makes it in over 125 breweries in 70 countries, employing over 80,000 people, and selling 300 local, regional, national or international brands. Heineken, the main brand, is the fifth best-selling beer in the world, available in more countries than any other beer. Without Heineken's global vision of brewing, selling and exporting lager far away from its Dutch breweries, the beer world might not be quite the way it is.

In 1864 Gerard Adriaan Heineken bought the Den Hoybergh (the Haystack Brewery) in Amsterdam. Heineken didn't know much about brewing and his brewery was in decline, but he was confident he could do something great. Within a year he had brewed 5,000 barrels of ale. Within two years he'd bought a plot of land on the then-outskirts of Amsterdam to build a bigger brewery powered by steam. Within five years he'd hired a German brewmaster, Wilhelm Feltmann, and made a big decision: that *Hollandsch bier*, a range of mostly dark, low-alcohol, often sour ales that he and his compatriots were making, was not the future – a decision made after a sobering experience at an international exhibition in Amsterdam where the clear and sparkling newness of the Bavarian *lagerbier* a neighbouring Dutch brewer was offering presented an unwelcome contrast to Gerard's flat, cloudy ales.

In February 1870 Heineken released a new lager called Heineken's *Beiersch* (that means "Bavarian", and it was a dark lager similar to Bavarian *Sommerbier*), a "full-bodied, clear, particularly tasty drink," it was reported at the time, "that appeared to combine the good qualities of Viennese beer and Belgian beer". That same year they opened their new brewery on the edge of town, where they continued to produce Dutch ale alongside the new Bavarian beer.

Also in 1870, three wealthy families opened a competing brewery in Amsterdam, naming it after the river that ran alongside: Amstel. Their beer sold well in cafés and bars and they used the growing railway network to sell it beyond the city. The stories of Amstel and Heineken will come to intertwine.

By 1873, Gerard and brewmaster Feltmann had decided that they would brew lager, and only lager, in their Amsterdam brewery. The following year they established a partnership with the d'Oranjeboom Brewery in Rotterdam and together they built a new brewery.

Heineken were brewing several types of beer by 1880. *Gerstebier* was a quickly brewed and cheap bottom-fermented dark lager for the local market, and even into the twentieth century it accounted for half of the output from their Rotterdam brewery; *Beiersch* was the Dutch equivalent of a Bavarian dark lager; *Münchener Bier* was dark Munich lager sold domestically, whereas they had a Vienna beer for export (a sign, perhaps, of the renown of Vienna overseas), and a Pilsener Bier.

With the latter, it's a possibility that Heineken are responsible for this spelling of the style as the brewery say that brewmaster Feltmann didn't want the name to be confused with Pilsen beer, so he spelt it Pilsener. Whether true or not, from around the late 1870s we see Pilsner, Pilsen and Pilsener as spellings for the palest style of lager, with the word Pils coming later (Heineken's Pilsener would become their flagship beer and from the 1950s it's been the beer we simply know as "Heineken").

Heineken were one of the early adopters of ice-making machinery and artificial refrigeration, and in 1886, following some bad fermentations, they opened a laboratory in the Rotterdam brewery with a Dr Hartog Elion in charge. That year, Elion, utilizing Hansen's pure culture method, was able to isolate two yeasts, which they called A-yeast and D-yeast. Heineken were one of the first breweries after Carlsberg to isolate their own pure yeast, and the A-yeast is what they still use today.

Gerard died suddenly in 1893, at the age of fifty-one. By then Heineken were brewing some 200,000hl a year when the average Dutch brewery made 3,000hl. The brewery continued to grow under the stewardship of his wife and later, in 1914, Gerard's only son, Henry. It would be the inter-war years, through a series of partnerships and takeovers, that would come to define Heineken for the rest of the century and, ultimately, its place in the beer world.

Between 1919 and 1934 Heineken took over six Dutch breweries, mostly to use as depots; they bought Brasserie Léopold in Brussels (after failing to buy the Artois brewery); and they invested in Interbra, a company with large holdings in ten international breweries, which gave Heineken access to facilities in what's now Kinshasa (capital of the Democratic Republic of the Congo), Indonesia and Belgium. They also developed partnerships in the Far East, West Indies, England, West Africa and the United States.

Pieter Feith was Export Manager at this time, and was largely responsible for Heineken's global outlook. One of his early deals was with two Scotsmen in Singapore, John Fraser and David Chalmers Neave, who had started out as Bible salesmen and then moved into lemonade. Feith wondered if they'd like to expand into beer, and in 1932 their joint company, the Malayan Breweries Limited, started to produce Tiger Beer, which would go on to become south-east Asia's best-selling lager. Around this time they took over a brewery in Surabaya, Indonesia, where they started to brew a brand called Bintang. Today that beer is so dominant in its market that Bintang is effectively the Indonesian word for beer.

No other brewery was doing anything like this at that time. In the past breweries grew by exporting beer, but now advances in brewing equipment and technology meant it was possible to make lager fast and on a large scale anywhere in the world, which in turn made beer affordable for more people. Heineken introduced brewing into countries that had previously had no locally brewed beer, and the beer they made wherever they went was a light and refreshing pale lager, where they took a systematic approach by first creating or investing in a local brand to establish or grow a domestic market, and then later introducing Heineken as a new, premium lager, to be seen as a better beer choice over the weaker or simpler domestic brews.

After growing in the East, Heineken then looked West, to a market that hadn't drunk a (lawful) beer in a long time, and in March 1933 Feith, along with some beer as cargo, boarded the *Statendam* passenger ship from Amsterdam, arriving in Hoboken three days after America's Prohibition had been was lifted. Heineken became the first legally imported beer into the US in thirteen years (incidentally, it was on the *Statendam* that Feith met Leo van Munching, who would become the sole distributor of Heineken beer in the US).

Then the foreign partnerships increased in the mid-1930s as the Dutch beer market crashed and drinking declined. A post-war boom of expansion combined with anti-German sentiment (meaning the big German exporting breweries like Beck's and Löwenbräu were no longer sending their beer overseas) and saw Heineken quickly become the world's largest beer exporter.

That growth actually began during the war, when in 1941 the Archipelago Brewing Company, founded by Beck's Brewery in what's now Jakarta, and with another brewery in Singapore (brewing Anker/Anchor and Diamant/Diamond respectively), was seized by the Brits as "enemy territory". Heineken's joint-owned Malayan Breweries took the breweries over and used them to supply beer to Allied troops around Asia. After the war they used the company to brew beer for the recovering local markets, at a time when beer was becoming more and more accessible to growing numbers of people, giving the world a taste for fresh, cold lager.

In the late 1940s Africa became a focus. The United Africa Company, an arm of Unilever, basically traded in everything it could. Heineken approached it about a partnership to build a brewery in Nigeria, and in 1949 Star lager was released. Within five years it was the most drunk lager in the region.[51] In the early 1950s almost half Heineken's export profits were coming from Africa, mostly from Nigeria and Ghana, and, having created the market for lager in Africa, they went on to build several other breweries later in the decade, and even more in the 1960s and onwards.

By this time, Henry's son Alfred "Freddy" Heineken had joined the board. At first Freddy's unscholarly ways and extravagant lifestyle meant he wasn't seen as chairman material, so in 1946 he was sent to the US to work with Leo van Munching (in other words he was sent far away while the board figured out what to do with the heir to the brewery), and while he was there Freddy would see the future of beer.

Heineken takes over the world

Freddy Heineken returned from America in 1948, and almost immediately created a new advertising department, supposedly by writing "Advertising Department" on a piece of paper and sticking it on the door of an empty office. He proved to be an inspired brain behind the development of the brand. His experience in the US had shown him the changes that were coming with car ownership, supermarkets, refrigeration and advertising, and convinced him of the growing importance of the brand's image in a marketplace where consumers were being faced with ever more choice.

Freddy and the board made the decision that their main brand should now be called just Heineken, and not Heineken's Pilsener – they no longer needed variety, but rather one great beer. Then, in the early 1950s, he oversaw several small changes to the brand's appearance that collectively turned into something much bigger.

The branding was a green oval, much like it is today, and had "HEINEKEN'S" around the top of that oval, and a black rectangle through the middle with the beer type inside it (i.e. Pilsener). Freddy got rid of the 's in the name, then wrote it in script instead of capitals, with each letter *e* tilted slightly upwards so it

---

51   United Africa Company were selling Guinness in Nigeria around this time, and in 1962 built a brewery in Lagos. Today more Guinness is drunk in Nigeria than in Ireland.

looked like it was smiling. Then the newly formatted "Heineken" went into the black box of the label, becoming the name of both the brewery and the beer. It still looks the same today.

The 1950s and 1960s were good decades at home for Heineken. Dutch drinking increased from 10 litres per capita in 1949 to 45.4 litres in 1968, while Heineken's market share went from 21.7% to 39% in the same period, ahead of Amstel in second. They built a third brewery in Den Bosch in 1958 (to go with Rotterdam and Amsterdam); they were the first Dutch brewer to go into the grocery stores, soon followed by Amstel; and they started to advertise on the radio.

But by the 1960s, even with breweries in more than twenty countries, including places as disparate as Venezuela, Angola, Chad and Indonesia, the activities of other European brewing companies forced Heineken to react. In December 1967 Allied Breweries, one of the biggest in Britain, bought Oranjeboom, and then added De Drie Hoefijzers (The Three Horseshoes) a few months later, buying themselves 20 per cent of the Dutch market. Heineken feared that if Allied were to take over Amstel, the Brits would have a similar share of the Dutch market to themselves.

For almost a hundred years Heineken and Amstel had been rivals, and together they accounted for 60 per cent of the Dutch market. In 1968, a merger between the two old breweries was agreed, and they would go on to invest in what would become the largest brewery in Europe when it opened in 1975 in Zoeterwoude, south-west of Amsterdam (replacing the site in Rotterdam).

Amstel were already brewing under licence (meaning the Amstel beer could be made in other breweries around the world) in Curaçao, Jordan, Lebanon, Greece, Surinam and Madagascar when Heineken took them over. Then from 1968, at a rate of almost one per year, they started working on new breweries in England, Sierra Leone, Trinidad, Jamaica, Norway, Sweden, Saint Lucia, Tahiti, Haiti, Ireland, Italy, France, Morocco, Greece, South Korea, Japan, China, Spain, Vietnam, Poland, Switzerland, Bulgaria and Slovakia.

They looked to South America now as well. Brazil had long been dominated by the brands Brahma and Antarctica, who both also sold soft drinks in a kind of cartel agreement that said customers had to buy both beer and soda. There were Coca-Cola bottling plants in the region and the bottlers built breweries in Rio de Janeiro, São Paulo and Belo Horizonte, and when Heineken discovered that there were 7,000 delivery trucks on the road in Brazil at any one time, they acquired small stakes in them. By 1987 Heineken were brewing four million hectolitres of a lager called Kaiser – it's still one of the top brands in Brazil. In 1984 Heineken also took stakes in the Quilmes Group, who had breweries in Argentina, Uruguay and Paraguay.

They grew further in Asia in the late 1980s and into the 1990s, just as China was emerging as the world's largest beer market. Altogether this enabled Heineken, or a Heineken-owned brand, to become a local beer in most of the world. There was just one area they hadn't yet come to dominate: Europe.

Fortress Europe

From as early as 1873, Heineken had been on sale in Paris, and now Freddy wanted to take control of the French market. In 1961, they appointed Moët & Chandon as their general importer, selling the premium lager alongside their premium champagne. In wine-drinking France, where beer was blue-collar, Heineken used the slogan "*La bière qui fait aimer la bière*" ("The beer that makes you like beer"), which was a successful campaign, but to get to be the number-one brewer they were up against Kronenbourg.

In June 1664, Jérôme Hatt started brewing at Brasserie du Canon in Strasbourg (they moved to the district of Cronenbourg in 1862), but we can jump forward a few generations to when the Hatt brewery was a contemporary of the Sedlmayrs in Munich, the Jacobsens in Copenhagen and Gerard Heineken in Amsterdam,[52] and had become a progressive, innovative lager brewery, growing to become France's number-one beer. A century later, Jérôme Hatt VI was in charge of the family business, and from there Kronenbourg and Heineken followed relatively parallel trajectories.

In 1947, Hatt changed the name of the brewery to Kronenbourg, taking the German spelling of his town's name from when Alsace-Lorraine was annexed to the German Empire. From there he started a series of innovations: in 1952 the brand 1664 was introduced as a premium, more bitter, stronger lager; he introduced sturdier 330ml and 250ml bottles with crown caps and packaged them in cardboard; there was a new red and white logo, accompanied by more extensive and expensive advertising; they introduced a six-pack in 1963 with the expectation of increased beer sales in the growing numbers of hypermarkets; and they opened a second brewery in Obernai. But in the process they over-extended themselves financially, and ended up joining the Boussois-Souchon-Neuvesel group, which later became part of the Danone group. They continued to grow, however, and by 1983 the French beer battle was between the red of Kronenbourg and the green of Heineken.

---

52 These brewers regularly corresponded with one another, and it makes me wonder what they'd say if they were resurrected in a modern bar today and saw their beers lined up next to each other. They'd still see famous brands like Heineken, Kronenbourg, Carlsberg, Stella Artois, Amstel, Löwenbräu, Pilsner Urquell, Guinness, and probably some others – the world has changed a lot, and beer has changed with it, but there's a remarkable thread of names with significant longevity.

Today, Heineken is still very strong in France, leading with its main brand, while also owning Pelforth and the tequila-flavoured Desperados. Kronenbourg remains the most famous French beer and the market leader, and is owned by Carlsberg (though in the UK it's brewed and distributed by Heineken) – the brewery in Obernai is Carlsberg's largest in Europe.

****

Spain took a while to become beer drinkers. In the 1950s per capita beer consumption was just 3 litres, but by the late 1970s beer drinking had jumped to 50 litres per person. In 1986 Spain joined the European Union and that's when it became a good time for Heineken to have a presence in the market.

El Águila (The Eagle) brewery made Spain's best-selling beer, the only nationally available one, with 20 per cent of the overall market. But they had tried to grow too aggressively and by the 1980s were in trouble. In 1984, Heineken took a 32 per cent stake, but then discovered that many of El Águila's seven breweries were falling apart and there was no standardized beer production. Heineken spent a lot of money and in 1994 launched Águila estilo Amstel. Over the next decade the branding evolved, first to Aguila Cerveza, then Aguila Amstel, then Amstel Aguila, then Amstel Cerveza. In 1999, the Guinness brewery group decided they no longer wanted a brand called Cruzcampo, so Heineken bought it. Heineken is now the second-largest brewing company in Spain (behind Mahou-San Miguel),[53] holding around 30 per cent of the market. In 2017, Spain was the eleventh largest beer market in the world and the fourth largest in Europe.

In Italy, Heineken invested in Cisalpina in 1960, a company with five breweries who also had the rights to the Dreher brand. Heineken was brewed in Italy from 1976; in the mid-1980s it was second to Birra Peroni; and in 1996 they bought Birra Moretti to increase their strength in the market.

Greece basically had no beer market in 1960. It's thought King Otto of Greece introduced beer into the country in the nineteenth century: he was a member of the Wittelsbach family, and his parents' wedding was the one that started Oktoberfest, and even into the 1960s there existed a *Reinheitsgebot*-like rule that only 100 per cent malt beers could be brewed in Greece. The limited

---

53 San Miguel, that famous Spanish beer, was actually first brewed in Manila, the Philippines, in 1890. It was south-east Asia's first production brewery and used artificial refrigeration and produced its own ice to brew lagers, including its own Pale Pilsen. They introduced their beer into Spain in 1946 and set up a separate company there in 1953, linking up with Mahou brewery, also founded in 1890, in Madrid. They became Mahou-San Miguel in 2000. Estrella Damm is the other main lager producer in Spain. The brewery was founded in Barcelona in 1876 by August Küntzmann Damm, an Alsatian brewmaster, who made a lighter lager for the Mediterranean climate.

domestic brewing, mostly by the brand Fix (launched when King Otto was in charge), was protected by a 600 per cent import tax.

But the increase in tourism made Greece an attractive market. In 1965 Amstel licensed the Athenian Brewery to make their beer; by the end of the decade it was the best-selling beer in Greece. Together, Heineken and Athenian opened a new brewery later in the 1970s, and then Heineken was introduced into the market, brewed locally, in 1981. Mythos became the most famous Greek lager brand after its introduction in the early 2000s. Today Mythos and Fix are both Carlsberg brands.

Heineken was exported to the UK as early as the 1880s, but drinkers took a long time to transfer from their ales. After World War II the British beer market still wasn't ready for lager, but Heineken were already there trying to kickstart a love of it. They began to brew it in Britain, lowering the ABV to just 3 per cent, and over the years, via some smart mergers, and by running a large estate of 3,000 pubs, they've grown to become the market leader, largely thanks to Foster's, one of the best-selling brews in Britain.

Fortress Europe was a success, and by 2015 Heineken were market leaders in volume share in the Netherlands, the UK, Italy, Austria and Hungary, and second in almost every other country apart from Germany and the Czech Republic. Now they cover the world in beer, whether owning a local brand, brewing Heineken under licence or exporting it there.[54]

Beer is now a global drink, and since 1989 lager has been the best-selling beer type in every country. Heineken's significance lies in how they took beer around the world, introducing themselves and local brands into countries that didn't yet have beer. Heineken taught the world to drink beer; they taught the world to drink lager.

BELGIUM: HOW LAGER REPLACED (MOST OF) THE REGIONAL ALES

Belgium is one of the great beer nations, and a country outwardly famous for its fantastic variety of beer: the white beers, the amber ones, the red ones and the brown ones, the fruit beers, the sour beers, the strong beers and the beers

---

54 A footnote on the beer itself. Heineken and Amstel are both all-malt, meaning no adjuncts like rice, corn or glucose. Both brands also have a specific yeast unique to them. And for a brewery to make Heineken they need to install horizontal lagering tanks and can't use the now-common vertical cylindrical vessels. It also takes up to 28 days to make Heineken (other lager brands are made in half that time), and all batches are taste-tested against each other to make sure there's no variation. One of the best Heineken breweries in the world, often out-scoring the home brewery in Holland, is the one in Ho Chi Minh City, Vietnam (Heineken are massive in Vietnam and have six breweries where they produce their main brands as well as Tiger and Larue).

brewed by monks, all served in their own unique glass. What that colourful variety doesn't tell us, however, is that 70 per cent of the Belgian beer market is simple, indistinct, uniformly priced pale lager.

Towards the end of the nineteenth century, as lager was beginning to spread from Bavaria, Vienna and Pilsen, the beers of Belgium were the antithesis of the clean character of a good bottom-fermented lager, with many brewed using rustic techniques, in rustic breweries, with a low alcohol content and a variable and often sour taste – acidity and vinous qualities were sought-after by drinkers.

Beers were typically 3–4 per cent ABV and lots of regional and local variation existed, often specifically from a certain town: Gerst from Antwerp, Uitzet from Ghent, Wit and Peterman from Leuven (both sour wheat beers), Hoegaards from Hoegaarden (which would inspire a local postman in the 1960s to re-brew the town's famous wheat beer), Saison de Liège, Mechelse Bruynen from Mechelen, while the Brussels area was particularly famous for Lambic.[55]

Altogether it made Belgium a country of beer drinkers. Taxes on beer were low, so it was affordable in comparison to wine, and a law from 1919 prohibited the sale of liquor in pubs, increasing the focus on beer (incidentally helping to create the stronger ales Belgium is famous for now, with new, more powerfully flavoured beers becoming popular alternatives to the now-unavailable spirits).

Lager was first brewed in Belgium in 1877 when a Brussels brewery, Brasserie Bavaro-Belge, introduced a lager in its range of beers; in 1884 Wielemans-Ceuppens brewed Bavière Wielemans, the name meaning "Bavarian", and it was a beer type that straddled Belgium and Bavaria, being a dark lagered beer at a Belgian strength of 3.5 per cent ABV; in 1886 the Grande Brasserie de Koekelberg opened in Brussels and were the first brewery to focus specifically on bottom-fermented beers, brewing a dark Munich-style lager, a *petit Bavière* (a low-alcohol dark lager), a Bock and later a Pilsner; in 1893 the Artois brewery had built a separate brewery capable of making lagers, where their "Nouvelle Brasserie" was a specially built Czech-engineered facility and they produced three kinds of bottom-fermenting beer: Bavière, Bock and Munich (their "Anciennes Brasserie" continued to make the old-style Leuven wheat beers); and at the Belgian International Exhibition of 1897, one third of all beer sold there was lager, giving a clue as to what was to come, but at the turn of the

---

55 Lambic is still a famous beer of Brussels today, and it's "spontaneously fermented", meaning that yeast present in the brewery will naturally inoculate the wort and start the alcohol production. It's then left to mature in wooden barrels for up to three years, after which time different barrels are blended together, it's bottled, left to carbonate and sold as Gueuze. The beer sold unblended and uncarbonated, often at 12-18 months old, is known as Lambic. Historically, Lambic was a stronger brew while Faro was weaker, but together they were the standard beers (like *Braunbier* in Munich or porter in London). Blended Lambic (Gueuze) was sold to the wealthy, whereas the Faro was the working man's beer in Brussels – it was sometimes sweetened to balance the rougher acidity, but it wasn't served as a "sweet" beer.

twentieth century lager remained as a small-scale beer type that was mostly drunk in the cities by wealthier customers.

World War I marked a definitive change in Belgian brewing. A lot of breweries were demolished or dismantled during the war (between 1913 and 1919 more than 1,000 breweries were lost) and, while some subsequently returned to their old traditional brews, for others it was an opportunity to invest in new equipment capable of brewing lagers, helped by retribution payments to compensate for their lost equipment.

The inter-war period is when lager took hold in the damaged Belgian market. Post-World War I beers were clear, sweet (compared to the sour ones, anyway), more uniform in terms of taste, with better consistency, stability and shelf-life, and as modern drinks were initially expensive, which made them more desirable.

The most popular beers were brown-coloured Bocks, stronger than old-style Belgian beers at 4.5–5 per cent ABV. Then came the paler lagers: one of the first was introduced by the Caulier brewery as their Perle 28. They spent a lot of money to advertise it and it quickly became the most popular Belgian beer, forcing other breweries to react by also brewing pale lagers and then spending money to promote them – this changed the rules of Belgian beer and the business approach, and whether the other brewers wanted to or not (most did not), if they were to be successful they were now playing a new game and had to spend money on marketing.

A succession of Pilsner recipes followed and in 1928 what could be considered the first "proper" Belgian Pils was released, a beer called Cristal by Alken brewery (the first to be very pale and bright, as the sparkle of the name suggests). Before the end of the 1920s lager had taken over half the Belgian beer market; by the 1950s Pilsner had increased to around 70 per cent of the market.[56]

A star is born

Stella Artois like to tell their story all the way back to 1366, when a brewery named Den Horn in Leuven can be dated back to. In 1708 a Sebastian Artois became the brewmaster, buying the brewery outright in 1717 and renaming it Brouwerij Artois. We've seen how they were brewing beers from 1893 and in 1926, Artois released a lager called Stellamass as a seasonal special. It would become their flagship.

Artois became the largest brewery in Belgium in the late 1920s, and by the early 1970s had surpassed four million hectolitres. To increase their market

---

56 The growth of lager saw a general update to Belgian brewing with a move away from the tart taste of old towards a drier, cleaner beer (though the sour beers remain and have grown in popularity with the surge of craft brewing). This had the impact of reducing some of the regional varieties, while new kinds of lighter blonde ales emerged, and alongside them stronger golden ales.

power, in 1971 Artois partnered with the Piedboeuf brewery, whose main beer was called Jupiler. Oddly, the deal was a secret, confined to just a few executives, meaning the two breweries' sales teams were competing against each other. Jupiler soon became more successful, at the expense of Stella Artois, and by the end of the 1970s had actually overtaken it by volume. When the Piedboeuf brewery was short on capacity Jupiler was even brewed in Leuven under the codename "Lager" and then tankered to the Jupiler brewery to be bottled.

In 1987 the merger between the breweries became official, and the new company came to be called Interbrew. As individually large companies, Artois and Piedboeuf had already been taking over other breweries in Belgium, meaning Interbrew had ten brewing facilities and around 60 per cent of the Belgian market, but with the beer world merging and consolidating they faced a decision: sell up or buy?

They bought. Bigger than anyone had done before.

There was Hoegaarden, Leffe and Belle-Vue, giving them a broad and distinctive portfolio of Belgian beers alongside their lagers, with a spicy-refreshing white beer, some abbey ales, and lambic and fruit beer. Then they started looking at the leading breweries in countries around Europe and trying to buy them.

In 1991 Interbrew bought the Hungarian Borsodi Sogyor; in 1995 it was the Canadian brewery Labatt; in 2000 they bought Whitbread and Bass in the UK; in 2002 they bought the German brands Beck's and Spaten, followed a year later by Löwenbräu. That made Interbrew the third-largest beer company in the world, but only for a year or so, before they merged with the Brazilian company Ambev to become InBev, the world's largest brewing company. They now had breweries in all the major and emerging world markets. Then came the biggest of the big moves: in 2008 InBev bought Anheuser-Busch for $54.8 billion to become AB-InBev.[57] And then came an *even bigger* move, a move that couldn't be made any bigger, when AB-InBev joined with SABMiller. The world's biggest brewery got even bigger.

The Belgian beer market itself has been in domestic decline for around thirty years, but it's been compensated by export growth, and that's where Stella Artois has been so successful. When Interbrew was created it was decided that Jupiler would be the beer for Belgium, while Stella Artois would be the beer for the world; Jupiler now holds around a one-third share of the Belgian market, while Stella is one of the world's largest beer brands, with over half its production exported.

---

57 This one was the real shock to the beer world. Anheuser-Busch, the brewers of Budweiser, were a huge company, but their short-sighted strategy of dominating the American market saw them lagging behind the more globally invested brewing companies like Heineken, Carlsberg and now InBev. In a way, Anheuser-Busch needed to merge with InBev to gain worldwide coverage at a time when the other large breweries had already achieved it.

The story of lager in Belgium runs like a precis of the story of lager in general. It started on a small scale with a few breweries experimenting or attempting to introduce a dark Bavarian-style beer onto the market, but it took a long time to happen. When it did happen, World War I had left a shattered beer market and created a period of change that saw old-fashioned, dark, sour, weak and inconsistent regional ales replaced by fresh, bright, clean, consistent and stand-ardized lagers (which would be sold at a relatively standardized price – today they still are all similar prices). For breweries to survive they had to grow, making use of new travel networks (basically delivery trucks) and advertising, which progressed them from local brewers to national brewers to international ones, with lots of mergers and consolidation in between, all while the liquid itself became less important than the business side (for the lagers, anyway; the idiosyncratic and parochial smaller Belgian brewers have managed to thrive alongside them and increase in numbers). Belgium might be one of the most varied brewing nations in the world, but look next to that curvy bowl-like glass of Trappist ale and there's a straight, small glass of pale lager.

HOW IT TOOK BRITAIN A HUNDRED YEARS TO LOVE LAGER

In the middle of the nineteenth century, Britain was the world's greatest brewing nation with the largest breweries in the world. It had grown with the Industrial Revolution and with the extended benefits of a worldwide empire where a lot of beer was exported. But that beer wasn't lager: the breweries had initially grown with a dark ale called porter, which was later joined by mild, bitter, pale ale, India pale ale and stout as the main kinds of beer. Lager would eventually transform the beer market, but it wasn't until 1989 that lager sales overtook ale sales, making Britain the final beer-drinking country in the world to move to lager.

The story could've been very different had a brewer in Scotland managed to keep some of Gabriel Sedlmayr's lager yeast alive in 1835, as we've seen, but that didn't happen, and it would take until the late 1860s for lager to return to Britain, and then another 100 years before lager gained any serious momentum. This is how it took Britons over a century to love lager. And the story begins in Paris with Anton Dreher's Vienna lager.

The Viennese beer hall reaches London (via Paris)
World Fairs were enormously popular and important in the mid-to-late nine-teenth century. These great exhibitions brought together culture, technology

and science, showing the diversity of the world in one large space, with countries and companies building elaborate pavilions. Over the years, they gave the world the Eiffel Tower and the Ferris wheel, and showed off wonderful new technologies that had never been experienced before: the typewriter, the telephone, X-rays, electricity, colour television – they even helped popularize tomato ketchup in the US.

The International Exhibition of Paris in 1867 had 50,226 exhibitors from 42 countries, and over nine million visited during the seven months it was open. There was a Gothic cathedral and a Tunisian palace; an elevator was revealed to the world; the Egyptians built a temple, the Brits built a lighthouse – and the Austrians built a beer hall.

There were two bars in the Austrian Pavilion, one for a brewery in Liesing and the other for Dreher's Klein-Schwechat. Dreher's was an immense beer hall with "curious Austrian and Hungarian dishes", according to contemporary news reports, while "Blue-eyed *Mädchen* in national costume attend on the local visitors and contribute to *couleur locale*". Behind the large and elaborate bar were big wooden barrels from which cold lager was poured into glass mugs, showing off its brightness, its frothy foam and its pale colour. Such was the success that apparently a daily wagon-load of beer was being sent by train to Paris from Vienna to keep up with demand. By the end of 1867 several bars in Paris were stocking it, and the following year it reached Britain, with establishments on the Strand and in the City selling it.

Dreher's beer was described at the time as

> bright, of a nutty golden colour (darker than pale ale), and pleasantly
> brisk. The points in which it seems to differ from its English analogues
> are that it is very light, very soft, very clean on the tongue, though mark-
> edly saccharine; less bitter; and, though fairly strong, not yet heady, nor
> thirst-creating. (*Medical Times & Gazette*)

Lager "has really no counterpart among the different varieties of English beer", read an 1869 article in the *Daily Post* (average ale strength then was around 6 per cent ABV, whereas the lagers were typically under 4 per cent ABV), "and supplies what has long been recognized as a want – a light, pure, clear drink, of good flavour, but weak alcoholic strength".

This new beer might have been "Light! Sparkling! Refreshing! Exhilarating! Non-Intoxicating!!" but it was also Expensive! As Ron Pattinson explains in *Lager!*, it was three times the price of a pint of mild, the main beer of the time, making lager a curious luxury mostly only Germans drank. Dark Bavarian or

Munich lager was also imported, and then Bohemian Pilsner, which quickly became more popular than Vienna lager.[58]

Later Sedlmayr's Spaten was sending enough lager to London to open a distribution depot at 17 Phoenix Street, with their beer mainly sold in hotels, restaurants, clubs and bars. By 1894, Spaten also owned four restaurants in London and one in Manchester, the flagship London location on Piccadilly Circus having SPATEN BEER advertised on the roof – the building is still there and is on the corner of Shaftesbury Avenue.

The most famous of the London beer halls by the end of the nineteenth century was the Gambrinus Original Lagerbeer Saloon, at 3 Glasshouse Street. It had dark Pschorr brewery beer from Munich, Pilsner Urquell, and a lager from Kulmbach, a major German brewing city of the day. One day in September 1899, Lieutenant-Colonel Nathaniel Newnham-Davis, a leading restaurant critic of the time, was on his way home to cook a solitary dinner of a leg of mutton when he met a friend, and they decided to go to "Gamb's" instead.

"Gamb's is the Gambrinus," his American acquaintance, Miss Belle, explains:

> a queer old place where you get Dutch food – you over here call it German, but *we* call it Dutch – and where you get real cold *steins* of beer. We girls often go there by ourselves, for nobody says anything to us, and we haven't to dress up, and we are not stared at like we are in your real swell restaurants.

"Inside the first sensation is that everything is brown," writes the Lieutenant-Colonel. Brown wooden roof, four brown wood chairs at each brown wood table, a brown material on the floor, walls of a brownish yellow. It had a great lamp with wrought iron; a long window onto the street was stained glass with coats of arms and scrolls on it. Decorative mugs hung on pegs for the locals. There was an organ. Snacks were on the bar top including sprats and sausages. Dried hops hung from the ceiling. He ordered the "brown beer", which was "served stone cold in great glasses of the form of old-fashioned champagne glasses" (he thought it excellent) and "a sense of good humour pervades the place."

The beer halls survived until the onset of World War I, when there was a mass de-Germanising of Britain. In November 1914 a writer for the *Newcastle Journal* heads to "Ye Olde Gambrinus" for the "excellent Pilsener beer" to cheer

---

58 It wasn't just in London that Vienna became less popular, and even back in Austria the style was replaced by Pilsner. Even today if you go to Vienna you'll struggle to find a "Vienna Lager" in the tradition of Dreher. The Schwechater brewery is still there and does brew a Wiener Lager, but to me it tastes more like a recipe written from a modern construct and one inspired by what is expected of a contemporary Vienna lager and not one directed by actual history.

himself up after reading about the war, "but when I entered what a change!" It had become Café Brasserie, and "spruce Frenchmen" had replaced the Saxon and Bavarian waiters. He wanted a German beer ("I love German beer, and I had come with the hope of a long draught even at the expense of my patriotism"), but the waiter shakes his head. He's offered a Dutch lager instead.[59]

However, despite the de-Germanising (even King George V changed his surname from the House of Saxe-Coburg-Gotha to the more modern and English Windsor), lager didn't go away and by now British breweries were making their own, primarily to capitalize on the growing taste for lagers overseas.

The export challenge

Many specialist lager breweries failed in Britain from the 1870s through to the early 1900s.

One of them was the Austro Bavarian Lager Beer Brewery in Tottenham. It was built by Germans, brewed by Germans, and German was the working language in the brewery, which had vaulted lagering cellars, an enormous ice store and no fewer than 88 fermentation vats. It brewed Tottenham Lager, Munich, Pilsen and Bock. It was an impressive facility but it was ultimately unsuccessful. Lager brewing required specialist equipment, which British brewers were reluctant to invest in, and drinkers hadn't yet acquired the taste for it, with the Tottenham brewery's lagers described in the *Lancet* as having a "peculiar flavour", compared to garlic and even curry, an acquired taste to those used to it.

For a long time, British breweries had been virtually unchallenged as the great exporters of beer, sending barrels all around their Empire and spreading the renown of beers like India pale ale and porter. But as the nineteenth century progressed other nations had begin to ship their beer around the globe. "The Germans are seriously attacking our export trade in beer to South America, Australia, India and China, and other countries, in all of which at one time, we had no competition," said Professor Charles Graham in a talk to the Society of Chemical Industry in 1881. As drinking tastes shifted towards the lagers of central Europe, by the early 1880s German brewers were exporting more than British brewers. British beer, said a critic at the time, had "too much alcohol, too much sediment, too much hops and too little gas". As a result, British brewers started to make lighter ales with "a degree of brilliance and sparkle," but it wasn't enough to recover the previous export highs.

---

59 Carlsberg, who had been exporting their beer to Britain since the end of the 1860s, seem to have suffered from the anti-German sentiment. "Carlsberg Lager is NOT German, as someone with malicious intent is circulating," reads a notice in the *Scotsman* of 17 August 1914: "'Carlsberg' is brewed by the world-renowned Carlsberg Breweries at Copenhagen, DENMARK, where only DANISH labour is employed." There were several adverts like this at the time.

One of the first British lager breweries to have success overseas was Tennent's of Glasgow. Founded in 1556, in 1884 Hugh Tennent took over his family's business. He'd tasted lagers in Bavaria while convalescing from illness and this combined with awareness of the declining ale exports to encourage him to make Tennent's Lager in May 1885. Tennent's "have succeeded in producing a beer of the Pilsener type," reported the *Brewer's Guardian*, "and it will defy the most delicate palate to detect any difference between it and the best foreign-made article". In 1891, the year after Hugh died, Tennent's opened a German-made lager brewery and their Tennent's Lager, Munich and Pilsener beers sold well overseas, bolstering their ailing export ale sales, while back in Scotland they started to sell more lager straight from the ice cellars of Wellpark Brewery. Tennent's are Britain's longest-running and most successful lager brewery.

The Wrexham Brewery in Wales also benefited from export sales. The brewery's main beers were a dark lager, pale lager and a Pilsner,[60] the latter being a "beautiful pale colour, light and pleasant to the palate, and effervescing like good champagne," according to the *Wrexham Advertiser*. They didn't sell much beer locally, but they did sell a lot of lager on the shipping lines, going to places like India, Malay, China, Japan, Indonesia, Australia, Canada and the USA (it's reported that of the 20,000 bottles of beer loaded onto the *Titanic,* Wrexham's was the only lager). They continued to brew in their Wrexham brewery, via numerous different owners, until it was knocked down in the early 2000s.

In 1899, the first of the big English brewers invested in lager when Allsopp's built a dedicated lager brewery on the High Street in Burton-on-Trent. It was a large brewery capable of making around 100,000hl a year and it was more American-inspired than Bavarian, a sign of how American brewers were impacting the wider industry. It had twenty-six glass enamelled steel tanks sourced from an American supplier, while a Pfaudler "vacuum fermentation" system from Rochester, New York, enabled them to brew lagers and sell them within two weeks. They also built above-ground lagering tanks instead of digging cellars – the old Bavarian brewing traditions had been usurped by modern American techniques.

Allsopp's brewed lager in Burton, mostly to be exported, until 1921, when they sent their brewhouse to Archibald Arrol & Sons of Alloa, in Scotland, who then proceeded to make Arrol's Lager, Calder's Lager and Allsopp's Lager, the

---

60   These three types of lager were common at the end of the nineteenth century. Pilsner would've been lighter in colour, drier, low-alcohol and more bitter than the lager, which would've been more golden-amber in colour, sweeter, a little stronger and less bitter. The dark or Bavarian was the sweetest to taste, a brown colour and slightly stronger than the lager. Where we see Export in the name of a beer we'd expect it to be a little stronger again. Most lagers were in the 4 per cent ABV range at this time, with ales around 6 per cent ABV.

latter still brewed for export.

Barclay Perkins, one of London's largest brewers, opened a lager brewhouse in May 1921. To begin with there were three kinds of beer: a pale Export lager, a Dark and a Special Dark. They brewed 5,000hl in their first year, but that amounted to the same volume of just three brews of their best-selling Mild ale, called X.[61]

But by 1936 there were only six breweries in Britain making lager – Arrol, Barclay Perkins, Tennent's, Red Tower Lager Brewery in Manchester, Wrexham Lager Brewery and John Jeffrey & Co. in Edinburgh – and their combined production came to just 0.5 per cent of the overall output from British breweries in that year. Additionally there were several recognizable imports available like Beck's, Carlsberg, Tuborg, Pilsner Urquell, Löwenbräu and Artois. While exports might have helped to create a small lager market in Britain, no one was really succeeding with it and lager still wasn't selling. World War II and the post-war recovery and modernization would change that.

From flat to fizzing

There was no single catalyst for lager's eventual growth in Britain and it needed social, cultural, technological and industry developments to combine with the increase in mass-marketing to finally push lager consumption beyond ale.

Let's start in the pub. In the early eighteenth century there were several different kinds: inns were like the modern equivalent of a cheap hotel situated by the main road in or out of a city serving fairly crappy food and cheap beer, but it was somewhere convenient to stop for the night with space to leave your horse; taverns were for the finer folks who preferred to have a glass of wine over a mug of ale; alehouses were for casually quaffing beer. Into the nineteenth century and the beer house arrived and these were basic and barely decorated spaces where you just went to drink beer. Over time the name "public house" came to be a catch-all term for somewhere you went to drink.

The standard pub evolved to feature different drinking areas. The public bar was for the working classes, where their dirty language and dirty clothes couldn't spoil the dirty space, which had sawdust on the floor to soak up all the spit and spilled beer. The parlour, saloon, lounge or private bar would be carpeted and comfortable with upholstered seating for a finer middling class of guest. There, the choice of beer was the same as in the public bar, but it cost more.

The ale was drawn from hand pulls on the bar top. There were often six taps on a "beer engine" all connected to wooden barrels in the pub cellar (before the beer engine it was common for a pot boy to be employed to run up and down

---

61 Figures from Ron Pattinson's *Lager!*

to the cellars to fill jugs with beer). You'd likely find Porter, Stout, Bitter and Mild, and maybe a tap of ginger beer, too, with several different mixes of beers poured when ordered (mixing Porter and Mild, for example, or a "Shandygaff" of Bitter and ginger ale).

Through the 1800s, beer was as much for sustenance as it was for socializing and the pub was the central meeting place of a community, where it was often an escape of the discomforts of home (going to a place surrounded by other peoples' spit, slops and smoke was the better option) to get to the conviviality of the pub.

In the twentieth century going to the pub had become more of a leisure pastime, where drinking beer was now joined by numerous other activities like going to the movies or a football match, while the home itself got warmer and more comfortable, meaning the pub's value and importance changed as fewer people used it as a kind of second living room. As jobs were becoming less manual for much of the population, the restorative qualities of beer were less necessary and the beer changed, becoming lighter-looking and lighter-tasting, with the standard alcohol content dropping from 6 per cent ABV to around 4 per cent ABV, a decrease also impacted by World War I.

By World War II, pub opening hours had been restricted, beer prices doubled, average alcohol content went down to 3 per cent ABV, yet overall consumption went up around 25 per cent. Pubs regained their central importance to a community and they were a symbol of wartime resilience, a place of shelter, solace and comfort, somewhere familiar during the turmoil: if the pubs were still open, then things were still O.K.

Beer was important on the front line, too, as a stoic symbol of Britishness, and many barrels were flown over to the combat zones, where young men drank the pale, weak ales and become accustomed to their taste and their social and patriotic importance.

The pub of wartime was experienced as a place of relative comfort but in the post-war reality many were actually crumbling, worn, damaged and needing attention; analogous of Britain in general, a place that stood tall, dealt with all the troubles, got through it all, but now had to be rebuilt.

The 1950s saw a remarkable shift in society and the emergence of a new normal, an unfurling of freedom with no desire to go back to how things were; it was a time to move forward.

By the 1950s the "traditional draught" way of serving beer drawn from a wooden cask shifted to steel casks, and then pressurized steel kegs with carbonated beer inside them, which were easier for the publican to look after and a more reliable drinking experience for the customer. Kegged ale brands like Ind

Coope's Double Diamond and Watney's Red Barrel grew to have large market shares. As drinkers became more familiar with the characteristics of chilled, carbonated beer on draught (and in bottles), so the transition from the sparkling pale ale of Burton to the sparkling pale lager of Bohemia was becoming easier. But there was still resistance, with lager having just 1 per cent of UK beer sales in 1960 (and 86 per cent of that was imported). Just like we've seen elsewhere, domestic changes had a big impact on drinking in Britain.

Commercial British television began in 1955 (and Watney Brewery advertised their beer on day one), by which time television ownership was approaching 50 per cent of households. Refrigeration took longer to be adopted but by 1971, when we see a more concentrated shift to lager consumption, 69 per cent of British households had a fridge and 91 per cent had a television (more households had a TV than an indoor toilet, in fact). In the late 1950s there were 250 supermarkets in Britain; by 1979 that had jumped to 7,500. By then most of the supermarkets had off-licences to sell alcohol, while the number of shops with an off-licence increased from 28,000 to almost 48,000 between 1971 and 1990. As more people stayed at home to drink, breweries began to put more beer in bottles and cans, but bottled ale didn't taste much like the ale drawn from casks, whereas kegged ales like Double Diamond could taste just like the draught versions. Through kegs and bottles, people were getting more familiar with the taste and consistency of cold, crisp, carbonated beer.

Pubs began to install fridges, so their bottled lager could be served cold. Then they had draught lager. Then breweries began to advertise heavily, focusing now on their lager brands to coincide with changing consumers. By 1969 lager sales had risen to 6 per cent, and then to almost 30 per cent by the end of the 1970s (it was over 40 per cent in Scotland). Lager overtook ale in 1989, and it's since levelled out at around 70 per cent of the market.

PEOPLE TRY IT. . . AND LIKE IT!

Edward Plunkett Taylor[62] had a busy year in 1930. As a director of his grandfather's Ontario-based Brading Breweries Ltd he decided to buy a struggling local brewery called Kuntz. He bought nine more breweries by the end of the year, including Carling Brewing Co., and acquired 26 per cent of Ontario's beer output. By the end of the 1930s, his Canadian Breweries Ltd controlled over half of the region's beer, with Carling Brewing Co.'s Black Label one of his

---

62 Taylor also invented an electric toaster that browned bread on both sides at the same time. He used the royalties from this to fund his university studies.

most important brands.

In 1951, the managing director of Sheffield brewery Hope & Anchor, Thomas Carter, visited Taylor, to see if he might like to brew Hope & Anchor's dark, rich stout called Jubilee. Taylor agreed, on condition that Carter brew Carling's Black Label in Britain. It was a deal.

But it wasn't a good deal. They didn't want strong stout in Ontario, nor did they want light lager in northern England. Even the 200 pubs the Hope & Anchor brewery owned struggled to sell the lager, which was advertised with the slogan "People try it. . . and they like it!". Apparently not.

Taylor wasn't familiar with failure and he began another brewery-buying spree, taking over three British breweries, including the Hope & Anchor, plus their pub estate. He also did something unprecedented: he bought £25 of shares in every stock-exchange-listed brewing company in the UK to get access to their financial figures, so he could tell who was and wasn't doing well.

It was Taylor's belief that by the end of the century all beer in Britain would be lager, and he wanted to build a national beer company. By the end of 1961 his United Breweries had stakes in over twenty-five British breweries, owning eleven of them, and an estate of 2,800 pubs. By the spring of 1962 Taylor took over Charrington Brewery in a deal that would make him the third-largest pub owner in Britain, and then in 1967 he merged with Bass in Burton-on-Trent (who had themselves already merged with the brewer Mitchells & Butler) to form the biggest brewing and pub company in Britain, now known as Bass Charrington, and having over 11,000 pubs. This last deal certified Carling's prospective position as a national lager brand, and in less than eight years Taylor had transformed the British beer industry.

Tennent's were also doing well. Their lager was nationally available in Britain until 1963, when Taylor bought them. Three years later, Tennent's merged with Caledonian (another of Taylor's) to became Tennent Caledonian Breweries. Because Taylor wanted Carling to be his main beer in England, he essentially gave Tennent's their home market of Scotland, where their lager is an icon today, accounting for almost two in three pints bought in pubs.

In 1930 Allsopp's bought Arrol's (who they'd sold their brewery to a few years before). Then in 1934 Allsopp's merged with Ind Coope. Together in 1949 they bought the Wrexham Brewery. In 1961, Ansells of Birmingham and Tetley's of Leeds joined them to form Allied Breweries, becoming the largest brewing company in Britain at the time, with 11 per cent of the UK's pubs as well as reciprocal agreements with other companies, which meant they supplied almost half the licensed premises in the UK.

Arrol's were brewing a beer called Graham's Golden Lager, which changed its name to Graham's Skol and then simply Skol, derived from the Danish word for cheers, "*Skål*". Skol became the main lager of Allied Breweries and their many pubs, where it was brewed at Arrol's and Wrexham.

In a nascent lager market – just one per cent of British beer sales – Skol quickly established itself as the number one British-brewed lager, helped by quadrupling their marketing budget between 1959 and 1961. The early ads are simple and bold, often linking with the idea of Skol being the "new way to say lager". In 1960 they had full-page adverts in British newspapers with a headline of "What is Lager?" followed by a series of questions and answers about Skol repeating the words *light, dry* and *pure* to reinforce the idea that it was continental, clear and refreshing. The following year the message of the ads was that everyone was now drinking Skol. The implication was clear: why aren't *you* drinking lager yet?[63]

In 1960, an advert in the *Belfast Telegraph* announced the new "cool-brewed" lager from the Guinness brewery with the words: "HARP IS C-O-O-L", explaining that lager should be drunk at a temperature around 9°C (48°F): "Only then do you drink it *as it was brewed to be drunk*. That's how they drink lager on the Continent."

Harp was made by a German brewer, and early recipes are somewhere between a continental European lager and an American one with a bit of British reserve at the end: as Ron Pattinson explains in *Lager!*, they used a decoction mash (for some brews, anyway), sometimes maize or sugar, it had a cold fermentation of between 6 and 8°C (43–46°F), then it was lagered for between five and twelve weeks at 0°C (32°F) and left to carbonate naturally. One big difference was the strength: it was only 3 per cent ABV, a low-alcohol trend others would follow.

Harp was initially available in bottles, and after launching in Ireland it was trialled in the north of England. By the end of 1963, and thanks to lots of advertising and flooding the market with beer, it had surpassed Skol as the best-selling British lager, and was quickly exported out of Ireland in huge volumes, meaning that by 1965 it was already on sale in 73 different countries. "Everywhere they're drinking HARP," said a *Belfast Telegraph* advert from that year.

---

63 Skol's British success didn't last. It was overtaken by other brands, eventually being replaced as Allied's main lager in 1984 by Castlemaine XXXX (Australian lagers got cool in Britain in the 1980s). Instead Skol's great achievement was that in 1964 Allied Breweries signed a deal with brewers in Canada, Sweden and Belgium to brew Skol under licence. By 1967 Skol was being brewed in 20 breweries in 14 different countries and on sale in 36 countries. It was brewed in Brazil from 1967 as a lighter lager than others on sale at the time. It's now the best-selling beer in Brazil and the fifth-largest beer brand globally. Around the world it's a brand owned by different parent breweries and made to different strengths. You can still sometimes find Skol in the UK, where it's become a cheap commodity lager with only 2.8 per cent ABV.

In Britain, Harp was available on draught from 1965 and soon had a quarter of the lager market, largely thanks to it being sold by what became known as the Harp Consortium. This saw the Guinness, Courage, Scottish & Newcastle and Bass breweries link together to make Harp the main lager for all four companies, with it brewed in different breweries around the UK, including a new dedicated lager facility in Alton, Hampshire (now owned by MolsonCoors and continuing to make lots of lager today).

Alongside the British-brewed lagers there were the big continental brewers, each wanting success in the emerging market. "All around the world, millions of hands are raising millions of glasses," ran early British Heineken adverts, "and millions of palates are saying 'Hi!' to Heineken. Nothing like it. Once you've had a Heineken, you'll never simply ask for 'lager'. You'll remember the name. The world's most imported lager."

It might have been the "most imported lager", but in the whole of 1951, just 2,500 pints of Heineken were drunk in Britain. The brewery made the decision to reduce the alcohol to 3.4 per cent ABV – a compromise for their main brand (but a decision aided by the then-trend of adding lime cordial to lager, meaning drinkers couldn't taste the beer anyway). It was to the "glee and dismay" of the brewery bosses in Amsterdam that it was a success, writes Barbara Smit in *The Heineken Story*. In 1958 the ABV went down to 3 per cent, bringing it in line with British-brewed lagers. Now they just needed more people to buy more of it. In 1960 they linked with Whitbread, who had 15,000 pubs and six breweries. After a slow start (Whitbread were also selling Stella Artois, Skol, Carlsberg and Tuborg), the lager market began to open and expand enough to encourage Whitbread and Heineken to build a brewery together near Luton, where Heineken would be made under licence (back at 3.4 per cent ABV). Between 1965 and 1970 Heineken's volume jumped ten-fold.

Carlsberg, which had been on sale in Britain for 100 years, was available on draught from 1969, and from 1973 was being brewed at a purpose-built brewery in Northampton, co-financed with Watney Mann, and brewed to be just 3 per cent ABV. This new brewery had an initial capacity of one million barrels, which then doubled three years later. Aerial photos show what a beer "cellar" looked like now: a double bank of tanks, thirty-eight of them in total, each capable of holding about a million pints, running along the full 250m length of the outside wall.

Lager was now finally a popular British-brewed beer on its way to overtaking the sales of ale, but as more people started to drink it, and came to favour volume over flavour, so lager faced more challenges, specifically for the marketing department.

Wholesome and refreshing, lads and louts

In the early 1960s Brits still needed to be taught about lager. At a time when women were most likely to do the grocery shopping, the adverts of the early 1960s depict wholesome images of housewives pouring nice glasses of lager for their happy husbands, or use words like "light" to appeal to the more body-conscious drinker. This didn't work. Next, as more lager came to be served on draught (a move that aided its acceptance compared to when it was only available in bottles), breweries tried to appeal to the men, who were the ones actually more likely to drink beer in large volumes. Lager was celebrated as a new kind of sophisticated drink for a modern man, and spoke to a new kind of cosmopolitan chap who dressed smart and drank smarter.

The next shift in marketing came in the 1970s. Heineken had success with the slogan "Refreshes the parts other beers cannot reach", and Carlsberg introduced their iconic "Probably the best beer . . ." campaign. But then it shifted into a leery laddishness, replacing the wife or the starlet with a busty waitress to blatantly appeal to the blokes. Then the adverts got funny, mostly led by Australian brands like Foster's, where a new kind of machismo proliferated, putting lager in the hands of manly men and defining that generation's drink and drinkers.

The sophistication of the 60s had been replaced by lads gulping down eight pints a night. Lager was linked with yob culture, with the lads drinking a gallon of beer on the beaches of Ibiza, and feisty football fans fighting in the streets after three-too-many pints. By the end of the 1980s, we see the first uses of the term "lager louts", and this negativity had an impact on lager's image. It needed to re-brand itself as a better-quality drink.

This created a hierarchy of premium stronger lagers above a tier of cheaper and weaker ones. Heineken had been struggling with their reduced-alcohol lager, and so they introduced Heineken Export (brewed in Luton, not Amsterdam) at 5 per cent ABV. It was "Matured a little longer, to taste a little stronger", and Stephen Fry's narration on the TV commercial celebrated a "strong, silken lager that is smoother than a cashmere codpiece". Eventually they would stop making the lower-strength lager and just focus on their full-strength 5 per cent ABV beer.

There was also Stella Artois, at 5.2 per cent ABV, with the slogan, "Stella's for the fellas who take their lager strong," showing an image of a ripped-in-half phone book. It was stronger and it also cost a lot more, a problem the brewery capitalized on cleverly with their very successful "Reassuringly Expensive" campaign. Stella had stellar growth in the UK at a time when British lager drinking was still increasing and people were trading up to premium, stronger beers. The 1990s was Stella's decade. But then the premium-priced, premium-tasting, premium-strength Stella had to endure another link to the lager louts with its nickname of Wife Beater, an angry association that seems to have come from the brutish lad culture of the time.

Lager had half the British beer market by 1989 and British drinking habits had irrevocably changed. The brewing industry had also changed with takeovers, mergers and consolidations – integration or disintegration, as one brewer put it – and there were then six big brewing companies in Britain who between them owned more than half the 60,000 pubs in the country. New legislation said that with the vertical integration of the brewing, supply and pub businesses the Big Six had too much of a monopoly, and couldn't own more than 2,000 pubs each (meaning that Bass, the largest pub owner, would have to get rid of 5,300 pubs). The result was more than a shedding of pubs, and the beginning of the end for the large brewing companies, most of whom decided to sell their breweries and become leisure and hospitality companies, in turn creating large and powerful pub companies on one side of the industry and large brewing companies (like Heineken and Carlsberg) on the other. British beer integrated, then disintegrated, then became an entirely new landscape, one now dominated by lager brands with many of the famous old ale breweries shuttered.

Today the lager market is still dominated by well-known brands: Carling, Foster's, Carlsberg, Heineken, Amstel, Stella Artois, Budweiser. But there's also been a move towards super-premium, with lagers like Pilsner Urquell, the Czech-brewed Budvar, Asahi Super Dry, Peroni and Camden Town Brewery's Hells Lager all able to grow and shift the market again.

Brits became lager drinkers just like every other nation, but it took a lot of interlinked or knock-on effects for it to happen: pubs changed, our homes changed, beer-drinking habits changed, new generations of drinkers wanted new things, breweries invested heavily in new lager brands and advertising campaigns, lager got cheaper, more prevalent, more accepted, more British, more trusted, more loved, then more hated, more scorned, but certainly more integral to the British beer and pub industry.

Burton and Carling

Burton-on-Trent had long relied on exports, often around the Baltic Sea, but as that trade disappeared in the early nineteenth century so did the breweries, and in 1822 there were just five small brewers in the town. Then, with staggering growth, over the next forty years Burton's brewers surpassed London's to become prodigious exporters, making its name, and the name of its most famous beer, India pale ale, known around the British Empire.

To me, Burton-on-Trent is an evocative place. Not many people will say that, especially if they've actually been there, but this was a town totally dominated by beer, breweries and ancillary industries: malthouses, cooperages, joiners, and a lot of pubs. A map of Burton in the 1870s shows almost the entire town covered by breweries, brewery depots and buildings, all intertwined by railway lines, which transported beer and ingredients in all directions. Burton then had between 30 and 34 breweries, 100 malthouses, 80 stores for the beer and 20 cooperages, as well as 160 pubs for all the thirsty workers.

Perhaps the most striking thing about Burton is how the old breweries disappeared; none of the once-great brands like Bass or Allsopp's remain. We look around the beer world at other famous names like Carlsberg, Heineken, Anheuser-Busch, Pilsner Urquell and Guinness and they're still in their home-town and have been able to continue to succeed, but that didn't happen in Burton. In fact, only one major brewery has remained in the middle of the city.

Yet still, it's impossible to avoid the presence of beer in Burton, and if you walk out of the railway station the first thing you'll see are enormous silver tanks dominating the skyscape. Most of those giant beer tanks – each capable of holding over 650,000 pints – are filled with Carling, which has been Britain's best-selling beer since the 1980s. In the background a tall black chimney chugs with the word "Coors" wrapped around it. MolsonCoors is now the most important brewer here.

As you explore the old red-brick town today, you'll find numerous old buildings that used to be breweries, including Bass, Allsopp's, Salt & Co and Truman's. In the centre is Coopers Square, the shopping centre, and in the middle of that is a monument to the brewing past: the Burton Cooper statue. He's a thickly-built man clad in heavy boots, an apron, a waistcoat, shirt with sleeves rolled up, neck-tie, flat cap, and he's hunched over a barrel and perpetually about to hammer into it. It's a reminder of the manual industry that was here before beer modernized, when all beer was fermented, and served from wooden barrels, making the job of the cooper one of the most important and common in the town.

MolsonCoors' Burton brewery covers the site where Bass and Allsopp's used to be and annually produces around *one billion pints*.

Carling accounts for almost two thirds of their output, and they also make Coors Light, Staropramen and Cobra, illustrating just how global lager has become now, and how a big lager brewery needs to be able to make beers with very different profiles.

The brewing process for Carling begins with the grain. Carling only uses British barley and it's grown by a co-operative of 150 farmers – it's a variety specific to Carling, with certain flavour profiles the brewery want. The barley is malted just down the road and sent here by the truckload: up to 12 deliveries arrive every day, each carrying 28 tons of malt. And every ton that comes in is a ton that goes out at the end, with spent grain going to feed cattle.

In the brewhouse there are two brewing streams side by side and each makes around 530hl at a time. One batch of Carling takes six hours to brew, but because the liquid moves forward into subsequent vessels they can start a new batch every two hours, for a total of 24 batches a day between the two brew streams. That's over two million pints a day (which, because it's high-gravity-brewed, makes more like four million pints at "sales volume").

Carling is around 97 per cent British malt, plus it uses a small addition of glucose. It's brewed with hop pellets and, when I was there, it was just one German hop variety and only used to give bitterness, not flavour or aroma. It ferments at 15°C (59°F), which is much warmer than the 8°C (46°F) of nineteenth-century lagers, and it takes about five days to get to its high-gravity 8 per cent ABV, using a Carling-specific yeast. It's then centrifuged to remove most of the yeast[64] and moved into a conditioning tank where it's held at 1.5°C (35°F), typically for two to three more days. Then it'll be filtered, "liquored back" with water to the sales percentage of 4 per cent ABV,[65] and then packaged and pasteurized, where they can fill kegs at a rate of 700hl an hour alongside almost 100,000 cans an hour.

After my tour of the Burton Brewery I want to drink a couple of pints of Carling to see what makes it so popular. My pint comes in a tall glass with a frosted design on it that looks like an illustration of an old building, perhaps an old brewery. At the bottom of the glass it says *Burton-on-Trent. Great Britain.* It's on the amber scale of yellow with pure white foam, which looks good. It tastes good, too: crisp, refreshing, dry, and no particular grain and hop flavour; it's

---

64 There's always a lot of yeast left over at the end of fermentation. In 1902 the Marmite Food Company was founded in Burton, less than a mile away from the Bass brewery. There they concentrated down the surplus yeast and added salt, spices and other flavours to give a thick and savoury spread. Later, vitamins like folic acid, vitamin B12, thiamine and riboflavin were added to increase its healthfulness. About 50 million jars of Marmite are made annually in the UK. Australian Vegemite is made in a similar way. Both are good on toast.

---

65 Carling got in trouble in 2017 when it was discovered that the beer was often actually around 3.7 per cent ABV. In British law, a beer that is 5.5 per cent ABV or under has a tolerance of +/-0.5 per cent ABV, so if you see a beer advertised at 4 per cent ABV then it can legally be anywhere between 3.5 per cent and 4.5 per cent. For smaller breweries that allows them some leniency and natural batch variation; for a bigger brewery which uses high-gravity brewing they should always be getting their percentages accurate. So to sell a beer at 3.7 per cent ABV when it's labelled as 4 per cent is probably not an accident. Does it make a difference? Yes, as you can probably drink an extra pint of 3.7 per cent beer compared to, say, 4.3 per cent, and if one of their tanks holds over 650,000 pints of 8 per cent beer and it's supposed to be "liquored back" to 1.3 million pints of 4 per cent beer, by going to 3.7 per cent they'll get quite a few more pints out of that same tank, and more pints means more money. In 2012 AB-InBev made the decision to reduce the alcohol content on several brands in the UK, including Stella Artois and Budweiser (i.e. change the packaging and add more water); as well as getting more beer from the same tank they also saved millions of pounds in taxes because beer in the UK is taxed per 0.1 per cent ABV.

perfectly inoffensive in the best way, making it easy-drinking, unchallenging, and giving it the classic taste of just "beer".

As I look around, most people are drinking lager and there are branded glasses of golden beer all around the pub. There are eleven different lagers available on draught, including seven of the top ten best-selling draught brands: Carling, Foster's, Carlsberg, Stella, Coors Light (brewed up the road), San Miguel and Kronenbourg 1664 – the missing two are Peroni and Amstel, while additionally on tap here are Heineken, Staropramen (brewed in Burton), plus Bud Light and Guinness's Hop House 13. But most people are drinking Carling.

Carling is Britain's best-selling beer, available in over 40,000 British pubs, and it sells about the same as the second and third best-selling draught beers combined (Foster's and Carlsberg). In the off-trade, it's the fourth best-selling beer after Stella Artois, Budweiser and Foster's. Carling is a powerhouse of a brand, which dominates through the Midlands and north to Scotland, but it's a Burton beer: it's long been brewed in Burton and MolsonCoors are continuing to celebrate Burton as a great brewing town, only now Burton isn't a town of ale, it's a town of lager.

THE WORLD'S MOST GLOBAL DRINK

At the turn of the twentieth century, 79 per cent of the world's beer was of European origin, but by 2017 Europe accounted for just 27 per cent. Central and South America made 18.6 per cent, the United States and Canada 12.6 per cent, Africa 7.8 per cent, while 32.5 per cent of world beer was now brewed in Asia. And between us all we drink a lot of beer, with the average adult consuming over 60 pints of it annually (that's back-of-a-beer-mat maths but it's indicative enough), and most of that is lager.

What makes lager an appealing drink to examine is how it was able to spread to become the most global drink, something with universal similarity yet subtle local variation. Wherever it went it required people to adopt it (and sometimes adapt to it or for the beer to adapt to them). Once it became naturalized and affordable then it could become accepted, essentially becoming a local drink wherever it went: Mythos lager is quintessentially Greek, Bintang is basically the Indonesian word for beer, the blue and white Quilmes logo is iconically Argentinian.

As lager became a part of different cultures it was – and is – consumed in different ways; we don't all drink alike and we open a beer in different social and private situations, while there's often an underlying economic impact on how, where and why we drink beer. This separates lager from other global drinks like Coca-Cola, or foodstuffs like a Big Mac, or things like tea and coffee which are more habitual than social in most cultures. We can have a personal or emotional investment in a beer in a way that we don't with a glass of soda, juice or even wine or spirits.

Despite the global spread of local and national beers, there are some ubiquitous brands that are available internationally and today the top ten best-selling brands in the world make up around 22 per cent of all beer drunk. (Think you know what the 10 best-sellers are? And the top ten beer-producing countries by volume? Answers in the footnote below.)[66] The big brands really are very big. We've already met several of them and next we're going to meet a few more, to see how beer was able to develop in places like Mexico, South Africa, Australia and China, before we look at the unique lager-drinking cultures in Vietnam and Japan.

IN MEXICO THERE IS NO BAD BEER

Mexico exports more beer than any other country in the world, with one in four of all exported beers originating in Mexico, while in the US, two in three imported beers come across the border to the south. This helps contribute to Mexico being the world's fourth-largest beer-producing nation. But they don't just export the beer – Mexicans are the fourth-greatest consumers of beer.

You've probably seen many of the exported brands, including Modelo, Sol, Pacifico and Dos Equis, but the most famous beer outside of Mexico is undoubtedly Corona, which originated in Mexico City in the 1920s and is now drunk in 180 countries, making it one of the most widely available beers in the world and something synonymous with Mexico.

****

In 1890, Cerveceria Cuauhtémoc opened in Monterrey and it's considered to have been Mexico's first large-scale professional brewery, initially capable of filling 1,500 bottles a day. Their brand Bohemia, first brewed in 1905, became one of the best-known beers in Mexico, with several variants including a Pilsner, a Vienna and a dark Bavarian lager.

---

66 The top ten best-selling brands (in descending order) are: Snow, Budweiser, Tsingtao, Bud Light, Skol, Heineken, Harbin, Yanjing, Corona and Coors Light. That's four Chinese brands, three American and one each from Brazil, Mexico and the Netherlands. By overall country volume (again descending), the biggest brewers in 2017 were: China, United States, Brazil, Mexico, Germany, Russia, Japan, United Kingdom, Vietnam and Poland. These figures are by volume and not value – China might brew a lot of beer but much of it is low-profit, with around 85% of the total volume being cheap lager and not premium or imports.

German-born brewmaster Wilhelm Hasse was making beer in his eponymous Cerveceria Guillermo Hasse y Compañía in Orizaba from 1894, soon renaming it Cerveceria Moctezuma. In 1899, to celebrate the new millennium, Hasse brewed an amber lager called Siglo XX (that's "20th Century") and the two Xs became a symbol of the brewery, eventually leading them to rename their main brand Dos Equis.

Cerveceria Modelo was established in 1925 in Mexico City, and supposedly named as a "model" of an Austrian or Bavarian brewery, with a German brewmaster responsible for the first recipes, including a beer called Modelo Especial and a lighter lager called Corona.

From the 1930s, Cuauhtémoc, Moctezuma and Modelo became the Big Three of Mexican beer and they began to vertically integrate. Modelo, for example, made malt, glass bottles, crown caps, corks and cardboard. With these three bigger companies trying to grow, the 1930s also saw the beginning of a period of takeovers, consolidation and mergers that has left the Mexican beer market as a duopoly between AB-InBev and Heineken.

Modelo bought Cervecería Toluca y México and their main lager brand is now known as Victoria. Then they bought Cerveza Pacífico Clara in 1954, a brewery that had been founded by three Germans in 1900 in Mazatlán, on the Baja coast. Modelo Especial was their main beer but it was the export success of Corona in the US that saw Grupo Modelo's growth surge in the mid-1980s, when they jumped from exporting 1.6 million cases of beer in 1984 to 12 million just two years later. In 2017, enough Corona was shipped to the US for 320,000 bottles to be drunk *every hour*. As the imports were growing, the big brewing companies took notice and then they took out their chequebooks, attracted to the lucrative and large market with huge export potential, and this led to Modelo being bought by AB-InBev in 2012.[67]

Cuauhtémoc merged with Moctezuma in 1985 to become Cerveceria Cuauhtémoc Moctezuma. Between them they own a brewery and brand called Tecate; an old amber lager brand called Indio; Sol, which was first brewed in 1899 by a German brewmaster, and is now the group's best-known export brand; and their main brands of Dos Equis and Bohemia. Today Cerveceria Cuauhtémoc Moctezuma are part of Heineken.

Despite the duopoly (basically for export it's AB-InBev's Corona, Modelo and Pacifico versus Heineken's Dos Equis, Sol and Tecate) Mexico is not a Pilsner monoculture, and amber and darker lagers are also popular as standard kinds of beer in a way that we don't see in many other countries.

---

67 Corona is part of Grupo Modelo, which was bought by AB-InBev in 2012. To appease anti-trust laws, Grupo Modelo's US beer business was bought by Constellation Brands in 2013. So if you drink Corona in the US, it's made and distributed by Constellation Brands, but anywhere else in the world, including Mexico, it's made by AB-InBev. All Corona is brewed in Mexico and then exported.

In the brief overview above we can see how Europeans took lager to Mexico much like they took lager almost everywhere else, and there are some anecdotal claims that Vienna lagers inspired many of the Mexican brews, but that seems fanciful to me; by the time lager reached Mexico, Vienna was not a popular style, with Pilsner becoming the main export beer (Austrian-born Emperor Maximiliano I was in charge of Mexico from 1864 to 1867, so there is some backstory, but it's unlikely the ability to make lager existed in the Mexican heat). Instead the characteristics we expect of a traditional Vienna lager – amber colour, malty flavour, nice bitterness – are more likely to have been maintained because they work so well with the local foods that they're served with. And that was enough of a link for me to go to Mexico City to drink as much beer as possible, alongside as many plates of tacos as possible.

****

I meet Ana Paola Ortega Silva, a local beer and food expert, who is showing me several different places where Mexicans typically drink beer. I want to try all of the main lager brands in traditional places and our first stop is a typical cantina, a kind of old-school Mexico City pub. I order a Bohemia Vienna because I want to try to see if there is an old link to Vienna lager. The beer is a rich amber colour, it's toasty, a little sweet, and with a creaminess that's reflected in their branding – "la Crème de la Cerveza". Not many industrial beers are this good, which is the first surprise, and the second surprise is how the malt flavour in the beer works so well with spit-roasted pork topped with salsa – it somehow makes it taste more meaty. I also have a Bohemia Oscura, their dark lager in a modernized Bavarian style, and it's just as good with the food.

Next we head across the street to a modern cantina, a bar that could be a cool Mexican chain in a Western city, with bright yellow beer crates stacked up; orange, red and green hot sauces on the table; old posters and a young crowd. "It's part of our culture to have tacos and snacks in the middle of the table and you have beers," says Ana. You snack, you drink, you talk, you order more food, more beers, and you talk some more. I get a Dos Equis. I know this beer from home and it's a pale lager. "People have the lighter lagers first," Ana explains, "then the amber ones with food". It's refreshing, it's cool, and while it's not as interesting as the Vienna lager it's still really good.

Plates of tacos arrive. There's *al pastor* off the spit with a juicy chunk of pineapple in it, and there's spicy chopped pork, fat shrimps, chipotle chilli and cheese, all covered in salsas and onion and coriander and lime. A Dos Equis Ambar comes with it. This is my kind of foodie heaven right now, and the Ambar is excellent with it.

Next we go to Salon Corona, an old family-style cantina that's been open since 1928. There's an *al pastor* on the spit by the door, the tables are packed close together, there's football on TV, Jarocho music playing, and it's really busy. Here they have some draught beer, which is unusual in Mexico: most people drink beer from the bottle, sometimes direct, other times poured into a glass.

I get a Modelo. At home this always comes with a lime in the neck and that's become an iconic image of a Mexican beer, perpetuated by Corona. Should I put a lime in the bottle, I ask?

Ana laughs: "You could if you wanted, but Mexicans don't."

Where did the lime come from, then?

"It's only from the States and the movies," she says. "Some people will sip salt and lime, like with tequila, and then drink the beer, but we don't put lime in the neck."[68]

The Modelo is way better than I remember from Mexican restaurants in London – it's really surprisingly good. When earlier Ana told me that "Mexico is known as one of the best producers of industrial beer," I was dubious, but now I get it. "The kind of beer is as complex as the taste of the people. We want beers as complex as our food, even if it's industrial. These beers are simple but complex. They have their own personality. It's completely related to our food." When an octopus *tostada* comes I have a bottle of Pacifico, with some far away sentiment of seafood and the beach combining in my mind: another perfect combination.

"There is no bad taco, there is no bad beer," Ana says, and this has been a surprise: the industrial beers here *are* really good, especially with the food (I knew the tacos would be good). I had this pre-conception about Mexican lagers being overly bland and simple, but that's not true at all. Freshness definitely impacts this, especially as most Mexican lagers are exported (instead of being brewed under licence), but location is such an important part of drinking that it's almost impossible to dissociate the two; it's definitely better to travel to drink a beer, to see where it's from, than sit at home and pull a cold Corona from the fridge. Corona is undoubtedly an authentic Mexican beer, but without that local context it's just a bland lager.

---

68 So where did the lime come from? It could've been to cover up the taste of stale, old beer, where the tang of lime could overpower any odd flavours. Another theory says it was to keep bugs out of the beer, but we don't do that for any other beer, so why would we just do it for Mexican beers? Then there's the idea that it was a kind of bottle-neck disinfectant, but a wedge of lime that's been sitting on the bar top for several hours is probably way dirtier than the inside of a bottle. One story attributes the custom to a New York bartender who thought they could start a trend. Some say it's to give some flavour to a mostly flavourless beer. Whatever the genesis, it's become an almost-essential way of drinking Corona – you wouldn't drink one *without* a lime, and I find it interesting it hasn't been reverse-adopted in Mexico. One more thing: in 2018, Constellation Brands, the US distributors of Corona, announced they were to sell Corona-branded limes in the US.

I leave Ana and I have a spare hour before I leave Mexico City, so I take my remaining cash and walk a few blocks to a taco place. I have exactly – to the peso – enough for five *al pastor* and one beer. I get another Bohemia Vienna and the simplicity of spit-cooked pork, salsa, fresh onion and a cold, malty beer is an unbeatable match.

As I'm eating my last taco one of the heaviest thunderstorms I've ever seen crashes down – this is not the sunshine I associate with Mexico and now I'm stuck. I have no more money for a taxi. I'm a fifteen-minute walk from my hotel. I have no clean clothes to change into if I get soaked. I have one pair of trainers, which I'm wearing. And I left my umbrella in my bag. The thunder is heavy enough to shake the whole restaurant as white lightning blasts through the black sky.

Almost an hour later it eases enough for me to run in the rain to the hotel and call a taxi to the airport. It should be a thirty-minute drive but it ends up taking over ninety. I have to rush through security and to find my gate and I make it by ten minutes. I'm exhausted, stressed, damp, somewhere between drunk and hungover, and in need of a day or two without any beer.

In the shop near my gate I see cans of Corona. Little yellow and blue tins that look like the sun and sea. I've been talking about Corona all day, thinking about it all day, making notes on it *all day long*, but I haven't actually had one. I probably shouldn't leave Mexico without drinking one...

I fall back into the hard, cold airport seat and open the can. It's simple. It's refreshing. It's . . . pretty good. I'm in a weird juxtaposition of place, drink and association: Corona might be *from* Mexico City but it's not *of* Mexico City; it's a beer of the beach, and it's the exotic, happy, sun-kissed and chilled-out lifestyle that has been evoked and exported with the beer. I'm in Mexico but I'm not on the beach. I'm in an air-conditioned airport and it's approaching midnight. Outside it's hammering down with rain. It couldn't be further from the white sands of Acapulco, and while I'm not going to pretend that half a can of Corona sent warming rays of sunshine through me, I was certainly surprised by the taste of the beer (and I didn't even need any lime). These industrial Mexican beers *are* very good when you drink them fresh, while smooth amber and dark Mexican lagers with tacos is one of the world's top beer and food combinations.

BRAZIL'S BREWING BILLIONAIRES

Brazil is the third-largest beer-producing country in the world. There's an enormous market for lager in Brazil, which makes it important in its own right, but if we look at how the world of beer has been consolidated, merged and taken over in the past few decades, many of the changes were directed by a few Brazilian businessmen who became beer billionaires.

****

It was probably the Dutch who first took beer into the Portuguese colony of Brazil, as early as the 1630s, but it's unlikely they brewed it there – or at least brewed anything *good*. Domestic Brazilian production began around the 1830s and increased in the following decades, when it was led by Germans and other Europeans who had fled their homelands.

The oldest Brazilian brewery still around today was founded in Petropolis, north of Rio de Janeiro, in 1853. Petropolis was conceived and built by Emperor Pedro II, who decided to turn the grounds around his royal summer palace into a settlement, where German immigrants made up a lot of the work force. The hot weather and hard work led to a need for beer, and a Henrique Leiden built the town a brewery called Imperial Fábrica de Cerveja Nacional. The brewery was taken over by a Henrique Kremer 10 years later and was one of the first to grow with industrialized production. In 1898 they expanded and modernized and changed their name to Cervejaria Bohemia, brewing several European-inspired lagers, including Petropolis Pilsner, Bohemia, Munchen, Vienna and Bock.

Due to the heat and general lack of brewing infrastructure, it wasn't until the late 1880s when lager-brewing machinery was more available. From then the Brazilian beer industry really began to grow, and what became the two largest brands were launched: Cervejaria Brahma in Rio de Janeiro and Cervejaria Antarctica in São Paulo. For over a century, they were major rivals in the Brazilian beer market, though their status quo was disturbed in 1967 with the introduction of Skol, which grew to become the number-one brand ahead of Brahma and Antarctica. Twenty years later, the business of Brazilian beer – and world beer – was about to change forever.

In 1989, a group of three Brazilian investors, led by Jorge Paulo Lemann, bought Brahma, a decision supposedly made when Lemann was looking at who were the richest people in different South American countries and saw that several of them owned breweries. They were able to grow Brahma, making it more profitable with a series of cost-cutting moves, and then in 1999 they took over Antarctica, forming a new company called Ambev. As we've seen, Ambev later merged with Interbrew (the Belgian brewery behind Stella Artois) and became InBev, who then bought Anheuser-Busch, who then bought SABMiller, by which time Lemann was the richest man in Brazil and in the whole of South America. [69]

Skol remains the best-selling Brazilian beer and one of the best-selling in the world. I went to Brazil once and drank Skol and it's terrible. If the industrial lagers of Mexico are notable for being surprisingly good then Skol is the opposite. Anyway, that was just a short South American interlude before we jump to see where the South African part of the world's largest brewing company came from and how indigenous brews compete with international lagers.

AFRICA: WHERE LOCAL HOMEBREW OUTSELLS NATIONAL LAGER

The first great brewers were the Egyptians. Beer was a central liquid in their lives, a drink for nourishment and refreshment, for medicine, a liquid salary (four or five litres a day for the Pyramid builders), something social and ceremonial, and drunk by everyone from farmers to Pharaohs. Those early beers are barely comparable to what we know and drink today, but they did follow understandable processes, and they brewed with grains, although depending on who was making it, where and when, they might also have brewed with honey, grapes, dried fruits and spices.

****

A few thousand years later and in sub-Saharan Africa, hundreds of regional and local specialities of beer were developed. While unique, each was made in fundamentally similar ways: grains were soaked in water to germinate, then dried out, ground, mixed with hot water in a cast iron vessel over a fire, then moved to ferment in a large urn for a few days. The beers used barley and wheat but also other grains like maize, sorghum and millet. In some areas they also brewed with roots or starches like cassava. The final liquids were opaque, thick, a little sweet, a little sour, and typically with a low alcohol content. And it was always the job of the women of the community to brew the beer – it still is.

---

69   Lemann and his investors didn't stop at beer. They formed a company in 2004 called 3G Capital, which had great success taking over and merging companies, then cutting costs to increase profit margins and empowering and quickly promoting ambitious younger employees. They combined Burger King and Tim Horton's, then Kraft and Heinz, creating one of the world's largest food companies.

By the nineteenth century those homebrews gave small-scale commercial opportunities to the women making them, especially in the south of the country. During and around the apartheid years – even when homebrewing was banned and black Africans were not allowed to make or drink beer – the social importance of beer remained and women continued to brew, where "shebeens" opened as small (and illegal) shops selling sorghum beer. These local brews still make up a significant percentage of commercial beer sales, sitting alongside the beers of huge international brewing companies.

* * * *

What became the most important commercial brewing enterprise in Africa was founded by Charles Glass in the late 1880s. In his article "The Beers of Southern Africa", Ami Kapilevich writes that Glass's Castle Brewery "filled what was more a yawning abyss than a mere niche in the market during the South African gold rush," with thirsty miners "drinking raw potato spirits mixed with tobacco juice and pepper before SAB opened the first proper bar in the northern gold prospecting regions of the country."

SAB is South African Breweries, the name the company adopted in 1895 when it merged several breweries together. By this time they were producing Castle Lager, perhaps the most famous South African beer, now sponsoring the soccer, cricket and rugby teams, and a beer that still has Glass's name on the label. While Castle Lager is the best-known, the best-selling beer in South Africa is Carling Black Label (an off-shoot of the one E. P. Taylor took to Britain); at 5.5 per cent ABV it's a stronger lager than the 5 per cent ABV of Castle.

In the late 1990s, SAB started to spread beyond their home continent and in a major move they bought Pilsner Urquell in 1999. Then in 2002, in a play to strengthen themselves further around the world, they acquired Miller Brewing to form SABMiller. Then, of course, came the mega merger of 2016, which brought them together with AB-InBev, creating the largest brewing company in the world.

They may now be a global company, but Africa is still their home and SAB are dominant in the south and up the east coast of Africa. As well as their national lagers, one continental quirk of African brewing is the use of alternative grains and starches, utilizing local ingredients and professionalizing the homebrewed beers. In Mozambique there's Impala, which is brewed with cassava, while in Uganda they make Eagle Lager, which is brewed with sorghum. Eagle Lager is notable for working with local farmers to grow the brewing grains while also helping to provide fresh water, to give academic scholarships to the region and to provide HIV tests locally (although one side complication is that Ugandan farmers are now growing the brewing grains in place of certain food crops).

SAB is one of four brewing companies along with Heineken, Diageo and Castel, who between them account for over 90% of draught and bottled beer in Africa. Heineken are strong in the centre and the north of the country, with brands including Stella in Egypt, Tango in Algeria and Primus in the Democratic Republic of the Congo, as well as the Star Lager they introduced into Nigeria in 1949, which is still the country's best-selling beer.

Diageo are strong in Nigeria and Cameroun – especially with their Guinness Foreign Extra, a 7.5% ABV stout brewed with sorghum and maize. They produce Tusker, the beer of Kenya; they make Harp Lager in Cameroun; Serengeti is popular in Tanzania; in Uganda they make Bell, the oldest lager, and also Senator, which is brewed with sorghum and cassava.

Castel is a large French wine producer and distributor and they bought Brasseries et Glacières Internationales (BGI) in 1990 to take over their African beer business, leading with brands like Castel, Flag and 33 Export.

Pale lager still accounts for most of the overall beer sales in Africa, but Africa is the only continent that hasn't been completely globalized by the Western hegemony of lager. In 2015, 18% of commercial beer brewed in Africa was sorghum beer, but in some countries the sorghum beer is far more prevalent, like Malawi, Zambia and Botswana, where three times more sorghum beer is drunk compared to clear barley beer – and that doesn't account for the homebrewed sorghum and alternative-grain beers.

Bottled premium lager is expensive and in some African countries an average bottle of average lager might be the equivalent of an average day's wage. In the developed world, where beer is the drink of the working man, almost everyone is able to afford a beer or two at the end of their working day, but this isn't as universal in Africa and for a large number of Africans, homebrew is currently the only accessible and affordable beer they can drink.

Almost everywhere in the world, lager became a product of Western cultural imperialism. It was a drink taken around the world by Europeans, whether migrants or merchants, who told the world what beer was like, and everywhere it went, the local beers and alcohols were replaced by the crisp dominance of cold lager. But not so much in Africa and the big breweries have had to adapt, making their own sorghum beers and low-priced domestic brands alongside the national and international lagers.

There are still many places where you can go and drink local homebrewed sorghum or alternative-grain beers. Sometimes they'll also still be drunk straight from the urns and sometimes sucked up through large straws. Some old traditions are so embedded in the fabric of life that they won't change. Everywhere in the world has their own local beer cultures and sometimes it's not a glass of golden lager.

AUSTRALIA: YOU WOULDN'T WANT A WARM BEER

In Australia it almost certainly *is* a glass of golden lager that you'll find. Either that or a great craft beer from one of the many modern breweries. And the Australians are a nation of beer lovers, though it took them a while to become lager-drinkers.

****

On 13 May 1787, eleven ships departed from Portsmouth in the south of England, heading for the other side of the world. Some 1,400 people were on board, including military and government officials, sailors, skilled professionals, masons, cooks, civil officers, and a *lot* of convicts. Two ships belonged to the Navy, three held food and supplies, and six were filled with criminals being sent to found a new colony in Australia. Finally, 250 days and 15,000 miles after departing, and having suffered terrible weather, disease and deaths, they landed in an Australian bay and named it after the then-British Home Secretary, Lord Sydney.

On board one of the First Fleet ships was a man named James Squire. Two years earlier he'd stolen some chickens and other goods from his neighbour and was sentenced to two years in prison and then penal transportation to Australia.

Just over a year after arriving Squire was again convicted of stealing, this time from a surgeon. He had taken pepper and horehound, a tangy herb with hop-like qualities, and Squire first claimed he took them for his pregnant girlfriend, but later revealed that he had been brewing beer for two lieutenants, making him one of the country's first colonial brewers. This time his punishment for stealing was 300 lashes.

When Squire's seven-year penal transportation had been served, he was a free man, and all free men were allowed 30 acres of land. Squire saw that others hadn't claimed their allotted land, so he started collecting it on their behalf, and by 1806 he had acquired almost 1,000 acres. On that land he farmed barley, wheat, maize and successfully established a hop farm. He was probably also brewing beer, although Australian beer was almost certainly terrible back then.

Brewed on primitive equipment in the hot weather and using inferior ingredients, the thin and undrinkable colonial ale was called "swipes". It was "sugar-and-water sort of stuff" with a "colonial twang", as one English brewer described it. Because of the lack of ingredients, the beers often used lots of sugar in their production, sometimes as much as 50 per cent, and that cultivated an unusual yeast and gave a weird flavour. None of this was good in a hot country when there was surely a great thirst for a long, cold drink.

Things started to improve through the nineteenth century. One of the first successful enterprises was the Kent Brewery, which opened in Sydney in 1835 and would later become Tooth Brewery, one of the largest breweries of the time. In 1854, the Victoria Parade Brewery, founded in Melbourne by Scotsman Thomas Aitken, was making beer and would brew Victoria Bitter. In 1857, the Castlemaine Brewery was opened in the goldmining town of Castlemaine, Victoria, by educated Irish gentry and brothers called Nicholas and Edward Fitzgerald. They had extraordinary success and went on to open breweries in Sydney, Brisbane, Newcastle, Daylesford, Newbridge and Melbourne, although eventually the breweries ended up splitting off individually. The Coopers Brewery opened in 1862 in Adelaide. In 1864, Carlton Brewery was opened in Melbourne by an Edward Latham who had arrived in Australia from Liverpool, bought a dilapidated brewery and hired Alfred Terry, who was thought to be the best brewer in the colony. By 1871 the state of Victoria alone had 126.

Lager arrived later and it's thought the first lager brewery in New South Wales was Messrs Marks and Murphey, who brewed "American-type lager" from 1882. There were also increasing imports of beer from America: "Their beer is of the lager description, a lighter beer than the British article, and much more suitable for a warm climate," wrote the Australian *Brewers' Guardian* in 1889. "Experience shows that beer-drinkers will take lager in summer and the British in winter, and, as our winter is short, the lager is almost sure to increase in sale."

There was a lot of hope for this new kind of beer and in 1888 two Irish-Americans from New York, William M. Foster and Ralph R. Foster, arrived into Melbourne with a German-American brewer and an American refrigeration engineer. The Foster Brewing Company in Collingwood set out to brew cold lagers to compete with the warm ales. Their lager was brewed with only malt, and to begin with the Fosters only bottled their beer, with every hotel bar that ordered their lager also receiving a supply of ice to go with it, a smart marketing move.

But the Foster brothers didn't have enough money to make the business work, and by the end of 1889 they'd turned the brewery into a public company and sold it to a local syndicate before going back to New York almost one year exactly from the day of brewing their first batch of lager. "They came to Australia, gave us a famous name, and left," wrote Keith Dunstan in *The Amber Nectar*. Nothing more is known of the brothers.

A lot of lager breweries had opened and then closed in the latter years of the nineteenth century, but not before introducing modern American-inherited brewing technology like machines for accelerated fermentation, artificial carbonation and the equipment to make filtered, pasteurized lager. By 1897, however, the Australian *Brewers' Journal*, which had earlier been so excited about lager, was declaring the "experiment in lager beer . . . a complete failure in the colonies". The cost of lager brewing seemed to be the biggest barrier. It required special equipment to brew it and then all the additional power to store it cold for a long time, whereas at a time of general depression and low income for the working classes quick-brewed ales could be made easily and sold cheaply.

To help with the ongoing struggle, the breweries of Melbourne discussed merging into one new, large company, to be known as Carlton & United Breweries (CUB). In a deal signed on 30 June 1907, Carlton, who were the largest and most successful brewer in town, led the new company, which also included Castlemaine Brewery Co., the Victoria Brewery and the smallest in town, the Foster Brewing Co. They consolidated production to a few plants, with Foster's lager made in the Victoria Brewery, where the majority of the overall production was Victoria Bitter and Carlton Ale.

Most beer at the time was sold on draught in hotel bars and those bars were about to be impacted by the temperance movement. From 1916, restricted trading hours were enforced (in all states apart from Queensland, which was 1923, while New Zealand also had the same rules). Already hours had been shortened because of the war but now pubs had to close at 6 p.m. The thinking was that it'd mean less drinking time and therefore less consumption, but the reality was different: people tried to drink as much as possible between finishing work at 5 p.m. and the bar closing at 6 p.m., leading to the "6 o'clock swill". It became a one-hour speed-drinking competition and the need to neck numerous pints in an hour meant that bars were disembowelled and anything superfluous to hard drinking was taken away, leaving an empty room with an elongated bar, often decorated in brown, and with wipe-clean surfaces (inside and out). The six o'clock swill unintentionally institutionalized a hard-drinking culture (which arguably still remains today despite the licensing laws changing in the late 1960s).

The conversion to lager came after World War I, as more brewers began to modernize and develop their breweries. One of the first was Sydney's Tooth & Co., who transitioned to lager in early 1918. CUB, meanwhile, had several lager brands, including Fosters (soon to market themselves as "Australia's National Beverage") and a new beer from Castlemaine called XXXX.

The 1930s would be the decade that confirmed lager as the beer of Australia, and it would continue to grow through to the 1970s – the peak year of Aussie drinking was 1974–75, when per capita consumption was almost 140 litres. Foster's became the best-selling Aussie beer in 1977 and was being exported to 40 countries. That eventually led it to becoming one of the best-selling beers in Britain, via the now-familiar stories of mergers and necessary growth as the brand owners looked for a European brewing partner to increase international sales. When it was first brewed in Britain it was made by Watney's Brewery, in London, and had a lower strength than the Australian version.

The Australian market is now dominated by old state-based breweries like Victoria Bitter (VB) and Carlton in Victoria or XXXX in Queensland. And if you're in New South Wales you might see a craft beer brewed by James Squire, named after the country's original brewer. But you won't find a Foster's because the best-selling Aussie beer became obsolete in its own country and it's now mostly brewed in Manchester, not Melbourne.

CHINA: BEST IN SNOW

China is the world's largest beer market and the Chinese brew more and drink more than any other nation. But it's a remarkable and recent ascension for somewhere that in 1978 wasn't even in the top 100 of brewing countries and was making something like one in every 300 beers drunk globally.

Beer was still considered a luxury drink in China in the 1970s, and in 1978 there were only 90 breweries in the entire country, most of them small and local and fitting the old Maoist idea of necessity and not luxury, with per capita consumption just one litre a year. But the sleeping dragon was about to wake up and it was thirsty.

In 1978 economic reform opened up China to foreign investment and trade and helped to transform the country into the superpower it is today. "Literally hundreds of small breweries emerged from the rice paddies," wrote Junfai Bai. Most were state-owned, and a county's beer factory was often a status symbol, providing many jobs. By 1990 there had been a ten-fold growth in brewery numbers (to 900) and a fifteen-fold growth in volume brewed, putting China 26th in the world.[70] They became the world's number-one beer-producing country

---

70 China also planted hops, and in 2018 almost 5 per cent of the world's hops grew in China. That might not seem like much, but that puts it third in the world in terms of volume. Almost none are exported. The top two hop producers are the US with 41.9 per cent and Germany, 36 per cent.

in 2001 – a position they've held since. Today China brews one in every five beers drunk in the world, and four of the world's best-selling beers are Chinese.

****

It was a Prussian-Polish man named Jan Wróblewski who gave China its first brewery, which opened in the north-east of China in 1900. Wróblewski saw an opportunity to make some money selling beer to Russian railroad workers, and named his brewery after the Russian spelling of his name, Ulubulevskij. It was later renamed Gloria, then it became Harbin in 1932 when it came under joint control of the Chinese and Czechs, and was later state-owned. It's now an AB-InBev brand. The main lager is the eponymous Harbin, and the beer that started out as a drink for thirsty labourers has become the seventh best-selling beer in the world.

Germans and Czechs were close behind the Prussian-Pole in opening breweries in the early years of the twentieth century, brewing primarily for the growing numbers of merchants, officials and soldiers based in China. Unlike the Brits, Dutch and French, the Germans don't have a recent history of colonizing places, but between 1898 and 1914 they did have an outpost called Shandong in the eastern Chinese city of Qingdao. Wanting good beer, in 1903 the Germans built the Germania-Brauerei and produced German-style beers. When World War I began, the brewery was taken over by the Japanese brewing company Dai-Nippon (later divided to become Asahi, Sapporo and Yebisu), which was then taken over by the Chinese Nationalist Government. It was state-owned under the Communist government, and later privatized. In the early 1990s, the Qingdao brewery merged with three other local brewing companies to become the Tsingtao Brewery Company Limited (the name is pronounced "*Ching-Dow*", not "*Sing-Tao*"). Tsingtao is the third best-selling beer in the world and the Chinese beer that's most exported. If you've drunk a Chinese beer outside China it was probably this one.

The main beer of Beijing is called Yanjing. It doesn't have such a long and convoluted history and was first brewed in 1980. It's the eighth best-selling beer in the world. But no one really cares about the *eighth* best, do they? They want to know about number one.

China Resources Enterprise, or CR Snow, was only founded as a brewery in 1994 in a joint venture with SABMiller.[71] In 1998 their main brand, Snow, had under 3 per cent of China's beer market; today, it has over 5 per cent of the

---

71 When AB-InBev and SABMiller merged in 2016, CR Snow took back full ownership, before Heineken took a 40 per cent stake in 2018.

world's beer market, meaning one in twenty beers drunk in the whole world is a Snow. The beer is brewed in around 90 different breweries in China, combining to produce over 100 million hectolitres annually, which is more than double that of Budweiser, the world's second best-selling beer.

Snow was designed to be a very light beer, low in alcohol, low in flavour, to suit its purpose of accompanying a meal, because around half the beer drunk in China is served in restaurants – they don't have a culture of going to a bar. All the mainstream Chinese lagers share a neutrality in taste valued in contrast to the flavoursome food.

The Chinese beer market is interesting for being so enormous. The beers, however, are not that interesting. So let's go to Vietnam, where they have their own unique kind of lager and a special beer culture – and it starts on the street.

VIETNAM: *BIA HOI* IS CULTURE

I lower down, down, down, almost to the floor, almost to the point of falling over backwards, until I land on the wobbly shin-high plastic stool. My feet are in the street, surrounded by discarded peanut shells and dirty napkins. My knees are unable to get under the battered blue plastic table, which is pock-marked from cigarette butts. Scooter after scooter whizzes past. It's *really* noisy. The crash of beer glasses being clinked to say cheers, the plastic grind of chair legs on rough concrete, the tonal language loudly spoken, the call for attention of *"Em Oi! Em Oi!"* I've only just arrived into Vietnam's capital city of Hanoi, and it's intense and overwhelming and intoxicating.

"*Một bia hơi!*" I say. It's the only thing I can reliably speak in Vietnamese. *One bia hoi.*

A chunky blue-tinted glass of pale yellow beer is put on the table, and I'm so thirsty that the first two deep mouthfuls almost empty the glass. It's simple, cold and refreshingly wonderful. *Bia hoi*[72] might not win an award for the most complex-tasting beer, but drinking it in Hanoi is my favourite beer experience in the world. It's unlike anything else in terms of the actual liquid, its story and the crazy, street-side, real-life theatre in which you drink.

Hanoi is my favourite city. I love how thrillingly different it is from London where I live; I love the energy, the speed, the chaos; I love that I can never quite

---

72 The name translates as "gas beer". In the past, kegs were filled with unfiltered beer and left unpasteurized. Those kegs would've sat in the hot weather for a while, undergoing some additional fermentation, so when opened they'd have popped with carbon dioxide and the gas would've risen from the opening like smoke. The name *bia hoi* means both the drink *and* the place where you drink it, so you go to a *bia hoi* to drink *bia hoi*.

relax, that I'm always engaged, enthralled, on edge, always looking around, always wary or wowed. Most of all I love the smells: the fragrant aniseed herbs, the funky fermenting aromas of tropical fruits, the smoking fires under grills of meat or bubbling broths, the muggy heat of a busy city, the distant lift of incense.

I order another beer and I watch as this one is served. It's coming from a metal container about the size of a large household fridge that's so bashed-up and dented it looks like it's been attacked with a baseball bat. Coming out of this battered trunk is a hosepipe – just your standard garden hose – wedged upwards into a cork of some kind to stop it flailing around, and to the side is a tray of clean glasses. When someone orders a beer, the server pulls the hosepipe from the cork stopper, points it down into a glass, and the beer gushes out in seconds. I've drunk beer here at No. 2 Đường Thành[73] many times in the last few years, but I've never quite worked out exactly how it's served or its real story.

From *French bière* to Vietnamese *bia*

The French introduced beer into Vietnam, and *bière* became *bia* just as the French *pot au feu* became the Vietnamese *pho* or the French railway station, *gare*, became the Vietnamese *ga*.

In 1875 a retired marine engineer named Victor Larue started a company in the southern city of Saigon to make ice and soft drinks to cool down the hot officers. He soon moved into brewing and started the Cho Lon Brewery, selling his Bière Royale using a logo of a tiger. The company would become known as Brasseries et Glacières d'Indochine – Indochina Breweries and Coolers – and one of their most famous beers was 33.[74]

The first brewery in the northern city of Hanoi opened in 1890 under an Alsatian brewer called Alfred Hommel and was known as Brasserie Hommel. It started small but by 1916 the brewery was capable of producing 20,000hl a year and had a large staff of locals. It had steam and ice machines, and the yeast was supposedly coming from Copenhagen. They had cellars with six fermenters and 48 lagering tanks, so we can be sure they were brewing lagers. By 1926 they were using a portion of rice in the beer and they'd replaced the wooden fermenters with concrete ones. An early brand was called Blonde Spéciale and was sold in barrels and bottles – it's likely it was a Pilsner-style lager. In 1927

---

73 This is my fourth time in Hanoi and No. 2 Đường Thành is one of my favourite *bia hois*. Opposite is 50 Bát Đàn for another *bia hoi*, and then if you head north and follow the streets around there you'll find several more *bia hois*, all filled mostly with locals. And if you've read a couple of my other books then you'll know that I've written about *bia hoi* before (mostly because I love it), but this time I'm going much deeper into the story.

---

74 If you've been to Vietnam, or just to a Vietnamese restaurant, then you've probably seen the beer 333 or "*ba ba ba*". When the Vietnamese took over from the French they added one more three to the name, while the French took 33 to some of their other outposts, mostly central and northern Africa.

or 1928 Brasseries et Glacières d'Indochine bought most of the shares in the Hommel brewery. The descendants of those early breweries are Vietnam's two leading beer companies today: SABECO in the south and HABECO in the north.

Beer was drunk by the French officers and troops, "but it wasn't for Vietnamese people," says Dr Viet, Chairman of the Vietnam Beer Alcohol Beverage Association. The locals didn't initially have the taste for bitter beer, but in any case they couldn't afford it. Instead they had their cheap and potent rice wines.

Not much of the nineteenth-century history of the industry is known today – hardly surprising given how much Vietnam endured in the twentieth (the history section on the SABECO website starts in 1875 and then jumps straight to 1977), but there is some overlap between the wars and beer's place in Vietnam's fractured past.

Going back to 1802, the Nguyễn dynasty, with the help of the French, brought together a divided Vietnam that was often invaded (mostly by China) and often at war. The French remained and grew in power before they themselves invaded and took over land in the north, then the south, and then everywhere in between, while also forming Indochina by taking land in Cambodia and Laos. Whether ultimately good or bad, the French gave many things to Vietnam, like education, language (hence Vietnam's Roman letters, albeit heavily accented and tonal), travel networks and many buildings, like Hanoi's Opera House and Saigon's Central Post Office.[75]

The French ran their colony until World War II, when the Japanese occupied Indochina, though the French didn't fully retreat. By the end of the war Communist rebels in the north, known as the Việt Minh and led by Hồ Chí Minh, countered the Japanese and in 1945 declared the north's independence, but the southern-based French fought back in what became a seven-year war. Communist China and the Soviet Union helped out the Việt Minh, while the US helped the French. The north won, and then the Geneva Accords of 1954 decolonized the area, reassigning borders and giving independence to Laos and Cambodia, and separating Vietnam at the 17th parallel into Hồ Chí Minh's Communist north and the State of Vietnam in the south, with Bảo Đại as head of state and Ngô Đình Diệm as prime minister. It was decided that Vietnam would remain partitioned until 1956, when a democratic election would be held in what was essentially a vote for or against reunification.

When the French left the north in 1954 they relinquished the Hanoi brewery, but not before destroying machinery and burning important technical documents. A few years later the north had hired Czech engineers and a Czech

---

75   They also took a lot of stuff, like rice and rubber (the Michelin tyre factory owned a lot of land in Vietnam), tea, coffee, pepper, salt and opium.

brewmaster (as fellow Communist nations they been diplomatically linked for several years by now) to come and fix the place and teach the locals how to brew, releasing the first true Vietnamese lager in 1958 and naming it after the local lake, Trúc Bạch.[76]

The planned election of 1956 didn't happen. Instead, Diệm called a referendum to decide whether he or Đại should run the southern region. In a heavily rigged election Diệm got 98 per cent of the votes, including 605,025 votes in Saigon from the city's 450,000 registered voters. There wouldn't be a reunification, and the anti-communist Diệm, who established strong links with the US, would rule the south until 1963 when he was deposed in a coup and then later assassinated.

By then, the Việt Minh in the north and the Việt Cộng in the south were at war (the Việt Cộng were the army of the National Liberation Front, a mass political organization of south Vietnam). The US, fearing the spread of Communism and the threat of Cold War, came in on the side of the south and the Vietnam War (or American War as the Vietnamese call it) lasted until the Fall of Saigon in 1975, confirming the victory of the north and in 1976 creating the Socialist Republic of Vietnam, by which time some three million had been killed.

Beer became prevalent during the Vietnam War, primarily with American troops, who drank cans of imported brands like Budweiser, Pabst Blue Ribbon and Schlitz. Brewing continued in the breweries in Hanoi and Saigon, which were nationalized at the end of the war.[77] In the south, 33 was the main brand, but rumours that the local beers contained formaldehyde meant they weren't as popular with the troops as the imports.

It was during the war that beer also began to be drunk by the Vietnamese, mostly those working in the cities to provide support for the troops. But to get the locals to drink it they had to make it affordable, and they had to make it taste good.

"At that time I was very small," says Dr Viet, "but I remember the taste. It was very, very bitter, so we put some sugar in it." Beer was then the primary

---

76 Czechs taught numerous Vietnamese to brew beer, and today there's something like fifty small Czech- or German-inspired brewpubs throughout Vietnam, where they brew authentic-tasting pale and dark lagers (though many are variable in quality) and serve them in a setting that looks as though it's been lifted from a Prague backstreet.

77 The government's Ministry of Trade and Industry have run the breweries since then, but they've been gradually selling off percentages and privatizing them; they still want the taxes, but not the business of running them. SABECO, for example, sold a majority stake to ThaiBev in 2018 (ThaiBev own the Thai beer Chang, plus a lot of other drink brands), and one of the reasons they picked it was the desire to promote the name of Bia Saigon around the world – and soon the name was on the sleeve of Leicester City Football Club's kit. As of 1993, more global companies have been introducing their beer into Vietnam, including Heineken (who brew Tiger and other brands), Budweiser and Carlsberg, who own a stake in HABECO.

alcohol, as it was forbidden for people to make their own rice wine at home. "People adapted to it quickly," says Dr Viet. The new kind of lager wasn't like the beers the French had brewed, and neither was it like a classic Czech beer: it had less alcohol, fewer hops (it wasn't easy or cheap to get them in Vietnam), it used less malt and included rice, which was a cheap local ingredient, and these combined to make a very light beer.

The breweries were state-owned, and in this socialist country beer was closely controlled. In Hanoi, beer was only available in certain beer shops, which were allocated 50-litre kegs of beer delivered from 4 a.m. by cyclo-drivers on their pedal carts. The kegs were more like metal casks, and were unpressurized, with the beer simply poured out by gravity through a small hose or tap. The beer was also not refrigerated after it left the brewery, only maintaining a coldness from the brewery's tanks (probably held around 0°C), where it was filled just hours before being drunk.

The control of consumption meant that a token system was in place, and people had to line up, sometimes for many hours, to exchange their token for a glass of beer. From 10 a.m. the beer shops could start selling the beer, and locals would sit around small plastic tables, eating peanuts and fried tofu, and talk. "There was no discrimination, no classes, because everybody had to queue up," says Dr Viet, and when the keg of beer was empty, they had to go home: "you couldn't ask for more, as it was all allocated." That simple, social setting and the keg of beer was the beginning of a beer culture that continues today in Hanoi.

Since the turn of the twenty-first century Vietnam has really become a nation of beer lovers, with drinking growing rapidly (209 per cent between 2007 and 2017). Most of that is from the major brands like Bia Hanoi, Bia Saigon, 333, Tiger, Larue and Halida (the four main brewing companies operating in Vietnam – HABECO, SABECO, Heineken and Carlsberg – own around 95 per cent of the market). Any old imperialism is long forgotten because beer has been fully adapted and adopted and it's seen as a defiantly local liquid. It's unlikely anyone drinking a Bia Hanoi in the Vietnamese capital links that beer with the French. Rather it's a source of pride: this is my local beer. And the most local kind of beer in Hanoi is *bia hoi*, a specific kind of beer, sold and served in a special way.

The culture hasn't changed

There are many things that make *bia hoi* unique: it's still served in almost exactly the same way as when it was introduced during the Vietnam War, with a keg delivered and drunk in a day in simple surroundings; it needs to be drunk very fresh because it's filtered but left unpasteurized; it's brewed quickly and sold very cheap (10,000vnd a glass on average, which is £0.33/$0.43);[78] it's low in alcohol at typically less than 4 per cent ABV; and it's only a draught beer, with the drinking culture meaning it's usually served in small street-side *bia hoi* or larger *quan nhau* restaurants,[79] where people drink beer after beer and share plate after plate of food. The better-known branded beers like Bia Saigon and 333 are typically only served in bottles, are pasteurized and are more expensive.

The *bia hoi* you're most likely to find in Hanoi is Bia Hoi Ha Noi, made by the large HABECO brewery in the city. All around Hanoi you'll see bright yellow or red awnings with the words "Bia Hoi Ha Noi" printed in bold across them, and beneath it small blue plastic tables and chairs. Inside those bars, or on the streets outside, you'll see battered, dented and scuffed-up old steel kegs, each with a red band through the middle and the brewery's name in yellow.[80] The kegs are delivered either early in the morning or late at night, enough to last a day or two.

My translator, Phanh, is taking me to a *bia hoi* owned by the family of an old school friend. Bia Hoi *Anh Vũ*, at 138 *Lê Duẩn*, has been run by Mr Điểm since the early 1990s, and serves two or three kegs of Bia Hoi Ha Noi a day. There's a bare utilitarian simplicity to this *bia hoi*, probably much like a *bia hoi* was in the

---

78 *Bia hoi* is among the cheapest beers in the world, and that's despite Vietnam having a 65 per cent tax on beer, one of the highest in the world. A 50-litre keg, including delivery, costs about 600,000vnd (£20/$25). A *bia hoi* can make around 450,000–500,000vnd per keg if it's sold at 10,000vnd a glass. Most *bia hois* make more of their money from food, as most people who visit one go to eat as well. Local bottled beer in a bar is usually around 20,000vnd, while a local craft beer on draught will be 100,000vnd.

79 "Here in Vietnam, we drink in open areas. In the *bia hoi* it's always open," says Dr Viet. Most houses are small, hot and filled with people, and outside in the *bia hoi* it's cooler and more social, and elsewhere in this book we've seen beer and "pubs" (in whatever guise) functioning as a domestic escape, with the culture of drinking with others developing partly as a way of being out of the house. In Vietnam there are several different kinds of eating and drinking spaces and you can often tell them apart by the seating. A standard *bia hoi* is the equivalent of a boozer or dive bar. It's simple: they only do snacks and draught beer, and are usually in small shopfronts beneath someone's house, where you'll sit on small plastic stools, the kind a pre-school child might sit at when drawing. A *quan nhau* is a larger *bia hoi* with a more extensive food choice, and plastic chairs like a small garden chair, the equivalent of a normal pub. A *nha hang* is like a gastropub, and you'll sit on wooden chairs, have a more refined meal and drink bottled beer, not *bia hoi* (it's common for a group of people to order beers by the case, so if there's four of you you'll get twenty beers, drink five each, then decide if you want more – if you do, then you get another case). Then you'll find more formal and fancy restaurants, again without *bia hoi*, and the food there will cost more – you'll only go on special occasions. Finally there's the new idea of a cocktail or craft beer bar, where it's more of a Western experience and more expensive, and you'll sit on tall bar stools.

80 Look closely at the keg and there's an address on the red wrapper: 183 Hoang Hoa Tham. This is where the original Hanoi brewery from 1890 was built, and it's still where all of Hanoi's *bia hoi* comes from. It's 3.5km north-west of Hanoi's Old Quarter, and I walked up there to see it: there's a large distribution area, mountains of old kegs are piled up and the main building is an old French colonial-era villa. It's big, but there's not much to see (and I couldn't see a bar to go and drink in, but I did drink some excellent *bia hoi* at a place just down the street).

beginning: it's in the ground floor of his house, and there's a few tables inside and a few on the street outside. There's a small kitchen and toilet in the back, and old family photos and keepsakes are all around – it's like a second living room. The *bia hoi* has been in his family for many years, with his aunt running it during Communist times, and now Mr Điểm lives upstairs, running the *bia hoi* with his wife and sister, while his mother runs another *bia hoi* next door.

The beer is being poured out of a large silver container – imagine an old metal coffee urn that can probably hold 100 litres of water – with a tap on the bottom and a basic cooling system on top, complete with a little fan to stop it overheating. Inside the container is a 50-litre keg of *bia hoi*.

Next to this he has a large freezer, but it's not plugged into any power: instead it's a big salt-water bath with bags of ice to cool two unopened kegs – being unpasteurized it's really important the beer's kept cold and sold as fresh and as quickly as possible. When the keg needs changing, he'll take out the empty one from the large metal container and replace it with a fresh one out of this water bath. He then inserts some hosepipe where a keg coupler might ordinarily go and that hose links to the tap on the front. Everywhere will have their own way of storing and serving *bia hoi*, with some using larger walk-in coolers more familiar to Western drinkers and others just having an upturned keg on the street. The quality of the beer will vary wherever you go, so many locals will have their favourite places.[81]

Almost thirty years is a long time in a place like this, but other than a few small things, Điểm says that "the culture hasn't changed." Has *anything* changed? "The beer," he says. He thinks it used to taste better and be more bitter. The glass has also changed, he says: it used to be a half-litre with a handle; now it's a blueish-green chunky tumbler that holds around 400ml. It's heavy and recycled, imperfect, with air bubbles and an uneven rim, but it's robust, hardy, heavy, and almost every *bia hoi* uses it (all of these glasses are handmade in one small village around 60 miles south of Hanoi).

Điểm passes me another *bia hoi*. There's something intangibly great about this glass and the beer inside it: it's familiar and yet at the same time it's very

---

81 One of my favourite *bia hoi* memories is from 2016 when my girlfriend Emma and I passed an old woman selling beer from the front of her house. She had one keg with a hosepipe connected directly as the "tap", and there was space for about eight people to sit on tiny stools. It was only 5,000vnd for one glass, so I couldn't resist stopping. When a local man ordered a beer soon after us the beer didn't pour properly, so the woman sucked the end of the hosepipe to let the beer out, and then just gave the beer to the customer. We didn't stay a second longer (but she was still selling beer when I passed her in 2018).

Most *bia hoi* is made by the Hanoi brewery, but not all of it – or it might be totally unbranded. Some *bia hoi* is clean and refreshing, some noticeably bitter and well-carbonated, while others can be heavier, sweeter, low in fizz and have more unusual aromas and flavours. The simple way of serving this beer, the different brewers and the lack of equipment make for variation.

different, it's special and yet it's the most everyday drink you can find in Hanoi. It's also an enduring drink and culture.

Ngon!

As we say cheers on the first beer of the day at 11.15 a.m., Dai Vuong is explaining how his company, SABECO, has twenty-six breweries in Vietnam, including two in Hanoi, and they make around half of all Vietnamese beer, including Saigon Special, Saigon Lager and 333. They also make a small amount of *bia hoi*, mostly sold in the kind of restaurant we're in right now, a large *quan nhau bia hoi* where they have two double-door refrigerators branded in the bright yellow of HABECO (it was only at that moment I realized I'd invited the SABECO man to their competitor's place . . .) and a range of different food.

Dai's brewery – or "factory" as he calls it – makes Bia Hoi Sai Gon. How is it different from their normal lager? It's made more quickly, so it takes under two weeks compared to the three weeks it takes to make Saigon Lager; the brew uses more rice (about 25 per cent more – Bia Hoi Ha Noi uses around 40 per cent); it has fewer hops, it's always unpasteurized, and only in kegs. "What is unique is not just the beer but how it connects with the food and the culture," he says. "Good, cheap food. Delicious!"

Delicious is a word I know in Vietnamese, so to impress them I confidently say it. "*Ngon!*"

Dai stares blankly back at me.

I say it again, trying a different tone. "*Ngon.*"

Also here is one of Dai's colleagues, Ngoc, and my translator, Phanh. They don't seem to know what I'm saying, either.

I say it again, making a sound somewhere between a nasal "*Nom*" and the sound a Formula One car makes when it speeds past: *Nnnhhoooggnn*. They still don't get it so I finally just say it in English and Phanh saves me, correcting my pronunciation ("*Ngon*" is actually pronounced something like the noise you'd make if you were swallowing a boiled egg whole). For the rest of the meal we stick to just "delicious", which is an important word because the food is great. There's also a lot of it, spread out over two tables, with crunchy fried sweet potatoes, morning glory and garlic, tofu in tomato sauce, veal with stir-fried vegetables, lots of noodles, and then, when I think we're done, a whole fish, cooked in soy sauce and beer (that was really *ngon*). There's also a lot of *bia hoi*.

After lunch Dai invites me to visit his factory, so the next morning I take a taxi 45 minutes west of the Old Quarter to meet him and his colleague, Mr Quy. There aren't many people around, the canning line is shuffling along, the corridors are long and dark, there's hundreds of kegs stacked up, and it's just a big industrial brewery on the edge of the city where a lot of lager is made. I get the feeling I'm not really here to see the brewery, and that's confirmed when lunch is offered 15 minutes after I arrive and again we're drinking by 11.15 a.m.

Dai orders beer and food, and a few minutes later a 3-litre tower of Bia Hoi Sai Gon is brought out by a "Promotion Girl" in a tight-fitting Saigon-branded red dress. She pours us each a glass and we toast and drink. It's a little stronger than Bia Hoi Ha Noi and more malt-flavoured. It's good, and I finish my glass quickly and top it up.

The girl returns with an empty glass and an odd, expectant look. "She wants to drink a beer with you," says Dai.

Great, I say, please do, expecting her to sit. She pours me a beer, then one for herself, we say "Cheers", and then say it the Vietnamese way: "*Mot, hai, ba, zo!*" (One, two, three, drink!).

I take a big mouthful, audibly announce a refreshed *aaahhhh* and return the beer to the table, but she's still drinking. She's got two hands on the glass and she's *necking* it. I look to Dai and Quy.

"100 per cent!" Dai says.

Oh shit, I have to down it. I pick up my beer and drink it as quickly as I can, *gulp gulp gulp*. We empty our glasses at the same time. She shakes my hand and leaves. I feel like neither of us could say no to doing that, whether we wanted to or not.[82]

The food arrives. There must be nine or ten plates on the table, and we share everything while continually topping up our beer glasses. When one new dish arrives, Dai points at it. "Special to Hanoi. Traditional for beer," he says. It's cubes of white tofu with a bowl of thick violet-brown sauce on the side called *mắm tôm*, which is made with fermented shrimp paste. "If you no like, this is for you –" and he points to a second dipping bowl with just chilli, sugar and lemon juice without the shrimp.

I can smell this fearsome mixture of deeply fermented fish from across the table, but I see his *If you don't like it* as a challenge, so I dig some tofu in as if it's ketchup on a French fry and eat it in one go. It explodes in my mouth like a stink bomb. It's the definition of pungent, like the most intense blue cheese mixed with fermented anchovies and raw garlic. It's equally disgusting and addictively intense and the beer washes away the flavour perfectly, and now I see

---

82 Unfortunately Vietnam is behind the Western world in terms of this kind of thing, and there are a lot of young women employed as Promotion Girls, or PGs, wearing tight dresses with the job of encouraging men to choose their brand of beer. In the busier parts of Hanoi where the tourists drink you might see three or four different brands represented in this way.

why it's such a popular beer snack (tofu and *mắm tôm* was one of the original snacks sold in the wartime *bia hoi*s).

Their English isn't great and my Vietnamese is limited to counting to 99 and mispronouncing *ngon* (and Phanh isn't here to translate today), but despite the language difference we're talking about beer and food and football and travel and wives, and somehow we understand each other perfectly. The beer tower is about two-thirds empty and I'm feeling a bit drunk and I've eaten so much food that my stomach hurts. It's been a good lunch, and I'm preparing to leave when a second 3-litre tower arrives, and now I know the day is going to go in a different direction than I had planned.

We fill each other's glasses, we talk about all sorts of things, I eat a lot more *mắm tôm* because I see it as a test of my eating abilities in the same way that the tower has been a test of my drinking prowess. This is the Vietnamese way with beer and food: glass after glass of beer, with lots of shared plates spread across the table, and several hours socializing. It's brilliant.

"We drink two litres of beer!" Dai says, red-faced, looking at the small amount of beer left in the second tower. And then he asks me how much I can drink. I pause for a moment. I look at the tower, I look at my beer glass, I look at the time (1.20 p.m.!), I look back at the 2-litre tower, worrying that a third might appear.

"Two litres," I say.

I think they're almost as relieved as I am not to drink another litre over lunch.

The value of tradition

Bia hoi has changed. When I was first in Hanoi in 2014, I sat with my best mate Matt and we drank dozens of glasses of *bia hoi* on Tạ Hiện, or what's known in the tourist guide books as Bia Hoi Corner. We moved from bar to bar, eating snacks, chatting with people, seeing it fill up with tourists as the night progressed, and just loving the crazy outdoor fast-moving experience.

But returning just two years later, I found the place different. The old women who had been serving it from kegs in the front of their homes had been replaced by young promotion girls; neon signs now lit the street with words like Tiger and Tuborg; the old kegs of *bia hoi* had been replaced by new fridges full of bottles: draught *bia hoi* wasn't being drunk any more. Big Beer had bought the corner, giving bars fridges and the benefits for stocking their brands instead of *bia hoi*. The reality is that it's easier to sell bottles of lager than draught and bars can charge more money for them, especially in this touristy part of town. *Bia hoi* no longer made sense on Bia Hoi Corner.

But then *bia hoi* is not something for the tourists. They are always welcome to drink it, but this is a drink for Hanoians.

I came here again to try to understand *bia hoi* better, but also to see whether this great way of drinking might be in danger; if a one-off beer culture might be about to disappear. Vietnam is a country in transition. It's urbanizing rapidly, it has the fastest-growing middle class in south-east Asia and it has one of the youngest populations in the region, where over half of the 95 million population is under 30, and every year around a million young adults leave school and enter employment. Seemingly old-fashioned *bia hoi* doesn't necessarily fit with a young, modernizing population, but then Vietnam is one of the most traditional countries, especially when it comes to food, drink and the associated culture, and "the Vietnamese value traditions," Dai had said to me. "Whatever lasts long, becomes culture. *Bia hoi* is culture in Hanoi."

Bia hoi has preserved a unique way of drinking a uniquely brewed and served kind of beer, and that's special in a world where a drink like lager has become so uniform. This tradition doesn't go back to the French at the end of the nineteenth century: it goes back to the resumption of peace after all the wars, as the country was rebuilding itself and trying to recover from the catastrophic loses and changes. Beer – and especially *bia hoi* – became a symbol of recovery, a way of bringing people back together again, over one of the few things everyone could afford.

It's late on my final night in Hanoi, and I want a couple more glasses of beer, so I go, almost instinctively, back to No. 2 Đường Thành. This was my first stop four days ago. It was my first stop when I came here last year. And the year before that. It'll probably be my first stop when I return next time. It's not because the beer is the best, or the food: I come because it's a familiar space in a very unfamiliar city, and right here it seems like *bia hoi* is unchanged.

There are families and children in here; there's a group of guys in their twenties; another group in their sixties; couples sit chatting, others share tables covered in plates of fried chicken, vegetables, rice, tofu and *mắm tôm*. And then there's me. The only white guy, squatting uncomfortably on the tiny plastic stool, taking photos of my beers, writing in a small notebook, and happy just watching and listening and enjoying being here. I have no idea what's being said or what's happening, and yet I know *exactly* what people are saying to one another. I know because it's universal.

"Excuse me. Where you from?"

I talk to the local man next to me for an hour. He owns a restaurant near here, and has come for drinks with his friends. We talk about football, the weather, food. He wants to go to Wembley Stadium. I love *bun cha* noodles. He comes to this *bia hoi* most weekends. We laugh at one of his friends who has fallen asleep at the table. We drink more beer. I try to buy him a beer but he ends up paying – you are a guest in my country, he says.

And it's a country and a culture that I love and I especially love *bia hoi*, a beer that was originally produced in the easiest and most practical way possible and was able to unify a divided place, allowing the Vietnamese to come together socially. Today it still does exactly that only in much better circumstances. I stumble out of the *bia hoi* late at night. The dawn-rising city goes to bed early, letting me walk through the streets in relative quiet, filled with joy by my favourite kind of beer and favourite place to drink it.

JAPAN: PURITY LAWS, DRY WARS AND THE THIRD TYPE OF BEER

"*Karakuchi!*"

Gota-san keeps saying this, sometimes really animatedly and at other times almost whispering: "*Ka-ra-koooo-chiii.*" It's very important for Asahi Super Dry, he says.

I've just drawn up a chart to try to explain this, with "Flavour Intensity" on the Y-axis and "Elapsed Drinking" on the X-axis. There's a vertical arrow pointing directly up through the middle saying "Body" and another going down saying "*Kire*" (which means something like "crispness"). I've written the words "Power up, release," though I'm not sure why. According to my notes, *karakuchi* is like nothing else in the world. I am delightfully lost in the mathematical concept of how this beer tastes.

I'm also very thirsty, because I've seen so many photos of perfectly poured glasses of Asahi lager, so I'm extremely grateful when Gota serves me a beer with a thick, smooth foam on top.

As I drink it, Gota says the word again – "*Karakuchi*" – and the graph flashes into my head. I think they've successfully brainwashed me, but I also think I understand it, and I taste it like a chart: body and flavour first, which increases; then that drops right away to leave very little aftertaste and a clean, dry finish that just makes you want to drink more. It's Karakuchi!

****

I've been in Japan for two days, and so far I've been really confused by most things. I'm particularly puzzled by the beer fridges in the convenience stores, and I rarely pass a 7-Eleven without stopping to look at all the weird and exciting stuff: the snacks, the rice balls, the things sitting in some kind of hot broth, the cans of coffee (hot or cold), the rows of green tea bottles, the cardboard cartons of *sake*, the candies, and then the beer.

The beer fridges are impossible to understand. It's like there's no system to them, just dozens of eye-catching cans all in white or silver or yellow or blue; some cans are 350ml and others tall-boy 500ml; I half-recognize some of the brands, but it's all in Japanese so I have no idea what they actually are. Then there are cans with lemons on them and words like "STRONG" and "9%" and "ZERO" (lots of things have "0%" on them, yet most of them are high in alcohol), but those ones don't look like beers to me – they look like a mix between an energy drink and a rave that's got out of control. What *is* all this stuff?

Before I'd arrived at Asahi's global headquarters in Asakusa, opened for their centenary and a great glowing 100m yellow skyscraper that looks a little like a big glass of beer, I'd asked Gota, who is part of Asahi's global brand team, to help me understand the Japanese beer market. He leads me to a meeting room where there are four cans of beer on the table. There's Asahi Dry Zero, which is alcohol-free (I understand that one); a can called Clear is known as a *dai-san*; Style Free is a *happoshu*; and there's an Asahi Super Dry, the best-selling *beer*[83] in Japan. By the end of the day I finally (sort of) understand the complicated Japanese beer market, one that's unlike anywhere else in the world, but before I explain the beer, let me tell you who's buying it.

Japan's population, the world's eleventh largest, has been in decline for the last few years (-0.23 per cent), while the median age is increasing (46.7 years – in the US it's 37.8 and in the UK 40.3). The Japanese are living longer and getting older, and the younger ones are having fewer kids. The older drinkers still want beer, which means the over-fifties are the key demographic for the beer industry, whereas the younger drinkers are more likely to order another category of drink called *chu-hai,* a pre-mixed cocktail in a can. If you want to find *chu-hai* in the stores then it's next to the beer and is also made by the major breweries. *Chu-hai*s vary from highballs (whisky and soda) to the things I've seen with the words STRONG and ZERO and images of neon citrus fruit all over them, which are basically cans of vodka and diet lemon soda.

Chu-hai originates from post-war times when *shochu* (a distilled vodka-like spirit made from a variety of starch sources like sweet potatoes, barley and rice) was the cheapest and most available alcohol, and it would be mixed with soda and flavourings in the *izakaya* (basically pubs), where it was called a "*shochu* highball" and ended up losing the *sho-* and *-ball* from its name. Suntory's STRONG ZERO LEMON -196° is the best-selling *chu-hai* in Japan, and it's disgusting in a *that's gonna fuck you up* kind of way as well as tasting gross.

---

83 *Beer*, not beer, because in this chapter "beer" is not quite as easy to understand as in others… It'll hopefully make sense very soon, but if it's written as *beer* then know that it means a Japan-specific type of beer and is based on the taxes paid on it.

More than the terrible taste, it's irresponsibly strong and cheap, being 9 per cent ABV and about £1.20/$1.70 for a 500ml can. The -196° part is because they use nitrogen to freeze the lemon before adding it, for some reason, and the ZERO part is because most of these cans of rocket fuel are also aimed at the health-conscious consumer who wants zero sugar or carbs. The market for *chu-hai* is so great that in 2018 Coca-Cola introduced a lemon sour called Lemon-Do into Japan, making that its first alcoholic drink in the company's 125-year history.

Now on to beer. There are three distinct types of "beer", which are ultimately determined by ingredients, taxes and the price the drinker pays. *Beer* is categorized and taxed as being made with at least 67 per cent barley, and includes the main brands like Asahi Super Dry and Kirin Ichiban (Super Dry uses rice and maize to make up the rest of the fermentables, while Ichiban is just malt).

Happoshu (or "sparkling liquid", which was also initially called *daini no biiru*, or "the second beer") is technically anything under 67 per cent barley, but it gets cheaper as the malt goes down, so it'll more realistically be under 50 or even 25 per cent barley, with the rest of the fermentable sugars coming from alternative sources like corn, rice or sugar.

Then there's *dai-san* (or "the third beer", also referred to as "new genre"), which is cheaper still and contains less than 25 per cent barley and often no barley at all, with the alcohol coming from a spirit like *shochu*. Instead of barley it might use "protein-decomposed products made from soya, pea, or corn" and, according to a report called *Economic Prospects on Craft Beer*, "a beer-flavoured compound [is] added to the third beer-like beverage, which [is] colored with caramel". Basically: some *dai-san*s are fake-beer-flavoured drinks fortified with a barley-based spirit. Together, *happoshu* and *dai-san* account for some 40 per cent of the Japanese beer market.

All the beers are around 5 per cent ABV, pale in colour and look and taste like classic lager; all the breweries make all the different kinds of beers as well as canned *chu-hais*, and all of these look similar on the store shelves, so the easiest way to tell the beers apart is to look at the price, which is where tax becomes important. A standard 350ml (12.3oz) can of *beer* costs around ¥225, with ¥77 of that being tax; *happoshu* is ¥170 with ¥47 tax; *dai-san* is under ¥150 with ¥28 tax (there's ¥110 to a US dollar and ¥150 to the British pound).

These days, Japanese drinkers choose either proper *beer* when they want something good to drink (if they're in a bar or restaurant), or *dai-san* when they don't care so much about taste and just want something cheap (typically if they're at home). And this has led to an emerging sub-category called "functional" *happoshu* and *dai-san*: essentially low- or no-malt beers that offer additional health benefits (or at least reduced perceived badness). In the functional category there are several "diet" low-calorie beers, low-carb and no-carb beers, and ones without purine.[84] These beers are increasingly popular with the growing population of health-conscious over-thirties.

Using this new knowledge, the following day I bought a few beers to drink in my hotel. Firstly, the proper *beers*, like Asahi Super Dry and Kirin Ichiban, are excellent and I'd happily drink them any time. They're among the highest-quality and best-tasting mainstream lagers, and it's interesting that in general they are unpasteurized, which is rare for mainstream beer anywhere in the world.

Dai-san is largely disgusting. Just imagine beer-flavoured (and not even good-beer-flavoured) soda water with vodka in it. I also have a *functional happoshu*. "A lot of doctors recommend people drink this one because it's no sugar and no purine," the people at Kirin tell me about their Platinum Double brand. It's a can with lots of zeros on the front, and I go to the website while I drink it and learn that 91 per cent of consumers think it's delicious. I am one of the other 9 per cent. The can says it's purine-neutral, it's low-carbohydrate, there's something about nucleic acid and it's brewed using activated carbon. I don't understand this stuff, which is worrying. The ingredients include malt, hops and barley, which is a good start, but then it has saccharide, caramel pigment, alcohol, flavour, sour agent, emulsifier and a sweetener called Acesulfame K. What the hell am I drinking?! It's imitation beer with an oddly diet-like character and a fake sweetness that leaves an odd empty taste. If people are buying this for "health" reasons then maybe they should consider the difference between those ingredients and the much more natural list of ingredients on a mainstream Japanese beer: barley, hops, yeast, water, and maybe some rice and maize.

Now that you hopefully understand the oddities and complexities of the Japanese beer market, you need to know that by 2026 the taxes of the different beer types will become equal at ¥54.25 per 350ml can. This means that effectively *beer* and *dai-san* will get much closer in price, with the hope that it will increase beer (or *beer*) sales overall. But that's in the future.

Right. That was interesting, wasn't it? Now I'm going to go and get really pissed with Gota while you read the history of beer in Japan. By the time I return, I'll be drunk under a railway bridge with two old artists.

---

84 I see purine mentioned a few times. Purines are naturally found in food and alcohol and the body corrects them to uric acid. If we have too much uric acid in our body then it can crystallize and cause gout. A lot of Japanese food is high in purines and nucleic acid, and that acid can also turn into uric acid. No-purine is appealing for the potential gout sufferers, a sign of the aging target market for Japanese brewers.

Bitter horse-piss wine

The Dutch brought beer, badminton and billiards to Japan. Here, Jeffrey W. Alexander explains in his book *Brewed in Japan*, the drink was described as "like a barley *sake*" with a bitter taste. The word and Japanese script for beer ("*biiru*") had entered the Japanese language as early as 1810 in a Dutch–Japanese dictionary.

In 1854 a special Japan–America Treaty of Amity and Friendship saw the Americans arrive with three casks of beer. It was described as an "earthen colour with bubbles", and some called it "magic water" while others were less enchanted, calling it "bitter horse-piss wine." The treaty opened up the city of Yokohama for European traders, with a significant number of Dutch, French and British troops based there from 1863, and expensive imported beer, including Bass Ale from Burton-on-Trent and lagers from America and Germany, available to drink. By 1865 two chaps called Campbell and Langthorne had opened a brewery in the European district, building it next to a natural spring; it's thought that this was the first brewery in Japan, but it wasn't a lasting success.

In 1868, sea captain and merchant Marinus Johannes Benjamin Noordhoek Hegt opened the Japan Yokohama Brewery, with a German-born and US-raised brewer named Emil Wiegand hired to manage it. At around the same time, William Copeland, a tall and imposing man who was mild-mannered when sober but was almost always drunk, opened a brewery on the site of Campbell and Langthorne's failed brewery, calling it the Spring Valley Brewery.

Copeland brewed Lager Beer, Bavarian Beer and Bavarian Bock Beer, and possibly some English ale, mostly sold in casks to locals. He was in competition with the Japan Yokohama Brewery until 1876, when they decided to merge and brew everything in Copeland's brewery, turning Wiegand's into a malthouse (which burned down the following year). When the two brewers fell out Copeland ended up taking over everything, but that caught fire and he was bankrupt in the mid-1880s, though not so badly off that he couldn't return to business and open a beer hall and garden, which Alexander describes as "a truly pioneering effort", with four or five storage cellars and water drawn from a nearby pond to keep them cool. It was mostly drunk sailors who visited, which put off the local foreigners. When Copeland died in 1902 his obituary reflected that at the time of opening his brewery "the Japanese had not acquired the taste for beer and the venture was not attended with much success".

In 1886, Copeland's old burned-down brewery, sought after for its position next to the spring, was bought by a foreign investment firm and became known as the Japan Brewing Company. In 1907 it changed its name to the Kirin Beer Company after its beer called Kirin, itself named after the Qilin, a luck-bringing horned, hooved and scaly creature from Chinese mythology. The main beers in the early years were Bock and Munich beer (both light brown), a pale Lager and a dark Stout.[85]

Meanwhile, in 1872 a man named Seibei Nakagawa had travelled to Germany to learn to brew. He spent over two years at Berliner Brauerei-Gesellschaft Tivoli in Fürstenwalde before taking up a post as official beer brewer on Hokkaido, the large island off the north of Japan's main island, where, by now the country's default brewing expert, he was employed by the government as part of an industrial development plan and colonization initiative.

The Hokkaido Colonization Office Brewery opened in 1876 as a German-style brewery, roughly following the Bavarian brewing season, making German-style beers and using imported German ingredients, but it didn't have the best start. The German yeast they got didn't work, they struggled to get good malt, they had to import hops from America as well as Germany, and then when they were finally ready to sell beer in 1877 they realized they didn't have enough bottles to put the beer in, and there were no glass manufacturers in Japan at the time. At least they had a name: Sapporo Cold-Brewed Beer. But "the beer is poor, weak stuff that will not keep," reported *Nature* magazine in 1879. They managed to improve, and the brewery would later change its name to Sapporo. They also successfully managed to grow barley and hops on the island.

In 1888, a man named Hiizu Ikuta went to Germany to study in Weihenstephan, the world's principal brewing school. The following year he was appointed manager and technical director of a new brewery built on the edge of Osaka by *sake* maker Komakichi Torii. In 1892 the Osaka Beer Brewing Company launched a new beer named after the land of the "rising sun": Asahi.

By the 1880s, beer and *sake* were being sold on the streets by "swinging sellers". In the later 1890s and into the 1900s, stand-up bars became more common, and then came *biya-hōru* or beer halls, "cool drink bars", beer cafés and, in the summer, beer gardens. But through all this beer remained predominantly a drink for wealthy people in urban areas; everyone else drank cheap *sake* (something like 164,000hl of beer was brewed in Japan in 1902 for a population of almost 45 million people: that's roughly one regular beer can or bottle per person for the whole year).

One thing marks out the first decades of Japanese brewing: its pursuit of German-ness. It used German ingredients and processes, strictly followed the *Reinheitsgebot* beer-purity law, and often had German brewmasters and engineers or German-trained Japanese brewers, making it essentially a German product made in Japan. Indeed, to begin with it was seen as necessary to appear as German as possible to compete with the premium imports.

---

85 Fun fact about Kirin: they had Japan's first ever vehicle licence plate, and that went on a bottle-shaped car that drove around promoting their beer.

Hefty tax increases between 1901 and 1908 saw many breweries close, leaving just a few smaller ones alongside four larger brewers: Osaka Beer Company, who made Asahi; Japan Brewery's Kirin; the Sapporo Brewery; and Nippon, who made a beer called Yebisu. Because of the tax escalations, Osaka, Sapporo and Nippon decided to merge to form Dai Nippon ("Greater Japan"), with Kirin remaining independent.

World War I became an impetus for growth, because even though the reputation for German and German-style beer endured, any other associations with the country were bad. Then when the extensive exports German breweries had built up were suddenly stopped, Japanese brewers were in a great position to expand through Asia.

By the 1920s, Tokyo was changing and becoming more Westernized. There were an estimated 5,000 Western-style restaurants in Tokyo in 1923, with "Western-style" meaning that diners ordered the one dish they wanted rather than having an array of dishes presented to them and shared in the old Japanese tradition. Beer is what they drank in these modern and Western restaurants.

Beer halls were increasing in number and spreading beyond Tokyo, with beer served in German-style tankards and people drinking sitting on long, shared benches. Beer was starting to be a popular drink for men on their way home from work or for work colleagues out socializing. This beer-drinking culture became part of the white-collar lifestyle, and proliferated among the growing middle class.

The growth in Japan's beer industry saw the cost of beer decreasing, which in turn led to price wars, so in the 1930s Dai Nippon and Kirin formed a "co-operative beer sales company", with production and prices controlled, fixing their market shares and making it almost impossible for smaller breweries to succeed.

Then came World War II. Up until 1940, cheap *sake* was the main alcohol in Japan, selling more than four times the volume of beer, but a bad rice harvest and the diversion of the remaining rice into food saw *sake* production prohibited. Because barley didn't have the same restrictions, more beer could be brewed (there were, however, fewer hops, so the beers generally got less bitter and lighter). During this period rationing saw households allowed to buy only three large bottles of beer a month, and at a fixed price. It wasn't much, but it ensured that beer at least stayed around throughout the war, which was important on a federal level as well as socially, because the government needed the money, especially as they'd lost all the tax on *sake*.

When the war ended, there was a seven-year Allied occupation. Until the middle of 1949 the Japanese were barred from going to restaurants and beer halls, so could only drink beer at home. The re-opening of the beer halls to the Japanese became a symbol of recovery, and beer sales increased. Beer was now seen as an essentially Japanese drink brewed to suit the local tastes and wartime self-sufficiency in beer production permanently dissociated Japan's brewing culture from its German heritage. By the 1950s most people could afford beer, and the brewers used Japanese celebrities in their advertising to target younger and female consumers, which combined with the increase in domestic refrigerators, home heating and television, and beer overtook *sake* sales. After work it became common to buy large bottles of beer and share them among your colleagues, pouring it into small glasses – even today you'll still see people sharing many large bottles with a group.

Dai Nippon and Kirin were the only companies to have come through World War II and the Allied occupation. Asahi broke away from Dai Nippon, which became Nippon-Sapporo, and in the 1950s the three beer companies each held almost exactly one-third of the beer market. Kirin was the brewery that would come to dominate the market, taking over half of it in the mid-1960s and leading with its Kirin Lager. By the mid-1980s, Asahi was struggling with under 10 per cent of the market with Asahi Gold, while everyone was feeling competition from cheap *chu-hai* cocktails. Then Asahi did something that transformed Japan's beer market and started another war.

The Dry Beer War

In 1986, Asahi decided they needed a new flagship beer, so they asked 5,000 drinkers what made the perfect beer. Their answer created Asahi Super Dry, which was released in 1987. It had more alcohol, a sharper flavour and a quick, clean, dry finish, with no bitter aftertaste (*Karakuchi!*). Super Dry used a new yeast that more fully fermented the sugars, giving that drier, more refreshing character drinkers wanted. Younger drinkers in particular loved it, and within a year Asahi had gone from under 10 per cent of the market to over 20 per cent, selling 13.5 million cases of Super Dry in the year of its release.

Kirin countered with Draft Dry Beer, but copying the name "Dry" was a low blow and the beer didn't last long. Meanwhile Super Dry was selling out: Asahi employees couldn't buy it because it all had to be saved for customers, reported *the New York Times*. In May 1988, Kirin released Cool, Sapporo released Hardy and Cool Dry, and Suntory[86] sold Sae, all within ten days of each other. American celebrities were brought in to advertise the new beer: Gene Hackman promoted

---

86 Suntory started out in 1899 as a shop in Osaka selling imported wine. In 1923 they built Japan's first malt whisky distillery. They added a brewery in 1963. They continue to brew beer, but it's for other drinks that they are now best known, especially spirits: they are the third-largest producer in the world and own several global brands like Jim Beam, Maker's Mark, Laphroaig, Courvoisier, Sipsmith plus

Kirin's Dry beer, while Mike Tyson was Suntory Dry's man. And Japanese Dry beer also reached the US, leading American breweries to introduce dry brands.

There was only one winner in the short Dry War, and by releasing Super Dry, Asahi had irrevocably changed the market, creating a general trend towards a crisper beer with a sharper, drier finish. (Kirin eventually produced a new beer called Ichiban, which would quickly become their new flagship.) Asahi Super Dry created Japan's first true beer type, and in 2001 Asahi replaced Kirin as the market leader in Japan, a position it still holds.

That wasn't the end of the disruption. In 1994, Japan's *beer* consumption reached a peak of over 70m hectolitres but in that same year the taxes changed and *happoshu* was introduced, followed a few years later by *dai-san*. *Beer* sales have since dropped to under 27m hectolitres, while the overall beer and beer-like category is 50m hectolitres in total, meaning actual proper *beers* account for a little over half of overall sales.

More recently, Asahi and Kirin have ascended to be truly global brewers, taking stakes or ownership in several large breweries around the world. In 2016, as a result of the AB-InBev and SABMiller merger, Asahi bought Pilsner Urquell, Peroni (where Asahi Super Dry is now brewed in Europe), Grolsch and several other large lager brewers. It also has a stake in Tsingtao, the sec-ond-largest brewery in China. Kirin have focused more on craft beer, with stakes in Brooklyn Brewery and Lion, which has many Australian and New Zealand brands, including Little Creatures of Fremantle, Western Australia, and the lager brewery Castlemaine XXXX, plus they have several British craft breweries. Outside Japan Asahi Super Dry and Kirin Ichiban are popular premium lager beers, giving these global brewers many diverse brands and beers to sell all around the world. Thankfully they haven't tried to sell *dai-san* anywhere else, yet . . .

Sitting *sake* shop
"*Kanpai!*"

We cheers our glasses again. We're in a smoky little *izakaya* under a bridge in Ginza. I now drink with a Manga-like thought bubble forming with every gulp of Asahi Super Dry and containing the word "Karakuchi". I can taste it like the chart I'd drawn ten hours earlier. It goes up with flavour to begin with and then drops, almost vanishes, at the end – perfectly refreshing.

"Sitting *sake* shop" is the kind-of translation of *izakaya*, Gota tells me. We're sitting at wobbly tables, on small stools, literally under railway tracks in the open air, with old beer posters on the wall, red lanterns above us and small

---

some soft drinks, Orangina and Lucozade.

beer glasses in front of us. Behind us skewers of meat sizzle on a grill, flaring up occasionally, next to a bubbling stock pot.

Izakaya are the Japanese equivalent of pubs. They are mostly small and cheap and do a variety of foods, and while they often lack the comfort or finesse of a restaurant, they are welcoming, informal and inclusive. "The objective is for communication," says Gota, explaining that the *izakaya* is more than just drinking and eating: it's for being with others. It also has a cultural role in helping lowlier employees speak to their superior; it's an egalitarian place for everyone to belong and talk to each other, and get really drunk. And I am already really drunk.

We've just been drinking *sake* in the kind of place where you close the bathroom door and the toilet seat opens for you and starts playing classical music. Before that we went to a great bar in Ginza called Pilsen Alley that just served Asahi Super Dry and Pilsner Urquell. Before that we'd been to a traditional Japanese barbecue restaurant, cooking our own meat over fire, and sharing several bottles of beer ("It's normal to start at the front and work your way backwards," Gota says, as he places some beef tongue on the grill followed by fatty hunks of rump, and finishes by ordering some stomach). Before that we'd had a lot of sushi and beer, and before that I'd been pouring and drinking my own beer at Asahi's headquarters.

Gota opens another large bottle of beer and shares it out among our glasses. We raise our beers and toast again: "*Kanpai!*" It translates as "Drink direct" or "Drink all", but it means much more than that. It means we're equal, we're to-gether, we're drinking, and whether it's "*Prost*" or "Cheers", "*Salut*" or "*Kanpai*", it universally means the same thing.

The table is soon covered in plates of food. I told Gota to order me the weird stuff, and I'm dipping unidentifiable innards, charred and chewy from the grill, into sweet-savoury *tare* sauce. Next to us are two elderly artists who've been celebrating the opening of their new show earlier in the day. The artists grab some chopsticks and eat with us. They order a big bottle of beer and fill all of our glasses. Gota orders some lemon sours, the original kind of *chu-hai*, which is *shochu*, lemon juice and soda, and it's really good. We order more plates of food.

In much of Asia, but especially China, Vietnam and Japan, beer and food are inextricably linked: you wouldn't have a beer without ordering food, and you wouldn't go to a meal with friends without having beer. And the food always involves lots of plates of shared dishes, which you eat over a long period. In China it's important that the beer plays a neutral role, allowing the food to be the centre of the attention; so too Vietnam, only they'll probably drink twice what the Chinese do; in Japan the beer is more engaging, more actively involved as part of the meal, and designed to work equally well with delicate sushi, rich bowls of noodles and grilled meat.

By now it's late and there are tables of drunk people in here, swaying on their stools, and it's exactly the kind of experience I was hoping for when I came out to Tokyo: this friendly interaction, this drunkenness that leads to nonsense and takes on its own momentum, leading from drink to drink. There's nothing like drinking with the locals in the places they go to drink.

"This is a precious experience," says Gota. "It might not happen again. It's about the moment and the place. But it's deeper than that; a kind of drunk fate."

****

Dai-san and the Japanese beer industry fascinate me. It's a well-established beer market and a large beer market – the seventh biggest in the world. The main beers are well known and well regarded as good premium lagers, but the Japanese beer market has been in decline for almost twenty-five years, propped up only by the new categories of beer. They've gone from beers brewed resolutely to the 500-year old *Reinheitsgebot* purity law to beers concocted in laboratories, which are lager-like but not like any lagers you could find in Bavaria or the Czech Republic, or indeed anywhere else in the world.

And it leaves me wondering about the future of lager. What will we be drinking next? Is this a step towards a unique personalization of beer? Will we soon be able to walk into a bar and order our perfect composite beer, which is then mixed for us in the same way we can go into a burger restaurant and pick the bun, the patty, the sauces and everything else? Will there one day be a machine I can go up to and press a button for colour, another for flavours, one for the alcohol and so on, and it mixes it right there for me? Will people be drinking cheap beer-flavoured alcopops? Will robots be the new brewmasters? The technology certainly exists to be able to do the beer mixes, and if it's going to happen, it'll happen in Japan.

But those beers won't be on the tables in the *izakaya* next to all the great food. They might make new rules for what beer can be, but that established and socially-important culture of eating and drinking isn't going away just yet.

CHAPTER FIVE

LAGER: THE PRESENT AND FUTURE

WASPS, YEAST HYBRIDIZATION AND PURE YEAST

Dr Martin Zarnkow's office at the Technical University of Munich smells funky.

I'm sitting at his desk and next to me is a large glass jar. It looks as though it's half-filled with grain and topped with a layer of liquid, almost like a thick soup that's separated. Every few minutes a bubble rises up and pops at the surface with a waft of fruity sourness.

This is a re-creation of a 3,500-year-old recipe for beer: it's one-third crushed emmer wheat, which was one of the first domesticated crops, one-third barley malt and one-third baked sourdough bread, which is fermenting naturally with airborne yeast plus the yeast that was in the bread. Zarnkow, who is Head of Research and Development at the world's foremost brewing school situated at Weihenstephan, the world's oldest brewery, has made this beer with his students.

I'm here because I want to try to understand lager yeast better. As we know, lager originated with the combination of a specific yeast, cold cellars or caves and a long storage. At least to begin with, 500 or 600 or however many years ago, all three of these things were essential, though how they all actually came together hasn't been discovered – and will probably never be. We can understand the cold part: cellars were a consistent, cool temperature and a natural refrigerator that helped to protect, preserve and improve a lagered beer. What we don't know is how the specific yeast came to get into the cellars.

There are two primary families of beer yeast, and they define the difference between ale and lager:[87] *Saccharomyces cerevisiae,* which makes ale, and *Saccharomyces pastorianus,* which makes lager (and was named after Louis Pasteur). Within these families there are numerous strains of yeast, each working in different ways and producing different characteristics, with most linked to a style of beer. For example, with *S. cerevisiae* there are specific yeast strains for brewing German *Hefeweizens,* there are numerous strains for pale ales, others for Belgian Trappist beers and many for British ales.[88]

The story of *S. pastorianus* is most interesting for this book. At some point in history it was formed as a hybrid of *S. cerevisiae* and another kind of yeast known as *Saccharomyces eubayanus. S. eubayanus* has never been found in Europe, but has been discovered natively in Patagonia, Tibet and West China. A sister yeast of *S. eubayanus* known as *Saccharomyces uvarum* was also found in some of those areas.[89] It's unlikely that the yeast got into Europe from South America, given the timeline of lager's first brew happening before Christopher Columbus's voyages in the 1500s, so it seems more feasible that *S. eubayanus* arrived from the far east of Asia, along the old spice trail. Though not everyone thinks that.

"I think it's bullshit it's coming from Tibet or Patagonia," says Dr Zarnkow, who says that "we have more genes in common with a pig" than *S. eubaynus* has with the non-*S. cerevisiae* genes of today's lager yeast. That might be hyperbole, but it's also reflective of a lack of general understanding of how *S. eubaynus* came into beer, and then how a hybridization event took place that evolved or bred it into what we now call *S. pastorianus.*

---

87 Historically, anyway… Today there are several hybrid kinds of beers that sit between the traditions of ale and lager. For example, in Cologne they brew a light, crisp, cold-stored beer that is brewed with an ale yeast – it's known as *Kölsch.* Other brewers around the world also use this yeast and process to make beer, but some of them call it a lager because it looks and tastes like a lager. Likewise, there are mainstream lagers produced with ale yeasts for speed and efficiency. Also, the old idea of ale yeast being top-fermenting and lager yeast being bottom-fermenting is now less relevant, because in modern breweries the beer typically ferments in a tall, closed tank with a conical base (as opposed to the old days when it was done in an open-topped wooden vessel), and all yeast has been evolved and trained to ultimately fall to the bottom of those tanks.

---

88 Beyond those two *Saccharomyces* yeasts, there's "wild yeast", commonly known as *brettanomyces,* which will give a range of qualities from leathery to farm-like to pineapple – they do exist in the wild, but more typical is to add a "domesticated" wild yeast (the brewer can order it from a yeast supplier like any other kind of yeast). *Brettanomyces* translates as "British fungus" as it was discovered in British beers – it was seen as an integral part of their flavour profile for many years (especially in long-matured porters), which is one reason why it took the traditional British brewers longer to change over to pure yeast compared to their European counterparts. Wild yeast accounts for a third family of beers.

---

89 In 2016 Heineken brewed a "wild lager" with S. *euyabanus* yeast. It was slow to ferment the sugars, and gave some characteristics that you don't typically want in a lager, like a spicy-phenolic aroma. This clove-like spiciness has been largely and deliberately bred out of yeast over the last centuries.

"I believe the hybridization is happening in the intestines of wasps."

The fermenting jar next to me burps out a bubble that smells like tart apples, and I'm momentarily distracted, but, yes: Dr Zarnkow definitely just said the words *intestines of wasps*. It takes me a few minutes to get all this understood, but basically, different yeast strains can meet, germinate and mate in the guts of hibernating wasps, a natural environment that has the perfect pH and temperature for yeast to live. I promise I'm not making this up.[90]

Nothing happens by accident in nature. Just imagine an old orchard in autumn, the wet grass covered in browning apples, and the air is fragrant with a warming fruitiness, which is the smell of airborne yeast fermenting the sugars in the fallen fruits into alcohol and different aromas. "Aromas are a communication. It's calling a bug for help," says Dr Zarnkow. Those fruity fermenting aromas attract the bugs, which fly in to see what smells so good, landing on the fruit or liquid, picking up the tiny yeast cells on their legs or wings or swallowing it, before flying on and transferring it to somewhere new, meaning the yeast can carry on fermenting something else – yeast just wants to carry on living, metabolizing sugar and multiplying.

"Wasps are the only insect which can bite the skin of an apple or grape, which is a perfect place for yeast to proliferate. So that orchard, with its flies and wasps, is a farm of countless invisible yeasts, each moving from one fruit to the next, spending time insides the intestines of wasps where it's possible or probable that they were able to hybridize."

If multiple different kinds of yeast meet in the belly of a wasp then it's possible they could mate and form a new hybrid yeast (yeast can reproduce both asexually and by mating, apparently) and this kind of thing could have happened many, many times, over many, many years, with those yeast cells transferred to different regions or trees or fruits or maybe wine or beer, perhaps in wood or on other ingredients. Somehow the *S. cerevisiae* and *S. eubayanus* hybridized, and then somehow that got into beer barrels in the cellars of northern Bavaria sometime around the fourteenth century.

Dr Zarnkow's wasp idea is just a theory, an opinion, because the reality is that it's unknown how, where or why a hybridization event took place, and perhaps it doesn't even matter, because what is more significant is that the yeast evolved in the brewing environment.

Two things become significant now: that yeast is adaptive in a Darwinian way (surviving and evolving), and that the *S. euyabanus* part of the hybridized lager yeast gave it a tolerance to cold temperatures that *S. cerevisiae* doesn't have.

---

90 Here's an actual science paper about it: www.pnas.org/content/113/8/2247. Wasps are a *Saccharomyces* mating nest.

So once the hybridized *S. pastorianus* yeast was proliferating, the environment became important.

If we consider that once upon a time any batch of beer contained a slurry of different yeast and bacteria strains in a competitive environment (a fight for food – sugar – and survival), then it's a battle for who gets to eat and reproduce. The warmer the environment gets, the faster everything is going to work, while things mostly slow down in the cold.

Now, imagine one batch of beer is split into two barrels with the same slurry of yeasts added into each. One batch goes into a cold cellar at 8°C (46°F) and the other is at the ambient temperature of 18°C (64°F). Fermentation begins in both of them. *S. cerevisiae* likes the warmth, so in the ambient conditions it's going to fight well, whereas the *S. pastorianus* doesn't like the heat and will be out-competed by the *S. cerevisiae*. If, somehow, there was a dramatic change in weather and it jumped to 28°C (82°F), then the *S. cerevisiae* yeast would get stressed, having to work too hard, starting to produce more negative characteristics, with any wild yeast or bacteria benefiting from the heat. In the barrel in the 8°C cellar, *S. cerevisiae* and bacteria don't like the cold, and they'll essentially hibernate or work so slowly that it's out-competed by the *S. pastorianus* (it's a bit like putting milk in the fridge so it stays drinkable for longer).

In the past it was typical for a bucket or two of fermenting beer or active yeast to be passed from one vessel to another, which would have the impact of starting the next fermentation. Say a brewer had three barrels of fermenting beer in his cellar and one was better than the others, then he'd use the good one in the next batches. A week or two later he'd have to make the same choice, again selecting the best-tasting to progress. Years later and this would still have been going on, gradually evolving out any bad characteristics. This enabled the yeasts to become domesticated through human selection, just like the domestication of animals, fruit and vegetables.

But still that yeast was always a mix of different cultures ("Everything before [Emil Christian Hansen] was mixed fermentation – without exception," says Dr Zarnkow), which was the reason for spoiled fermentations and a general inconsistency in beer: cold conditions can only help to a certain point and beer, like fresh food, will always eventually go off. It was only when Emil Hansen figured out how to cultivate a pure, single strain of yeast that brewers could eliminate a lot of the lack of control that had impacted them for millennia. After Hansen, brewers were just having to try to control one strain of yeast, not several.

Once the yeast got pure it then started to show its own variation, based on its natural adaptation to the brewing environment and how brewers have manipulated it, which is where different *S. pastorianus* strains have evolved from. Most lagers have a neutral yeast character that you can't taste, but there are some distinctive strains, like the Coors yeast, which is fruity and sometimes a little banana-like. Budweiser gives some apple-like aroma; Heineken is a little like pear drops. These larger breweries will manage their own proprietary yeast strains and have a constant healthy supply ready to be used (with back-ups stored in several places around the world just in case of some kind of disaster – for Heineken and others, the yeast is integral to their beer).

Most breweries buy from the yeast labs, and the most-used yeast strain in the world is probably W34/70, or Weihenstephan lager yeast. It's a great and relatively neutral all-round lager yeast.[91] In those yeast labs they have a dozen or two different lager strains that have been isolated. Brewers can just place an order and have the yeast sent to them (and don't need to hope that some wasps are flying by with some mating yeast in their bellies).

The unknowns of lager yeast's origins are so far in the past that we can overlook them and focus on the specifics of the environment that helped to progress the yeast through to new generations.[92] Scientists now have the ability to change a strain of yeast based on its genetic make-up, which is leading us towards the present and future of brewing. And where Carlsberg were the first to isolate pure yeast, they remain at the forefront of brewing research.

The laboratories of lager

You might imagine that the world's largest brewers are the least agile. The big brands, with their worldwide reach, have a dominance that suggests scale over suppleness, like an ocean liner's slow turn compared to the jet ski's fast spin, but in several important examples you'll see how the global brands are able to have a far more significant impact on the present and the future of brewing, whether it's with their research or their focus on sustainability.

Lager is a stored beer, a matured beer, but slow fermentation and months of maturation contradicted Big Beer's priorities of making beer in larger volumes faster, with greater efficiency and for less money (while still tasting good). Yeast is still a temperamental ingredient that always produces some odd flavours, and it was the long lagering process that was able to eliminate those negative characteristics. Think of it like this: yeast eats sugars, burps out carbon dioxide

---

91 The yeast "W34/70" originally came from Hasen-Bräu, a brewery in Augsburg, Bavaria.

92 Here's something else I learned from Dr Zarnkow: ale yeast stops working at 40°C (104°F), whereas lager yeast stops at 37°C. That would seem a pretty small difference, but it's an important one: the human body is around 37°C (98°F), so in an unfiltered lager the yeast becomes inactive in your belly, whereas an ale yeast can remain alive, potentially continuing to ferment. This adds – or added in the case of bright, filtered beers – to the drinkability of a lager, which perhaps helped its success.

bubbles, pees alcohol and poops a load of weird stuff.[93] Give the yeast long enough, though, and it'll mop up the crap and leave a cleaner beer. But what if the yeast never pooped in the first place?

In front of the original Carlsberg Laboratory in Copenhagen is a copper statue of J. C. Jacobsen that has turned green with old age. He hooks his right hand into the chest pocket of his waistcoat and stares off into the distance. Behind him, the building looks like an old Victorian school house with *Carlsberg Laboratorium* in golden letters at the top.

I'm here to meet Birgitte Skadhauge, Vice-President of Carlsberg Research Laboratory; Erik Lund, head brewer at the Research Centre; and Zoran Gojkovic, Director of Brewing Science and Technology. Birgitte and Erik, both in a shirt and white lab coat, share a quiet, considered and scientific approach. Zoran wears a T-shirt depicting "Beer is Good but Beers are Better" written on a bottle top, and speaks in colourful analogies. Together they are leading one of the world's most important brewing laboratories. Throughout the research of this book there's been one question I've wanted the answer to, so I ask them.

How did we go from it taking six months to make a lager to being able to do it in under two weeks?

At exactly the same time all three of them say: "Yeast."

Since the era of Emil Christian Hansen, Carlsberg have been collecting yeast, filling frozen vaults with as many as 40,000 different strains, and in 1934 they had a major scientific breakthrough when Øjvind Winge, then the Director of the Laboratory's Department of Physiology, developed a technique for breeding yeast. Prior to this, scientists thought yeast could only be grown, but now they were able to breed specific characteristics into or out of their beer.[94] Breeding "was a revolution in optimizing yeast", says Zoran.

One of the flavour compounds a brewery wants to avoid in lager is known as diacetyl. It's a buttery aroma and flavour given out by the yeast during fermentation, leaving a slick kind of mouthfeel that takes away from the essential crispness of a lager.[95]

---

93 The "weird stuff" is actually natural compounds with a wide range of different flavours and aromas, not all of them good in your glass: eggy sulphur, appley acetaldehyde, clovey phenols, bananary esters, buttery diacetyl.

94 Later they were able to sequence the yeast's genome and then transfer DNA from one yeast to another. With this they created the ability to make genetically modified yeast, though as a company they made the decision not to take any GM-yeast into production.

95 Diacetyl can be tasted at 0.1 parts per million: it'd be like being able to taste one teaspoon of salt in 5,000 litres of water. Diacetyl is one of those flavours some people are "blind" to, meaning even if it's unquestionably present they cannot taste it. Of those who can taste it, some like it while others do not.

"In the good old days it took one year to get rid of [diacetyl], because yeast will make a lot and then slowly eat, eat, eat, until it's gone," says Zoran. It requires a chemical reaction to remove it, and at a very low temperature that takes a long time, so the long lagering period was necessary. But, says Erik, "We don't see a flavour benefit of keeping a beer for six to nine months.

"We have tried to find yeast strains which are not producing so much diacetyl," he goes on, "and if they do they are faster picking it up. And we have also increased the temperature tolerance, so instead of fermenting at 6–7 degrees, we're doing it somewhat higher, which helps." (Lager brewers elsewhere will do a "diacetyl rest" where in the final day or two of fermentation they increase the temperature, which kicks the yeast into extra action and encourages it to metabolize the diacetyl – old Bavarian brewers weren't able to add a few degrees to their cellars, so they just had to wait longer for it to naturally go away.)

Carlsberg were able to isolate the diacetyl-producing DNA and remove it from their yeast, while it was also made to work well at a warmer temperature, speeding up the process. By doing this Carlsberg have been able to breed the lagering out of lager, overall creating "a cleaner, crisper-tasting beer", says Erik, and a beer that can be made in "one to two weeks".

Alongside the yeast, Carlsberg's research focus has been on the other raw ingredients of brewing, and in 2017 this led them to unlock the full genome sequence for barley, revealing its full DNA. It took over ten years and involved many international scientists, and the benefits include the ability to develop barley strains resistant to diseases or climate changes; growing barley in more extreme conditions, or with less intensive farming; and breeding strains that contain better nutrients for human or animal consumption. This has enabled scientists to study every individual barley gene and how it might have an impact at any stage in the process, from barley field to malthouse to brewhouse to bottle of beer.

One of the most important discoveries in the genome were the "Lox" enzymes. These are involved in degrading fat in the barley when malting: when those (fatty) lipids oxidize with age they produce a papery flavour – if you've ever found an old can of lager in the back of the cupboard and opened it then you probably tasted something drying and paper-like. When the Lox enzyme isn't there, the fat isn't degraded (the fat would also give foam-negative components, so without the Lox there's better foam stability). "Simply by reducing or eliminating one enzyme activity," and "through completely traditional breeding," Carlsberg's scientists and brewers have been able to keep the beer fresh for a longer time – "up to 75 per cent longer". With beer that might travel a long way, or potentially sit on shelves for weeks or months, this is a significant development. The base "Null-Lox" barley is now being bred further to look for other positive impacts (one variant they've bred requires less water in the field, for example, and then less time and heat energy in the malting process).

They don't just look to the future. In 2016 a few very old bottles of JC-era Carlsberg were discovered deep in the brewery cellars. Birgitte applied to the Carlsberg Foundation, which still oversees the brewery, for some funds to analyze the yeast, and they set out to try to brew an old style of Carlsberg beer, using grain similar to that of the 1880s, the old brewing processes and the original yeast.

That beer brought back from the cellars has since been modernized for today's drinkers and is now sold in Denmark as 1883. It's toasty and bready, like the old beer might have been, but finishes light and dry, a modern update. It's not easy for a big brewery to introduce a brown lager to yellow beer drinkers, but it's been very successful.

Having genome-sequenced yeast and barley, the Carlsberg team will now turn their attention to hops. As well as breeding yeast, Øjvind Winge bred hops designed specifically for Denmark, a country too far north to naturally have reliable hop harvests. This research will work alongside hop research all around the world, which is constantly looking for new varieties with interesting aromas, flavours and agronomic qualities.

Carlsberg are acutely aware of their place within the world and the need to secure a better future for the planet. "If we're to be here for another 170 years," says Simon Boas Hoffmeyer, Carlsberg's Director of Sustainability, "which big decisions do we need to make *now*? What would JC have done? We think he'd be a burning environmentalist if he were alive today, and he'd want to act on it. The Foundation was Sustainability 1.0 of its time." Brewers are completely reliant on the natural world for their ingredients, Simon explains, so "if the world isn't working we won't be able to sell beer."

A priority is Towards Zero, a programme aimed at achieving a zero carbon footprint, zero water waste, zero irresponsible drinking and zero accidents. It's not just a top-down dream: the culture has to be pervasive in all breweries. Since 2015 Carlsberg have reduced water consumption by 9 per cent, and have done trials of brewing with waste water. All their western European breweries are using renewable electricity, and almost half their overall energy use across the world is renewable; they are reducing plastic waste, introducing a six-pack held together by glue instead of the plastic rings, and they're working on a bio-degradable beer bottle made with wood fibre: "We don't know how to do it, but we're going to do it," says Simon. Selling in over 150 countries requires different local solutions, and affects the entire supply chain all the way back to the field.[96]

---

96 Will Carlsberg be the beer young and informed drinkers turn to when they're looking for a more sustainable product? They are certainly better on an environmental level than, say, the small craft brewery in your town.

One of Carlsberg's Towards Zero goals is for no irresponsible drinking, and alcohol-free beer is something every major brewer is looking at as more people are moving away from alcohol or reducing their consumption. Alcohol-free beer[97] opens up the possibility of new drinking occasions (at breakfast or your desk at work, for example), of putting beer back on the lunch table (at Carlsberg's Copenhagen head office, staff are encouraged to have an alcohol-free beer with lunch), and giving people who can't or don't want to drink alcohol an option in the evening. Previously a maligned category, it's now growing in variety and quality, and there's a suggestion that alcohol-free beer could be seen as a new kind of soft drink.

There's another kind of alcohol-free beer that might have its moment in the coming years: cannabis beer. Not some novelty light lager with hemp seeds or flavourings in; this is alcohol-free beer with added THC (that's tetrahydrocannabinol, the psychoactive cannabis compound that gets you high). While still small-scale and limited to American states where marijuana has been legalized, these new drinks might appeal to a drinker looking for a different kind of high. There's even THC-infused hopped soda, made by Lagunitas Brewing Co., which is alcohol-free, carb-free and calorie-free, adding an additional body-consciousness to the offer. Who knows whether these drinks will challenge beer, but with weed legalized in some of America's most prominent craft beer states (Colorado, Vermont and all up the west coast), it's a new liquid option on the shelf.

And there's research into a synthetic-alcohol substance that recreates the good feelings of drinking alcohol (sociability and relaxation) without the bad ones (hangovers and health issues). We've seen the functional benefits that come with the composite beers of Japan, so perhaps here's another area of growth.

In the Carlsberg laboratory I asked what the three scientists thought was the future for lager.

"No question, we think it will be there," said Zoran. "There is no other style that came from the beginning and took over the world; two hundred years of lager and eighty per cent of the market." The trouble, he thinks, is that there is no respect for lager: the price has been driven so low, and it's such an accessible commodity, that people don't see it as special any more. "If you have a bottle of Dom Perignon for €1 then people will love it but they will not respect it."

---

97 There are two ways to make alcohol-free beer. One is to restrict the brewing process, using fewer ingredients and chilling down the yeast, making it inactive before it's converted sugars into alcohol. The other is to produce a regular beer and then take the alcohol out. Since alcohol boils at a lower temperature than water (78°C/173°F), by heating it and holding the beer at that temperature the alcohol can be boiled out. Another way to remove alcohol is to use reverse osmosis, effectively filtering the booze out.

Birgitte, Erik and Zoran all think there will be more variety, both within the lager category and around it. And maybe it's craft beer that has the best chance of celebrating greatness and diversity in lager.

CRAFT BEER DOES LAGER: RENEWING OLD TRADITIONS AND MAKING NEW RULES

Big breweries basically ruined lager for a lot of people. To most American drinkers, lager means Bud-Miller-Coors, and craft beer became the antithesis of them. Lager was what craft beer drinkers rejected when they started buying flavoursome, impactful IPAs and other styles. This meant that for a while "lager" became a kind of beery swear word, but recently craft beer has gone so far in the opposite direction in trying to distance itself from lager that it's alienated a lot of drinkers, while at the same time more and more brewers want to make better versions of classic lager styles.

"We're a three-malt, two-hop and one-yeast brewery, and we make beer-flavoured beer," says Ashleigh Carter, co-founder and brewer of Bierstadt Lagerhaus in Denver, Colorado. Ashleigh explains that she and Bill Eye, the other co-founder and brewer, wanted to build a place "to make lager and lager only". So they borrowed money from her dad and went to Germany, where they found a brewhouse that was still being used, meaning they knew it still worked. They took as many photos and notes as possible, dismantled it, and packed it into crates and shipped it to Denver.

It's a handsome old Bavarian brewery built in 1932. It has two main copper vessels, which you can see from the brewery's taproom, and it's the brewhouse equivalent of a classic car. "It's really fucking cool and I love it!" says Ashleigh.

"We are as slow and traditional as we can be," she says, explaining that it takes three brews to fill one fermentation tank, and that those back-to-back-to-back brews take 26 hours, which Ashleigh and Bill do straight through – much of that time is because they use a traditional decoction mash which alone takes over three hours, but it gives the beers an intangible and special malt flavour.

The beer will ferment for two weeks at 47.5°F/8.5°C before moving into a squat cylindrical lagering tank (shaped like an old wooden barrel) for a min-imum of eight weeks, far longer than most lagers brewed today. "I think lager is like sandpaper," says Ashleigh: "the longer you leave it, the smoother it gets." The horizontal vessel helps the yeast to settle out and leave a clearer beer, yet despite that, they still filter the beer, just as you'd find in Munich. "I think of unfiltered beer like cookies and cookie dough," she says: "I love cookie dough but I can eat, like, forty-five cookies. I prefer the finished beer."

Using just Pilsner malt, Munich malt, Vienna malt, plus Mittelfrüh and Hallertauer Tradition hops, and their lager yeast, they make three year-round lagers – a Pilsner, a Helles and a Dunkel. "Pils should be about the finest hops. It should be just enough that you want to take another sip without it being too much." The beer is called Slow Pour Pils, and gets its name because it takes five minutes to pour a glass. While you sit at the bar, the beer is crashed into the glass, creating lots of foam. As the foam drops, the beer is topped up, gradually building it up, knocking out carbonation, meaning by the time you get the beer it's a tall, lean glass of gold with a thick, tall, blooming white foam on top. It's beautiful – in appearance and taste. "I like to think it's one of the most photographed beers in America."

"Helles walks the line between bland and sublime," says Ashleigh. "It's the perfection of malt. You can't understand it until you've had two half-litres and then you realize you want another one." It's malty without being sweet, complex with the decoction mash steps, then the kind of balance that means it's almost impossible to stop drinking it.

My favourite is their Dunkel. "It's my least favourite of our beers . . . I love it!" says the bartender when I return to the brewery later that night. It's copper-coloured with a thick foam on top, and it's nutty, toasty and deeply satisfying. I only popped in for one quick beer and I've ended up drinking a Pils, a Helles and two Dunkels. In many ways these *are* just "beer-flavoured beers" in that they're recognisable to all drinkers and have a simplicity about them, but they are also some of the most considered, complex and exceptional lagers I've tasted anywhere in the world.

"There's a craft lager resurgence," says David Deline of Denver's Prost Brewing, who have been making lagers since 2012 using a German copper kettle built in 1963 – it's another very attractive old brewhouse. David talks about the current craft beer market as being a "Rotation Nation": always seeking something new – the latest one-off release, the next big style, another IPA or sour beer. "Lager is about continuity and consistency. This is a tribute to five hundred years of lager brewing."

At Prost they make authentic versions of traditional styles with a Pilsner, Helles, Dunkel, Märzen, Doppelbock and more, plus some German-style beers. "There's no reason that lager has to be this diluted beer. People are learning that you can get a high-quality lager with complexity." They want the flavour but also the easy drinkability of a lager: "We're that middle ground between macro and IPA – craft yet approachable," says David.

In Chicago, I stand in front of yet another good-looking old copper Bavarian brewing vessel. This one is in Dovetail Brewery, and was built for the Weihenstephan brewery in 1905. "It was cut in half, and we were silly enough to buy both halves not knowing if we could put it back together again," says brewery co-founder Bill Wesselink. He and Hagen Dost met over a "slaughter plate" in Weisses Brauhaus, Munich, while they were studying brewing (that's the bar that used to be Mäderbräu where the Munich Beer Riot started).

Alongside the old tank they have had a bespoke vessel built for their decoction mash and they use the Weihenstephan copper as a holding tank. "I like making beer a certain way," says Bill: their kettle is direct-fired from below; they use a cooling tray to cool the beers, something very rare in modern breweries; they have open fermenters (just as lager used to be fermented in big open-topped wooden vessels); and they lager their beer for a minimum of five weeks in big yellow horizontal tanks. It's a traditional – even old-fashioned – way of making lager.

"Lager is the beer we dream about. If we had only one beer to drink, this has got to be that beer," Bill says of their flagship beer, called simply Lager. It's a beer *I* dream about now, too, along with all their other beers: a Czech-style Pilsner, a Helles, a Vienna lager, a Dunkel. The beers are so deeply interesting to drink and yet they don't arrest your attention and distract you from things like talking to friends, and you can drink a few without falling off your bar stool. They are balanced in every way.

I'm fascinated by how Dovetail, Bierstadt and Prost are using old brewing equipment and processes, the kinds of equipment and processes that had been phased out with the modernizing of the brewing industry, and concentrating on classic lager types. Maybe it's my lager-loving romanticism, but they have an elusive greatness about them, a depth of deliciousness rarely found in any mainstream lager or even craft-brewed ale.

****

To most drinkers, lager is essentially one kind of beer. One flavour, if you like. But near Boston, there's a brewery showing the world just how varied lager can be. "People would come into the taproom and say, 'I don't like lager' before even trying anything," says Jack Hendler of Jack's Abby in Framingham, Massachusetts, who have been brewing since 2011. "What is people's perception of lager? Is it just light, fizzy beer? I love light, fizzy beer, but lager isn't a *style* of beer, it's a category." The brewers and taproom staff would give tasters to people, and "it was really rewarding seeing people coming with a negative attitude and leaving saying, 'Wow, I didn't know you could do that!'"

In some ways, even Jack didn't know what could be done with lager, and didn't expect to be a lager-only brewery: "We didn't have money to buy an ale yeast so we just kept on brewing lager," he says. "I wanted to brew ales, but after four months we'd solidified this reputation for brewing great, creative lagers, and we wanted to see where that could take us." Jack's Abby have since made over 100 different kinds of lager.

When I'm there in May 2018 there are 20 on tap, including classic lagers like their House Lager, some hazy *Kellerbiers*, a bitter German-style Pilsner, a smooth toasty Vienna lager, a couple of dark lagers, a *Rauchbier* smoked lager. Then there's the lagers more aligned to American craft beer: a blood-orange wheat-based lager that has become the taproom's top-seller; there are sour lagers and strong ones aged in old bourbon barrels, sucking up a vanilla and bourbon flavour from the wood; and there's Hoponius Union, which is a lagered version of an IPA that's strong, bitter and bold with citrusy hops.

"IPA is king, and we knew we needed to have a hoppy beer, but we didn't have ale yeast, so we racked our brains about how to make it," says Jack. Hoponius Union is probably the beer they're best known for and, while Jack's reluctant to say they invented the style, they certainly did more than any other brewery to turn lagered IPA, or India Pale Lager (IPL), into a category. For me, the joy of their IPLs is that they maintain the essential balance of a great lager but are bursting with bright hop flavour, and because of that cold fermentation and maturation it is smoother, sharper and cleaner than a lot of IPAs.

If Jack's Abby made ales instead of lager "we'd double our capacity, but it's just great to be able to get a beer like this at the end of the day," he says of their House Lager. "You almost have to travel to Germany to get beer like this." But what do Germans think when they visit? "Germans don't know what to make of us," laughs Jack. "On one level they're intrigued, on another level they're appalled!"

****

I've just been handed the best-looking beer that I've ever seen. The glass is small, straight with a slight curve at the top. The beer is lemon yellow, lightly hazy; the foam on top is so thick and so smooth that I just want to lick it like an ice cream. In many ways it looks like a regular glass of lager, but there's something just unquantifiably *better* about it.

"When you get a beer that looks like this chances are it's been brewed, fermented and cellared really well," says Dan Suarez, who runs Suarez Family Brewery, a "mom-and-pop production brewery" in upstate New York, with his wife Taylor.

I drink the beer in seconds and need another right away. It takes a min-ute or two to pour it, in which time I literally feel my mouth watering. Most breweries I've visited while writing this book are huge international factories, making millions of pints a day, but it's beer like this that excites me. Palatine Pils, the brewery's main lager and the one I'm drinking, has a sharp precision of flavour and a rare brightness and brilliance; it's like seeing the world through new glasses when previously it's all been a bit blurry.

Dan describes that beer as an unfiltered classic German Pils. "It's striving for something classic, but I went to Germany and came back and tasted our lagers and was like, 'These don't taste anything like those lagers!' But I wouldn't call them modern, either. It's not an adjunct brew or new-school hops."

I sit in the taproom and drink a few beers. It's a sparse Scandinavian-styled space with white walls, huge windows looking out to green fields, wooden benches lined up convivially. It's open, it's welcoming, it's understandable and understated. In so many places in America – bars and brewery taprooms – you find 30 taps and 15 big screens tuned to several different sports with music overlaying everything. It's overwhelming, disconnecting, and somehow reflects the short attention span of America and of craft beer in general: the neon lights and knock-out hops, the big screens, the dozen burgers and too much choice on tap, like a restaurant that serves pizza *and* noodles *and* curry *and* fine patisserie. At Suarez Family it's a stripped-back simplicity, which belies the extraordinary complexity of the beers and the warmth of the brewery. They've reinvented lager but not turned it into something different or unique or esoteric; they've just made lager better.

To most craft beer drinkers, lager is the thing they turned their back on when they chose to have an IPA. But that undermines the huge possibilities of lager. Lager can be a canvas for creativity, whether that's a progression on the classics or something completely new. The complementation between old and new means that lager can now be the most varied and exciting type of beer as well as the most prevalent.

AMERICAN *GEMÜTLICHKEIT*, NEW OLD RECIPES, A TUBA AND A KIND OF EPILOGUE

What did Gabriel Sedlmayr's Munich lager taste like in the 1830s? How was that first glass of Pilsner Urquell in 1842? What were American lagers like in the 1860s, and then how did they change in the 1880s and then in the years before and after Prohibition? These are questions no amount of recipe-reading or speculation could answer. But then I heard about an event called Lagerfest.

Held at Urban Chestnut Brewing in St Louis, Lagerfest features around twenty breweries (including Bierstadt Lagerhaus and Dovetail), each pouring one or two lagers based on historic American, German and British recipes.

I start with what's called 1910 St Louis Lager – it's basically Budweiser's recipe and is brewed by the host brewery, which is run by Florian Kuplent, a German brewer who worked for Anheuser-Busch before moving across town to open a lager brewery and German-style beer hall. On a Sunday in April, the beer hall is full, there's German music playing, people drink lagers and eat German-style food, and it's wonderful.

As for the beer, how different do you think Budweiser is today compared to 100 years ago? Do you think old-fashioned beer would admit a halcyon glow, or would it taste sweet and rich? Imagine a burger joint wanted to create a tribute to the Big Mac: a legit copy of the burger, just better-tasting. Well, this beer is like that: a more interesting and complex version of Bud. It's excellent.

There's a Munich *Bockbier* based on a recipe from 1866, which is sweet and then roasty with malt. A 1896 lager recipe uses just Munich malts, like the one Gabriel Sedlmayr pioneered, and it's a bright chestnut colour with a deep toasty brown bread flavour – Munich beer was commonly made with just this malt for a long time, so it's fascinating to get an idea of what it might have been like (even if the old Munich version would've been much sweeter). Dovetail has brewed a Bohemian Pilsner from 1870, and it tastes much like Pilsner Urquell, with a satisfying richness and bitter-sweetness. There are two recipes from London's Barclay Perkins, one from 1930 and the other from 1939, and they're golden and ale-like with some fruity hops.

This is the closest I'll get to trying those old lagers. It's impossible to know just how similar these attempts are, especially with modern processes, techniques, equipment and yeast, but they are a reflection and a sip of history.

Bierstadt Lagerhaus have also brewed the recipe for a 1910 St Louis Lager. I take a large glass – because the best lagers should be drunk from large glasses – and then sit in the beer hall to get a few minutes to myself, have a snack, listen to the music, take the whole event in and write some notes. But I'm immediately distracted.

The band have been playing for a while now, although I've been too absorbed in the beer and chatting to people to pay attention to the music,which is something like upbeat brass-band. As soon as I do listen and look up I'm transfixed by the tuba player. He has thick, luscious, long hair, tousled with sweat. He's wearing lederhosen, showing off thick quads and the kinds of calves of some-one who only runs up really steep hills. He's athletically playing high-tempo party-polka punk covers on a tuba, which is a magnificent instrument, perhaps the *most magnificent* instrument I've ever seen, and while he's playing it he's gulping golden lager from a litre glass. Yes, while he's *playing a massive and magnificent tuba* he's drinking a stein of beer.[98]

Alongside this effigy of testosterone dancing with the great golden beast of a tuba is a bloke playing the drums and another singing while playing an accordion. Together they're making an enormously entertaining sound with their Teutonic covers of American songs alternated with drinking songs, like *Ein Prosit* (an especially popular song is "You Are My Beer Stein", which they sing to the tune of "You Are My Sunshine"). This is exactly the kind of music I want to listen to in a big beer hall while I'm drinking great lager, and the sort of music that gets more fun the more you drink, and all through the beer hall people are singing and dancing along. When the band's set ends everyone stands and cheers, and when I next look up my emasculation is confirmed as the tuba player has unbuttoned his shirt and his sweat-glazed chest is chiselled like a Roman emperor's.

As I sit here in a German-American brewery in one of the most German-American of cities listening to German-American music, I eat a big American version of a traditional German pretzel and drink a modern re-creation of the most famous old German-American beer. After a few darker, richer and heavier lagers earlier, I wanted this lighter, fresher beer, and it's easy to see how pale, bright, golden lager was able to change the beer market in America and then the rest of the world: it's pleasing to drink, easy to drink, refreshingly dry, and I want to drink glass after glass of it.

Lager has changed a lot over the last 500 years, and it's changed a lot since Budweiser was first brewed in 1876. But it hasn't changed *that* much. In this beer hall I can see everyone from toddlers to retirees sitting at long communal benches. Most adults have half-litres of lager, some have full litres, while others sip from smaller glasses, wanting to try as many of the historic lagers as possible. People drink, eat, chat, laugh.

This is American *Gemutlichkeit*, and it's just the same as the German one, even if it might be a bit louder and have more tuba than most American bars. There's a suggestion of Old St Louis, where Germans and Americans (and Brits and the Irish and Italians and everyone else) came together in a new way, out of the dark bars and into the bright beer halls. It's Sunday afternoon, and the same Sunday afternoon in St Louis 140 years ago might have been similar to this – glasses of fresh beer, music, families, food. And all around the world people are doing the same: sharing food and glasses of cold lager with friends and family in their own local way.

---

98 I've just done an online search for the band to make sure it wasn't just beer goggles, and there's a video of the tuba player crowd-surfing while still playing. Crowd-surfing with a tuba. Incredible. They're called the Bolzen Beer Band, by the way.

There's a wonderful universality to lager. It's an equalizer, a sympathizer, a simplifier, a friend (and sometimes a foe). It's a way to belong and a way to escape. It can warm us up and cool us down, inspire and incite, help us talk and let us listen better. It creates friendships and it fortifies them.

The constant evolution of lager has marked its more-than-500-year lifespan. Beyond the empirical understanding that laid the foundations of lager, the combination of brewing science, technological invention, agricultural advances and liquid engineering have long been coming together in practical ways to give new processes, equipment or ingredients. It's that perpetual forward momentum, driven by whatever greater purpose – quality, cost, efficiency, speed, sustainability, innovation – that is always seeing lager progress.

Lager – and beer in general – is something people have strong feelings about. We're emotionally connected to some and instantly dismissive of others; we have our favourites and we have those we'd never buy. And whether mainstream lager is the beer you drink all the time, or whether you pick classic Pilsners or Munich-brewed *Helles*, or even if lager is something that you rarely buy, preferring wheat beers or IPAs or stouts, then it's hard to deny the pleasure that comes in the consistent, knowable reliability that comes with simple, accessible lager. More than preference or prejudice, lager shouldn't be a divisive drink because as it spread and became the world's local beer, it became the liquid that we were most likely to share socially with others. *Let's go for a beer. Do you fancy a pint?* It means more than simply drinking. And beer has always been more than just a drink. Today it continues to evolve, but there are many things about it that will never change.

BIBLIOGRAPHY AND REFERENCES

Abrams, Lynn. *Workers' Culture in Imperial Germany: Leisure and Recreation in the Rhineland and Westphalia*. Routledge. London. 2002.

Aerts, Erik, et al (Eds) *Production, Marketing and Consumption of Alcoholic Beverages since the Late Middle Ages*. Leuven University Press. Leuven. 1990.

Alberts, Brian. "Beer To Stay: Brewed Culture, Ethnicity, and The Market Revolution" Doctoral Thesis. Purdue University. May 2018.

Alexander, Jeffrey W. *Brewed in Japan: The Evolution of the Japanese Beer Industry*. University of Hawaii Press. Honolulu. 2014.

von Altenbockum, Annette. *The Munich Hofbrauhaus. The Place, the Beer, and Other Articles of Faith*. Prestel Verlag. Munich. 2008.

American Beer: Glimpses of Its History and Description of Its Manufacture. United States Brewers' Association. New York. 1909.

Anderson, Ray. "The Transformation of Brewing: An Overview of Three Centuries of Science and Practice." *Brewery History Society* 121. p. 5–24. 2005.

Appel, Susan K. "Artificial Refrigeration and the Architecture of 19th-Century American Breweries." *The Journal of the Society for Industrial Archeology*, Vol. 16, No. 1. p. 21–38. 1990.

Arthur, John W. "Beer through the Ages: The Role of Beer in Shaping Our Past and Current Worlds." 29 September 2014. Online: http://anthronow.com/print/beer-through-the-ages-the-role-of-beer-in-shaping-our-past-and-current-worlds

Austin, Gregory A. *Alcohol in Western Society from Antiquity to 1800: A Chronological History*. ABC-Clio. Santa Barbara. 1985.

Bamforth, Charles W. "A History of Brewing Science in the United States of America." *Brewery History Society* 121. p. 81–93. 2005.

Barbour, Neil. *The Arup Journal*. December 1979. Carlsberg Brewery. Northampton. 1979.

Baron, Stanley. *Brewed in America*. Little, Brown and Company. Boston. 1962.

Barrows, Susanna and Robin Room (ed). *Drinking Behavior and Belief in Modern History. University of California Press*. Berkeley. 1991.

Behringer, Wolfgang: *Die Spaten-Brauerei 1397–1997. Die Geschichte eines Münchner Unternehmens vom Mittelalter bis zur Gegenwart.* Piper. München. 1997.

Benbow, Mark. "German Immigrants in the United States Brewing Industry (1840–1895)." 1 Feb 2017. Online: https://www.immigrantentrepreneurship.org/entry.php?rec=284

Bjerager, Anna-Lise. *The People's Brewer*. Gyldendal. Copenhagen. 2011.

Boak, Jessica & Ray Bailey. *Gambrinus Waltz*. Kindle Edition. 2014.

Boak, Jessica & Ray Bailey. *Brew Britannia: The Strange Rebirth of British Beer*. Aurum Press. London. 2014.

Booth, David. *The Art of Brewing*. 2nd Edition. London. 1834. Online: https://play.google.com/books/reader?id=9xgZAAAAYAAJ&pg=GBS.PP7

Bowden, Sue and Avner Offer. "Household appliances and the use of time: the United States and Britain since the 1920s." *Economic History Review*, XLVII. p. 725–748. 1999.

Brignone, Daniela (trans Christopher Evans). *Birra Peroni: 1846–1996. A Hundred and Fifty Years of Italian Beer*. Electa. 1995.

Brown, Pete. *Man Walks Into a Pub: A Sociable History of Beer*. Pan Books. London. 2010.

Bryson, Bill. *At Home: A Short History of Private Life*. Doubleday. London. 2010.

Butler, R. H. *Brewing in North America. A Record of a Visit to American and Canadian Breweries*, 1947. Mitchells and Butlers. Cape Hill. 1947.

Carlsberg Archives Online: http://carlsbergarchive.com/jacobsenfamily/Pages/Notes.aspx

Carpenter, Kim Newak. "'Sechs Kreuzer Sind Genug Für Ein Bier!' The Munich Beer Riot of 1844: Social Protest and Public Disorder in Mid-19th Century Bavaria." Phd Georgetown University. 1998.

Carpenter, Kim. "'We demand good and healthy beer!' The nutritional and social significance of beer for the lower classes in mid-nineteenth-century Munich." In

Cowan, Alexander and Steward, Jill. *The City and the Senses: Urban Culture Since 1500*. Ashgate. Farnham. 2007.

Christensen, Jens. "Consolidating the Global Brewery Industry, 1992-2012." *Brewery History Society*, Issue 157. p. 20–44. 2014.

Corran, H.S. *A History of Brewing*. David & Charles. London. 1975.

Cornell, Martyn. *Beer: The Story of the Pint*. Headline. London. 2004.

Cornell, Martyn. *Amber, Gold and Black*. The History Press. Stroud. 2010.

Cornell, Martyn. Twitter update 28 April 2019: https://twitter.com/zythophiliac/status/1122599997411921921

Cowan, Ruth Schwartz. *A Social History of American Technology*. Oxford University Press. Oxford. 1997.

Cuervo-Cazurra, Alvaro (ed). *Mexican Multinationals: Building Multinationals in Emerging Markets*. Cambridge University Press. Cambridge. 2018.

Dare, Robert (ed). *Food, Power and Community*. Wakefield Press. Kent Town. 1999.

De Baets, Yvan. Lagers in Belgium – a short history. Personal notes from author. 2019.

Davidson, Eloise. Beer in the American Home. Published by United Brewers Industrial Foundation. 1937.

Dering, Florian and Ursula Eymold. *Das Oktoberfest: 1810–2010*. Munchner Stadtmuseum. Munich. 2010.

Doward, William L. *Dictionary of the History of the American Brewing and Distilling Industries*. Greenwood Press. Westport. 1980.

Dunstan, Keith. *The Amber Nectar: A Celebration of Beer and Brewing in Australia*. Viking O'Neil. 1987.

Engels, Frederick. *The Northern Star*. No.341, May 25, 1884, first written mid-May 1844. Available: https://www.marxists.org/history/etol/revhist/otherdox/beerriot.htm

Fischer, Claude S. *Made in America*. University of Chicago Press. Chicago. 2010.

Fleming, Alice. *Alcohol: The Delightful Poison*. Delacorte Press. New York. 1975.

Francks, Penelope. *The Japanese Consumer*. Cambridge University Press. Cambridge. 2009.

Gaab, Jeffrey S. *Munich: Hofbräuhaus & History – Beer, Culture, & Politics.* Peter Lang. New York. 2006.

Gantz, Carroll. *Refrigeration: A History.* McFarland & Co. Jefferson. 2015.

Garavaglia, Christian and Johan Swinnen. Ed. *Economic Perspectives on Craft Beer: A Revolution in the Global Beer Industry.* Springer International. Cham. 2018.

Gately, Iain. *Drink: A Cultural History of Alcohol.* Gotham Books. New York. 2008.

Glamann, Kristof (translated by Geoffrey French). *Jacobsen of Carlsberg: Brewer and Philanthropist.* Gyldendal. Copenhagen. 1991.

Glamann, Kristof and Kirsten Glamann (translated by Geoffrey French). *The Story of Emil Christian Hansen.* The Carlsberg Foundation. Copenhagen. 2009.

Gourvish, T.R. and R.G. Wilson. *The British Brewing Industry 1830–1980.* Cambridge University Press. Cambridge. 1994.

Hardwick, William A. (Ed) *Handbook of Brewing.* Marcel Dekker. New York. 1995.

Hawes, James. *The Shortest History of Germany.* Kindle Edition. 2017.

Heineken Archives Online: https://www.heinekencollection.com

Heineken History. Heineken N.V. Amsterdam. 1992.

Herbst, Henry, *et al. St. Louis Brews: The History of Brewing in the Gateway City.* Reedy Press. St. Louis. 2015.

Holian, Timothy J. "The Hudepohl Brewing Company of Cincinnati, Ohio: a case study in regional brewery prosperity and decline." *Brewery History Society,* Issue 141. p. 12–53. 2011.

Holt, Mack P. (ed). *Alcohol: A Social and Cultural History.* Berg. London. 2006.

Hornsey, Ian S. *A History of Beer and Brewing.* Royal Society of Chemistry. Padstow. 2003.

Hornsey, Ian S. "Of Spaten and Sedlmayrs." *The Brewer and Distiller International.* December 2007.

Iverson, Martin. *Mapping European Corporations: Strategy, Structure, Ownership and Performance.* Ed. Andrea Colli et al. New York. 2012.

Jackson, Michael. *Beer Companion.* Michell Beazley. London. 1993.

Jalowetz, Prof. Eduard. *Pilsner Beer in the Light of Practice and Science.* Pilsner Urquell. 2001.

Jennings, Paul. *The Local: A History of the English Pub.* Tempus. Stroud. 2007.

Journal of the Society of Chemical Industry 16, no. 4 (1897)

Kamman, Michael. *American Culture, American Tastes.* Alfred A. Knopf. New York. 1999. Digital.

Kapilevich, Ami. "The Beers of Southern Africa." *All About Beer Magazine.* Vol 22, Issue 5. 1 November 2001. Online: http://allaboutbeer.com/article/the-beers-of-southern-africa/

Kejha, Josef, *et al. Plzensky Prazdroj: A Story That Continues to Inspire.* Nava. Prague. 2012.

Kellenbenz, Hermann. "Shipping and Trade between Hamburg-Bremen and the Indian Ocean, 1870–1914." *Journal of Southeast Asian Studies* 13, no. 2. p. 355-358. 1982.

Krennmair, Andreas. *Historic German and Austrian Beers for the Home Brewer.* Kindle Edition.

Kümin, Beat and B. Ann Tlusty (Ed). *The World of the Tavern: Public Houses in Early Modern Europe.* Ashgate Publishing. Aldershot. 2002.

Lang, Johannes. "The Reichenhaller Reinheitsgebot of 1493." Online: https://braumagazin.de/article/das-reichenhaller-reinheitsgebot-von-1493/

Lockhart, Bill. "The Origins and Life of the Export Beer Bottle." *Bottles and Extras.* 2007. Online: https://sha.org/bottle/pdffiles/ExportBeerBottles_BLockhart.pdf

McGovern, Patrick E. *Uncorking the Past: The Quest for Wine, Beer, and other Alcoholic Beverages.* University of California Press. Berkeley. 2009.

Meussdoerffer, Franz G. "A Comprehensive History of Beer Brewing" in Hans Michael Eßlinger (Ed.) *Handbook of Brewing: Processes, Technology, Markets.* Wiley VCH. Darmstadt. 2009.

Meussdoerffer, Franz. "Beer and Beer Culture in Germany" in Wulf Schiefenhövel and Helen Macbeth (Ed.) *Liquid Bread: Beer and Brewing in Cross-Cultural Perspective.* 2011.

Miller, Carl. *The Rise of the Beer Barons.* 1999. Online: http://www.beerhistory.com/library/holdings/beerbarons.shtml

Mittelman, Amy. *Brewing Battles: A History of American Beer.* Algora. New York. 2008.

Mohl, Raymond A. (Ed.). *The Making of Urban America*. 2nd Edition. SR Books. Maryland. 1997.

Musisi, Moses. "Africa Goes Sorghum: Challenges and Opportunities." Online: http://www.ibdlearningzone.org.uk/article/show/pdf/242/

Nelson, Jon P. "Beer advertising and marketing update: structure, conduct, and social costs." 2004. Online: https://pdfs.semanticscholar.org/79ed/ e1c07fbb72d1815295cb2bab2c8771bf6a4f.pdf

Ogle, Maureen. *Ambitious Brew: The Story of American Beer*. Harcourt. Orlando. 2006.

Oliver, Garrett (Ed). *The Oxford Companion to Beer*. Oxford University Press. New York. 2012.

Patterson, Mark and Nancy Hoalst-Pullen (Ed.). *The Geography of Beer: Regions, Environment, and Societies*. Springer. 2014. Digital.

Pattinson, Ron. *Decoction!* 5th edition. Kindle Edition. 2011.

Pattinson, Ron. "Heineken's Early Lagers." *Beer Advocate*. July 2014. Online: https://www.beeradvocate.com/articles/9875/heinekens-early-lagers/

Pattinson, Ron. *Lager!* UK. 2nd edition. Kilderkin. Amsterdam. 2014.

Persons, Warren M. *Beer and Brewing in America: An Economic Study*. United Brewers Industrial Foundation. 1937.

Pursue Perfection. The Carlsberg Foundation. Copenhagen. 2014.

Persyn, Damiaan, Johan Swinnen and Stijn Vanormelingen. "Belgian Beers: Where History Meets Globalization." LICOS Discussion Paper Series 271/2010. Online: https://core.ac.uk/download/pdf/34488604.pdf

Phillips, Rod. *Alcohol: A History*. University of North Carolina Press. 2014.

Pilsner Urquell. *Citizens' Brewery in Pilsen*. Small book published by the brewery.

Plautz, Jason. "The Time 'Ten Cent Beer Night' Went Horribly Wrong." *Mental Floss*. 4 June 2015. Online: http://mentalfloss.com/article/30826/date-1974-clevelands-ten-cent-beer-night-went-horribly-wrong

Powers, Madelon. *Faces Along the Bar: Lore and Order in the Workingman's Saloon, 1870–1920*. University of Chicago Press. Chicago. 1998.

Pozen. Morris A. *Successful Brewing*. Brewery Age Publishing Company. New York. 1935.

Rail, Evan. "On The Founding Of Pilsner Urquell." *Brewery History Society Journal* 149. 2012. Online: http://www.breweryhistory.com/journal/archive/149/Rail.pdf

Roberts, James S. Drink, *Temperance and the Working Class in Nineteenth-Century Germany.* George Allen & Unwin. Boston. 1984.

Rorabaugh, W.J. *The Alcoholic Republic: An American Tradition.* Oxford University Press. Oxford. 1981.

Salem, F. W. *Beer: Its History and its Economic Value as a National Beverage.* F. W Salem. Hartford. 1880.

Schiefenhövel, Wulf and Helen Macbeth (Ed.). *Liquid Bread: Beer and Brewing in Cross-Cultural Perspective.* Berghahn. New York. 2011.

Schlüter, Hermann. *The Brewing Industry and the Brewery Workers' Movement in America. International Union of the United Brewery Workmen of America.* Cincinnati. 1910.

Scheufler, Pavel. *Pilsner Urquell: 1842–1982.* Severografia. Liberec. 1982

Sismondo, Christine. *America Walks Into A Bar.* Oxford University Press. 2011. Kindle Edition.

Smit, Barbara. *The Heineken Story.* Profile Books. London. 2014.

Stack, Martin and Myles Gartland. "The Rise of Packaged Beer and the Reordering of the US Brewing Industry." *Brewery History Society.* Issue 141. 2011. p. 102–127.

Stack, Martin. "Liquid Bread: An Examination of the American Brewing Industry, 1865 to 1940. Part I." *Brewery History Society.* Issue 154. p. 32–78. 2013.

Stack, Martin. "Liquid Bread: An Examination of the American Brewing Industry, 1865 to 1940. Part II." *Brewery History Society.* Issue 157. p. 47-89. 2014.

Stack, Martin. "Liquid Bread: An Examination of the American Brewing Industry, 1865 to 1940. Part III." *Brewery History Society.* Issue 159. p. 55–97. 2014.

Swinnen, Johan F. M (Ed.). *The Economics of Beer.* Oxford University Press. Oxford. 2011.

Swinnen, Johan and Devin Briski. *Beeronomics: How Beer Explains the World.* Oxford University Press. Oxford. 2017.

Teich, Mikuláš. "The Industrialisation of Brewing in Germany (1800–1914)" in Erik Aerts, Louis M. Cullen & Richard G. Wilson (Ed). *Production, Marketing and Consumption of Alcoholic Beverages since the Late Middle Ages.* 1990.

Thausing, Julius E. (translated by William T. Brannt). *The Theory and Practice of the Preparation of Malt and the Fabrication of Beer, with especial reference to the Vienna Process of Brewing.* Henry Carey Baird & Co. London. 1882.

The Beer That Changed The Way The World Sees Beer. Pilsner Urquell. Brewery publication. Undated.

Unger, Richard W. *Beer in the Middle Ages and the Renaissance.* University of Pennsylvania Press. Philadelphia. 2004.

Van der Hallen, Peter. "Concentration in the Belgian Brewing Industry and the Breakthrough of Lager in the Interwar Years." Online: https://feb.kuleuven.be/drc/Economics/research/dps-papers/dps07/dps0728.pdf

Wahl, Robert and Arnold Spencer Wahl. *Wahl Handybook of the American Brewing Industry: Beer From the Expert's Viewpoint.* Wahl Institute. Chicago. 1937.

Weeks, Morris Jr. *Beer and Brewing In America.* United States Brewers Foundation. 1949.

Westheider, James. *Fighting in Vietnam: The Experiences of the U.S. Soldier.* Stackpole Books. 2011.

Williams, Craig. "An Examination of the Lemp Brewery Cave." *Brewery History Society.* Issue 155. p. 16–32. 2013.

Wolfe, Thomas. *The Web and The Rock.* Heineman. London. 1969.

Zalkind, Susan. "Southern Africa's Beer Boom: A Look at the Heart of Africa's Beer Scene." *BeerAdvocate.* 2012. Online: https://www.beeradvocate.com/articles/6816/southern-africas-beer-boom-look-heart-africas-beer-scene/

BLOGS

The following blogs each provided numerous articles and resources.

Cornell, Martyn: www.zythophile.co.uk

Garshol, Lars: www.garshol.priv.no/blog/beer

Hofer, Franz D: www.tempestinatankard.com

Krennmair, Andreas: www.dafteejit.com

Pattinson, Ron: www.barclayperkins.blogspot.com

NEWSPAPERS, ARTICLES AND WEBSITES

"A history of television, the technology that seduced the world – and me." Anthony, Andrew. *Guardian* (online). 7 Sept 2013. https://www.theguardian.com/tv-and-radio/2013/sep/07/history-television-seduced-the-world

"A Tragedy of War." *Newcastle Journal.* 28 November 1914.

"An Ideal Lager Beer." *War Office Times and Naval Review.* 31 Dec 1915.

"And Now From Japan, The Hot New 'Dry' Beers." *New York Times.* 10 July 1988.

"Beer Drinking in Munich." *The Wheeling Daily Intelligencer.* 19 August 1873.

"Beer Wars." *Tokyo Weekender.* https://www.tokyoweekender.com/1989/07/beer-wars/

"Brewery Provides Half Denmark's Tax." *Coventry Evening Telegraph.* 22 January 1954.

"Carlsberg Lager" Notice in the *Scotsman.* 17 August 1914.

"Cleveland Indians' Ten Cent Beer Night: The Worst Idea Ever." *Bleacher Report.* 22 March 2009. Online: https://bleacherreport.com/articles/142952-ten-cent-beer-night-the-worst-idea-ever

"Dreher's Vienna Beer." *Medical Times and Gazette.* 30 May 1868. P594-595.

"Eins." *New York Herald.* 21 July 1867.

"German Beer in England." *Birmingham Daily Post.* Wed 27 January 1869.

"German Sunday Amusements." *New York Herald.* 24 August 1857.

"Head Quarters of Beer Drinking." *Atlantic Monthly* v.14 1864.

"Helles" Wikipedia: https://de.wikipedia.org/wiki/Helles

"How Beer is Tested and Drank in Munich." *Manchester Courier* and *Lancashire General Advertiser.* 26 June 1876.

"How Lager Beer is Made." *New York Times.* 20 August 1881.

"On The Continent." *Isle of Man Times.* William Heap. 10 September 1881.

"Paris Exhibition of 1867." *London Daily News.* 18 March 1867.

"Pilsner and Vienna Lager Beer." *Nottingham Evening Post.* 18 May 1882.

"Pilsener Lager Beer." *Wrexham Advertiser*. 25 October 1890.

"Saving the Past: The Rescue of the Allied Breweries Archive." http://www.pubhistorysociety.co.uk/PDF-Dowloads/allied1.pdf

"Sunday in St. Louis." *New York Herald*. 21 July 1867.

The Brewers' Guardian. May 28 1889.

"The First Oktoberfest in 1810." http://wiesnkini.de/en/magazine/the-first-oktoberfest-1810/

"The Gambrinus." *Pall Mall Gazette*. 29 September 1899.

"The German Sangerfest." *New York Herald*. 17 June 1856.

"The Great Japanese Beer War." https://www.tofugu.com/japan/japanese-beer-wars/

"The Ideal Lager Beer." *War Office Times and Naval Review*. 15 March 1914.

"The Millions Beverage." *New York Times*. 20 May 1877.

"This is Where Hanoi's *Bia Hoi* Glasses Come From." *Saigoneer*. 19 October 2015. https://saigoneer.com/vietnam-news/5489-photos-this-is-where-hanoi-s-bia-h%C6%A1i-glasses-come-from

"Vienna Lager." *Cornhill Magazine*. vol XIV. 1866. p. 757–758.

INDEX

THANKS

I raise a massive foam-topped mug of delicious lager to the many people who helped with this book. Ron Pattinson for being an incredible source of information. Brian Alberts. Mike Stein. Trina Brown. Erik Brooks. Dan Scholzen. Heidi Harris. Tracy Lauer. Ashleigh Carter. Jack Hendler. J.P. Williams. Theresa McCulla. Hagen Dost. Bill Wesselink. David Deline. Dan Suarez and the rest of the Suarez Family, especially Mom and Dad for the ride back to town and the pizza. Ana Paola Ortega Silva. Sam Wainwright. Russell Jones. Kasper Juul Larsen. Erik Lund. Zoran Gojkovic. Birgitte Skadhauge. Flemming Besenbacher. Simon Boas Hoffmeyer. Angus Meldrum. George Kyle. Tom Robberechts. Guy Vanautgaerden. Jan Steensels. Special thanks to Yvan de Baets for his extended information on Belgian lager. Prince Luitpold. Eric Toft. Matthias Trum. Special thanks to Astrid Assél and Christian Huber for answering my many questions. Sabine Marthelmeß. Martin Zarnkow. Birgit Schmalohr. The Fütterers. Manfred Newrzella. Hamdi Ammar. Robert Lobovsky. Anna Perinova. Josef Krysl. Jan Fišera. Evan Rail. Michael Comerton. Phuong Anh Nguyen. Dai Viet. Dang Thuy Anh. Dr Viet. Caleb DeMarais. Gota Iribe. Chris McLardie. Andreas Krennmair. Andreas Urban. Silvan Leeb. Conrad Seidl. Ian Webster. Andy Runcie. Jo Dring. Paul Jones. Luca Lorenzoni. Jasper Cuppaidge. Simon Farnung. Jonny Garrett and Brad Evans. To my publishers and everyone who's worked on the book: Jo Copestick, Tara O'Sullivan, Graham Coster and Paul Palmer-Edwards – thank you all. Cheers to my mates and drinking buddies Chris Perrin, Lee Bacon, Mark Charlwood and Matt Stokes. To Frankie and Lucas and their brilliant mum (and my sister), Vicki. To Karen and John for welcoming me into your family and always being willing to share a beer and stories of Burton. To Mum and Dad: you're always positive, proud, excited and encouraging of everything I'm able to do – thank you. And to Emma for always making me smile and being my favourite person to drink beer with.